Fair

Simon & Schuster

Game

Valerie Plame Wilson

With an Afterword by Laura Rozen

NEW YORK   LONDON   TORONTO   SYDNEY

CERTAIN NAMES AND IDENTIFYING CHARACTERISTICS
IN THIS BOOK HAVE BEEN CHANGED.

Simon & Schuster
1230 Avenue of the Americas
New York, NY 10020

First Simon & Schuster hardcover edition October 2007

SIMON & SCHUSTER and colophon are registered trademarks of Simon & Schuster, Inc.

For information about special discounts for bulk purchases, please contact Simon & Schuster Special Sales at 1-800-456-6798 or business@simonandschuster.com.

Designed by Paul Dippolito

Manufactured in the United States of America

1   3   5   7   9   10   8   6   4   2

Library of Congress Cataloging-in-Publication Data is available.

ISBN-13: 978-1-4165-3761-8
ISBN-10:   1-4165-3761-9

To Joe

Contents

PUBLISHER'S NOTE

All employees of the Central Intelligence Agency must sign a confidentiality agreement that requires that they submit their writings to the CIA for prepublication review. Valerie Plame Wilson, whose work for the CIA entailed covert operations, of course abided by this agreement, and her manuscript was reviewed by the CIA and returned to her with numerous redactions—cuts—that the CIA determined were necessary. Many of these cuts related to material that would disclose Ms. Wilson's dates of service, information that has already been widely disseminated.

As has been reported, Simon & Schuster and Ms. Wilson brought a legal action against the CIA; we felt that the redactions required by the CIA went beyond any reasonable requirements of national security and impaired important First Amendment rights. A federal district court has disagreed, determining, essentially, that while Ms. Wilson's dates of service may be in the public domain, they cannot be reported by Ms. Wilson. Accordingly, Ms. Wilson's portion of this book contains only that information that the CIA has deemed unclassified and has allowed her to include.

The sections of *Fair Game* that have been blacked out indicate the places where the CIA has ordered cuts. Still, even with these substantial redactions, we believe the book conveys the power of Ms. Wilson's story, if, alas, not all its details.

To enhance the reader's experience Simon & Schuster has added an afterword by reporter Laura Rozen. Drawn from interviews and public sources, it provides historical background and recounts portions of Ms. Wilson's life and career that she was unable to include herself. When the afterword is read together with *Fair Game,* a full and vivid picture of Valerie Plame Wilson emerges. Ms. Wilson has had no input or involvement in the creation of the afterword, which she has not seen before the publication of this book.

Simon & Schuster has also added an appendix of relevant documents.

We thank you for your understanding and look forward to your enjoyment of this important book.

Fair Game

CHAPTER 1

Joining the CIA

Our group of five—three men and two women—trekked through an empty tract of wooded land and swamp, known in CIA terms as the "Farm." It was 4 A.M. and we had been on the move all night. Having practiced escape and evasion from an ostensible hostile force—our instructors—we were close to meeting up with our other classmates. Together we would attack the enemy, then board a helicopter to safety. This exercise, called the final assault, was the climax of our paramilitary training. Each of us carried eighty-pound backpacks, filled with essential survival gear: tents, freeze-dried food, tablets to purify drinking water, and 5.56 mm ammunition for our M-16s. The late fall weather was bitter, and slimy water sloshed in our combat boots. A blister on my heel radiated little jabs of stinging pain. My friend Pete, a former Army officer, usually ready with a wisecrack and a smirk, hadn't spoken in hours, while John, our resident beer guzzler, carried not only his backpack but at least fifty extra pounds of body weight. His round face was covered with mud and sweat.

When our point man gave the hand signal, we gratefully

stopped, shrugged off our backpacks, and slumped together for a moment against a small protected knoll. Then we fell into formation again and moved toward the landing zone. When we finally reached a clearing at dawn, I could barely make out the blades of an enormous helicopter rotating slowly, and the friendly faces of my other classmates, Sharon, David, and Tex. I heard Pete mutter, "Finally." We all surged forward, energized by relief and hope. I began to imagine the hot shower I would enjoy when this was over. Then suddenly the sharp firecrackers of light from magnesium flares exploded over our heads and the repetitive sound of machine-gun fire sent adrenaline rushing through my veins.

I dropped to the ground and crawled over to Pete, thinking he would know what to do. Despite three months of hard training, my idyllic suburban upbringing had not prepared me for incoming fire and the overwhelming physical sensations that accompanied it. Dragging me a few yards away to a crest of land, Pete pointed at the helicopter. "Get your ass over there!"

Before I knew it, we brushed aside any pretense of military discipline and made a dead run at the helicopter. As we careened down the hill at full speed, M-16s blazing, I caught the eye of a classmate running alongside me. His expression suggested a hint of enjoyment, or at least his awareness of the absurdity of the situation. Soon enough, I threw myself into the open door of the helicopter and caught my breath beneath the noise of artillery and the deafening sounds of the rotors and engines. I shrugged off my pack, and as we were lifted to safety, I marveled at how I came to be at the Farm.

As a teenager, I read William Stevenson's *A Man Called Intrepid*, about the Office of Strategic Services (OSS) days during World War II. The OSS was the predecessor of the Central Intelligence Agency. I loved the book and I found the history intriguing. I began to seriously consider what working for the CIA meant. If I joined, what would I be asked to do? Was it dangerous? Did I believe in what the CIA did? My family had always valued public service and kept a quiet patriotism. On Memorial Day and the Fourth of July we always put out the flag in a big flowerpot. My father, Samuel Plame, was a retired Air Force colonel. When the Japanese attacked Pearl Harbor in December 1941, he was studying at the University of Illinois in Champaign. He remembers that the next day the campus was a ghost town; all the eligible male students had left to sign up for military service. He was soon on his own way to enlist in the Army Air Corps—the Air Force predecessor—in San Diego. He served in the South Pacific during World War II and has a seemingly inexhaustible supply of corny jokes, stories, and songs from his time there. My brother, Robert Plame, older than me by sixteen years, joined the Marines in 1966 and was promptly sent to Vietnam. One day in 1967, as my parents and I returned home from some errands, the neighbors told us that two uniformed Marines had been knocking at our door. We learned that Bob was MIA. My stricken parents assumed the worst and, for a few days, we did not know if Bob was dead or alive. He was finally located on a hospital ship. During a reconnaissance mission behind enemy lines, he had been badly wounded in his right arm. He endured years of multiple, painful operations to restore some sensation in his limb. Incredibly, with just one working arm and hand, he went on to learn how to fly, ski, write, and tie shoelaces. He has been happily married to Christie, a nurse, for nearly thirty years and is the proud father of two bright and beautiful girls. I thought that if I served in the CIA it would extend a family tradition. Still, I had my nagging doubts. Hadn't the CIA tried to kill Castro with an exploding cigar?

"Imagine you are meeting an agent in a foreign hotel room and there is suddenly a loud banging at the door. You hear 'Police, let us in!' What do you do?" This question was being put to me by a kindly looking older woman wearing pearls and a surprisingly bright yellow blouse during my initial CIA interview in Washington. I ▮▮▮▮▮▮▮▮▮▮▮▮▮▮▮▮▮▮▮▮▮▮ had checked into a modest—well, seedy—hotel in Arlington, Virginia. I had no idea what to expect but the interview the next day, in a beige building in the suburbs of Washington, followed along the traditional lines of "What are your strengths, what are your weaknesses, why do you want to work for the CIA"—until now. This question veered off the conventional path and was more interesting. My immediate thought was that excluding espionage, there is only one good reason for an unrelated man and woman to be in a hotel room together. "I would take off my blouse, tell the agent to do the same, and jump into bed before telling the police to come in." Her barely perceptible smile told me I had hit on the right answer. I thought, This could be fun. I was ready for the next question.

██

███████████████████████████████████████but I thought if it didn't pan out, I could find something on Capitol Hill or in the Peace Corps. In the meantime, I found a job as a management trainee with a █████████████Washington department store ████████████████. Despite the 20 percent employee discount, I hated working in retail, but it was a way to pay the rent as I continued through months of CIA psychological tests, a battery of interviews, and an exacting, comprehensive physical exam. One question out of at least four hundred in one psychological test still stands out in my memory: "Do you like tall women?" I still have no idea if I got the right answer on that one. Later that summer, I was asked to take a polygraph exam. It was a weird, but relatively brief experience. █████████████ █████████████████████████ At the same time, the Agency was conducting a security background check on me. Several neighbors reported to my parents that "someone ████████████ ████had interviewed them to ask if I had any known drinking, drug, or other problems. ████████████████████████████

██
██████████████████████████ ████████████████
██
██
██

[REDACTED] I nervously settled into my chair in a nondescript government classroom in a bland office building in a congested Virginia suburb. I took in my ▮ classmates in our CIA introduction course. Many of the young men were clearly ex-military types, some still sporting regulation buzz cuts. Just less than half were women, but as I later learned, only a fraction of those were destined, like me, to work in the Directorate of Operations (DO). The rest were pegged to become analysts in the Directorate of Intelligence (DI) or administrative/logistical officers and the like in the Directorate of Administration (DA). A few were engineers who would ultimately work in the Directorate of Science and Technology (DST), the Agency's research arm. It looked like I was the [REDACTED] by far and this suspicion was confirmed when a tiny woman, nearly as wide as she was tall, took me and three other (male) classmates into her office during a break. She was the DO liaison to the Career Trainees (CTs)—in other words, she would be our den mother as we worked through the initial training. It was hard to believe that this matronly woman had actually been an operator in "the field," but she certainly knew a lot more about the CIA than any of us did. "[REDACTED]

[REDACTED] PCS meant "permanent change of Station," in other words, assignment abroad. As the acronyms flew around us, it was clear that a paramilitary culture reigned at the CIA.

During our lunch breaks, taken at our desks or in nearby cafes, I got to know my classmates. I couldn't help but feel intimidated—most either had gone to prestigious universities, or had at least a master's degree or some years of military experience. All seemed much more sophisticated, smarter, better traveled, and wittier than I was. Feeling overwhelmed, I vowed to keep my mouth shut and learn as much as possible. Perhaps no one would notice that I had precious little meaningful life experience and was educated at a state school. Over the next few weeks, an interesting dynamic emerged. We had all taken the Myers-Briggs psychological profile test during the interview process. Most of the future operations officers, myself included, scored varying degrees of "ENTJ"—Extrovert, Intuitive, Thinking, Judgmental. ENTJ personality types tend to be strong leaders and feel the need to take command of a situation. The Myers-Briggs description of an ENTJ says that "although ENTJs are tolerant of established procedures, they can abandon any procedure when it can be shown to be indifferent to the goal it seemingly serves . . . They are tireless in the devotion to their jobs and can easily block out other areas of life for the sake of work. The ENTJ female may find it difficult to select a mate who is not overwhelmed by her strong personality and will." ENTJs appear in approximately 5 percent of the population; apparently, that's what the CIA was looking for in its future operations officers. We were drawn to one another, not just because we would be doing the same training and ultimately the same job, but because we had similar personalities. Wherever the future case officers gathered on breaks, they were usually the loudest, most social, and I thought, most entertaining. The air seemed to crackle with excitement. I began making friends in the class and despite our different backgrounds, we began to form deep bonds. I looked forward to attending the CIA introductory course every day where we learned how the Agency was organized, how intelligence was collected and analyzed, and how the wider intelligence community functioned. One of the most gripping guest speakers was a woman who had served her first tour as a case officer in Moscow. She told us in harrowing detail how she had been surveilled by Soviet intelligence while picking up and setting down "dead drops"—fabricated rocks or other innocent-looking containers with notes, money, and instructions to an important Soviet double agent. She was thrown out of the country (declared persona non grata, or PNGed in CIA lingo) but her agent, the spy for whom she was responsible, was not so lucky. He was executed. We all sat in stunned silence as we digested the huge responsibilities and the consequences of making a mistake.

Finally, after about three months of "CIA 101," as we affectionately called the course, we were all sent on our way to our various "interims" to begin some on-the-job training. Being a CT on an interim at the Agency was comparable to pledging a sorority or fraternity: you were assigned the most tedious tasks and spent lots of time walking cables and memos to distant parts of the Headquarters building or waiting for a dossier in the vast underground space known as the file room ██████████████ , as I was beginning my first interim phase ██████████████

female case officers were either former secretaries who doggedly worked their way out from behind their desks to field work, or the wives of case officers who got tired of being the only ones at home with the children while their husbands were out having all the fun being spymasters. There were a rare few who did not fit into these categories, but these older, tough-as-nails women who had triumphed through the entrenched discrimination scared me. I occasionally came into contact with them during my early interims, and I admired their ambition and perseverance, but it was clear that they paid for it with their personal happiness. Most went home in the late evening to a cat. In my class of fifty or so, just fewer than half were female. Of that number, about four were destined to go into operations. Either through ignorance of youth or naïveté, I did not see myself in the vanguard of a new CIA; I simply wanted to do well at my job and did not expect to find any sort of discrimination because of my gender.

I was assigned to interims mostly in the European Division of the DO. I generally enjoyed my work, menial as it was, but was anxiously counting the days until we could go to the Farm for our paramilitary training. Finally, the time arrived for me to pack a few items in my car and head south with the other young CTs. I had more and longer interims than most of my original classmates— ▮▮▮▮▮▮▮▮▮▮▮▮▮▮▮▮▮▮▮▮ and as a consequence, I joined another training class. As instructed early on by the Agency, I had told my friends and family that ▮▮▮▮▮▮▮

██████████████ ███ my time away from Washington was for some vague, undefined "training." No one questioned this, or at least did so directly to me. All my friends outside the Agency were busy starting their own careers and so training was part of everyone's early professional life. Only my parents and brother knew where I really worked. My mother and I agreed not to tell my uncle: her brother was an early Air Force jet jockey and would have been so proud of my career choice he could not have kept it to himself. As I sped along the highway toward the Farm, I was looking forward to this next phase of training, one that would move me much closer to a field assignment as a case officer.

"Check your sizes, only take one, keep the line moving! Let's go!" barked the instructor in camouflage fatigues as we shuffled into a cavernous corrugated-tin warehouse in an open field at the Farm. In the dim light of the warehouse we picked combat boots, fatigues, webbed belts, caps, canteens, backpack gear, and other paraphernalia out of enormous bins. This stuff would see us through the next three months of military training. As our arms overflowed with equipment, the instructors, all ex-military types, took us next to the Quonset huts located deep in the scruffy pine woods. These would be our sleeping quarters. The women's barracks was lined on both sides with bunk beds and had a spartan bathroom at the end. I had never had to wear a uniform at school, but as I changed into my fatigues, I liked the idea of not having to figure out my outfit every day—which shoes and belt would go together—for the next few months.

Our training quickly assumed a pattern: up at 5 A.M. for physical training, which involved running or walking in formation while singing bawdy songs to keep tempo, just as military recruits have done for decades; followed by a quick breakfast, then a morning class in a military discipline. Lunch ████████ ████ a throwback to traditional southern cooking. Almost everything was dipped in batter and deep-fried, and a salad bar was considered newfangled. This was usually followed by an outdoor activity, then dinner—more deep-fried food—then some brief free time before lights-out at nine. There was naturally plenty of complaining—some good-natured, some bitter—among the class members, but the instructors, ██████████████████████ ██████ were more than capable of subduing a bunch of whiny suburbanites and kept us in line. For many the physical demands of the course were tough—running at least three miles in the morning, trekking through the woods with eighty-pound backpacks and an M-16 rifle—and more than one overweight trainee gave up in the middle of a march or quit well before completing the required sit-up reps. Fortunately, I had always been athletic, and though the physical requirements of the course were a challenge I was able to do them all. I began to see the Farm experience as camp for adults.

Each week was devoted to a different topic ██████████████ ████████████████████████████████████ ████████████████████████ and the instructors struggled to whip our class into shape and instill some military discipline. The Agency clearly understood that we were rarely, if ever, going to be called upon to use these skills, but the Farm paramilitary course remained a popular class for Agency recruits because management realized it forged an esprit de corps that would last throughout one's career. Moreover, it gave the Agency another opportunity to evaluate a new employee's strength of character, ability to work in a team, and dedication—all skills critical to success in the Agency, no matter what your career path.

One of our first sessions involved learning about weapons and how to use them. Unlike some of my ex-military classmates, my exposure to guns had been limited: I knew that my father kept his World War II service pistol strapped to the back of the bed headboard, in the event an intruder got into the house. Learning about ███████████████ guns was completely new to me and to my astonishment, I found I was pretty good at it ███ ████████████████████████████████████ Probably aided by beginner's luck, I simply followed the instructions: hold your breath steady, take careful aim, and pull the trigger slowly. I was apparently the best in our class ██████████████, which I am sure many of my male colleagues found unnerving. My proudest moment came when I managed to score very high on a handgun test, despite having to balance on crutches after spraining an ankle during a morning run in the dark.

As the weeks went by and we learned ██████████████ ██████████████████████████████████████ ██████████████████ skills perhaps more appropriate for an Army ranger than a CIA case officer lurking around bars, a vague understanding hung over us that at some point we would face an interrogation exercise designed to simulate POW captivity. From the beginning we had been taught how to build and sustain our cover and we knew that we would be severely tested toward the end of the course, but we had no idea where or when this would happen. Before dawn one Monday morning, after all the students had returned from their weekend break, we were awakened with war cries and curses and flashlights being shoved in our faces as we were pulled from our bunks.

Although we had known this challenging portion of the course was coming, it was unnerving to look around and not see our instructors' familiar faces. They were unknown authorities dressed in fatigues, most with black hoods with eyeholes. As I hurried to dress, I kept telling myself that this was just an exercise, but their rough taunts and shoves as we moved out of the Quonset hut to the woods were realistic enough to set off a surge of adrenaline. For hours in the dark, we were forced to crawl on the ground and do push-ups and sit-ups—and if you faltered in any way, you were kicked or subjected to brutal verbal abuse. After a long, exhausting march through the woods, each of us with one hand on the shoulder of the student ahead, we were thrown into a waiting army truck. We bounced over dirt roads and stopped at a small white concrete-block building surrounded by pine trees. The real fun was about to begin.

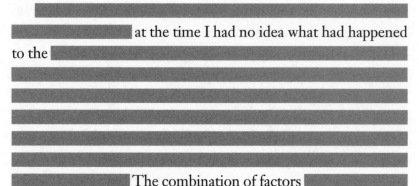 at the time I had no idea what had happened to the

The combination of factors really got to you psychologically. Your rational mind kept saying that this was just an exercise, one that you had known was coming, but another small voice in your head wondered what the hell was going on. It was certainly realistic.

At some point, hours later, I was pulled into my first interrogation. I struggled to keep my wits about me.

 As I sat down—a slight concession that they had given us a few hours earlier—I dared check my surroundings. To my delight, a classmate who had

become a friend had chosen that moment as well to defy the rules. The brief smile and eye rolls we exchanged renewed my confidence that I would get through this.

██

██
██
██
██

████████████████████ I fainted—from low blood sugar—and fell backward. When I came to, I was mortified to find myself being held by the elderly director of the Farm, someone I had only seen at a distance and when he addressed our class the first day. The good news was that at least I knew it was still an exercise. My relief was short-lived ████████████████████████████
██
██

██████████████████ I liked the quiet and dark of my new small wooden home. I began to think about who I should put on my Christmas card list that year and how much of each address I could remember. Finally, ████████████████████████████
██████████████████ we were "freed" by our regular instructors and after another bumpy ride in the back of an army truck, we arrived at our Quonset huts. We were filthy, disoriented, and famished. As I stood under the hot shower, luxuriating in being clean, the nightmarish capture exercise faded quickly to a surreal memory. I had passed another of the Agency's tests, had not ratted out my classmates, and after a good weekend of sleep, would be ready for the next challenge.

"One, two, three, *go!*" yelled an instructor in my ear, wind ripping around us, as my legs dangled out the airplane's open door. I was terrified beyond anything I had felt before, but the instructor had vowed when he checked our parachutes and tightened our webbing that if we went up in the airplane, the only way we would come down was by parachute. There was no backing out now and so I lurched forward—helped by a strong shove from instructor "Red"—and plunged toward the earth at 120 mph. As the instructors had predicted, my mind froze during the first jump, and that's where the training on the ground is indispensable. All the jumps from shoulder-high platforms and then from the tower, in which you hurtle toward a padded truck at the end of a long cable, forms muscle memory that takes over when the brain fails. As the parachute opened above me and I drifted slowly down, I reached up, grabbed the toggles, and tried to steer away from the electrical lines that were racing toward me at an alarming speed and land in the zone marked with white chalk. The jump instructors had drilled us to land on our feet and immediately absorb the ground's impact up the side of our body and then roll. At 118 pounds, I was so light that I could have just stayed upright on my feet when I hit the ground, but went through the motions of dropping and rolling so I wouldn't be chewed out by the instructors. My relief at being on the ground somewhere inside that chalk circle was overpowering and gave way to a huge surge of ego and pride. "I did it!" Only four more jumps and I would have my much-coveted "jump wings." It was exhilarating and I was sure I was having a better time at work than anyone else I knew.

When the paramilitary course ended, we were given the option of attending jump school—provided we could pass our physical tests and standards. I knew from the moment I heard about this opportunity that it was something I would try for. After nearly ten weeks of physical conditioning ▇▇▇▇▇▇▇▇▇ ▇▇▇▇▇▇▇▇▇▇▇ we felt we could eat nails for breakfast. Still, not everyone opted to jump and some of those who tried, failed. One woman, Karen, whom I had come to regard warily because of her overly ambitious nature, clearly wanted to jump. She was not a nemesis per se, but her superior airs got my competitive spirit going and I passed the test with flying colors, if only because I didn't want her to beat me. After a few days of training, we were told that we would make five jumps over a period of three days to earn our wings. I dared not tell my parents about my latest "job opportunity"—my mother would not have slept for the entire week.

The day of the first jump dawned gray and cool with light wind gusts. Our group of six went through the safety procedures and scrambled, two at a time, into the light aircraft with our craggy jump instructor, Red, who never went anywhere without a full cheek of tobacco. I was dismayed that my ultracompetitive classmate, Karen, was in the planeload with me. As I watched her tumble out first, again with a helping hand from Red, I thought, If she can do it, so can I, and a few minutes later, out I went, too.

Once everyone came down—from a speck in the sky to a heap of nylon on the ground—we cheered and high-fived one another, feeling cocksure and very cool. Then Red walked out from the airplane hangar with his unmistakable swagger. He had just heard that a storm was coming in for the next few days and he wanted to know if we were willing to complete all five of our jumps that afternoon. We all looked at one another—there was no question. We gathered up our parachutes without a word and hustled over to the hangar to prepare for our next jumps. We weren't about to leave the Farm without pinning those little silver wings on our fatigues.

I tapped lightly on the door at 7:30 A.M. and pushed it open a little way. I heard "come in" and stepped into the office for a meeting with my operations course adviser. ███████████████

██

 Dick sat behind his desk, smoking a cigarette. The heavy pall of tobacco already filled the small space. His salt-and-pepper buzz cut, short-sleeved plaid shirt, and thick glasses completed the look. Next to the ashtray was his customary can of Coke. Breakfast of Champions. "How's it going?" he rasped as his hand shook on the way to his mouth to take another drag. Dick was not a bad adviser, but he was not terribly effective. ▓▓▓▓▓▓▓▓▓▓▓

▓▓▓▓▓▓▓▓▓▓▓▓▓▓▓▓▓▓▓▓▓▓▓▓▓▓▓▓▓▓▓▓

▓▓▓▓▓▓▓▓▓▓▓▓▓▓▓▓▓▓▓▓▓▓▓▓▓▓▓▓▓▓▓

▓▓▓▓▓▓▓▓▓▓▓▓▓▓▓▓▓▓▓▓▓▓▓▓▓▓▓▓▓▓▓▓

▓▓▓▓▓▓ . Years of living abroad, dealing with agents, and juggling the demands of a demanding double life inevitably took their toll on officers' health, marriages, and families. The Agency's frequent solution was to send its troubled officers to the quiet of the Farm, which perhaps helped restore the officers' balance, but the result was that many broken-down officers taught the new, idealistic students that a life in the CIA was a tough one. Senior management periodically vowed to put only their brightest stars at the Farm and reward them with a promotion for their stateside tours so the junior officers could be taught by the best. But the reality was that most of the time the best and most effective officers wanted to be in the field recruiting spies.

Still, Dick had significant field experience and I asked him how to pace an upcoming exercise. He exhaled smoke over my shoulder and looked down through his heavy glasses to read my latest report, written late the night before

Although it was easy to make fun of the make-believe world ▮▮▮▮▮▮▮▮▮▮▮▮▮▮▮ passing the course was deadly serious if you ever wanted to serve in the field. Through short deadlines, sleep deprivation, constant surprises, and changes in the scenarios, the instructors ratcheted up the pressure on the student cadre. I felt like I was living under a microscope, and all my interactions—even in rare moments of relaxation—were under close scrutiny from the invariable edits on our reports to follow-up debriefing sessions with instructors after operational exercises, to the feeling that we were being watched by instructors even when we shared a beer with them in the evening. We knew we were being evaluated: Did we have "the right stuff"?

The kickoff exercise for the operations course a few weeks earlier had been surprisingly easy. ▮▮▮▮▮▮▮▮▮▮▮▮

██. Our job was to find our target person, chat up him or her, and secure another meeting. As I surveyed the crowded room ████████████████████████████████████ I saw that I probably had some relevant life experience that I could use in the exercise. As a Pi Beta Phi sorority sister at Penn State, I had lived through the frenzied "rush" weeks, and once I'd been accepted in the sorority, I attended many a crowded party where fitting in and exchanging easy banter with others was key to social success. Now, I smiled to myself, envisioning the room as nothing more than another fraternity/sorority party I dove in, trying to find my target, "Gary." Introducing myself, talking a bit, eliciting essentials, and moving on proved to be easy for me. I had a revelation as I worked the crowd in the club: the vast majority of people really only want to talk about themselves. Answering a query about yourself, especially if there is not a lot you want to give out, is a matter of providing enough to be polite, then deflecting the question back to the conversation partner. It was a lesson that would serve me well in the years ahead ████████████████ and the need to deflect attention from myself to my target became critical.

I took a quick break from my quest to find Gary and made a beeline for the bar, where I gave back my glass of wine and asked for sparkling water with a twist so it would look like a gin and tonic. Another early lesson: don't drink more than one drink on the job because it impairs your memory. I turned around and saw an instructor with dark hair and gray sideburns standing alone and thought I would try my luck. Bingo! It was Gary. ████████ ██████████████████████ "Oh, how interesting," I replied, as I turned on the charm. In no time we had agreed to meet in the next few days for lunch so that Gary could tell me more ████████ ██████████████████████████████████ Mission accomplished, I thought, as I left the party early.

Over the next few weeks, I met regularly with Gary and got to know more than I ever wanted ███████████████████. More important for the point of the exercise, I was learning what made him tick: his motivations, prejudices, and aspirations both personally and professionally. He was quite engaging and had obviously perfected the role of Gary. After much practice, he was great at tossing out details, some meaningful, some useless, to see how much I would pick up. After each meeting, I scrambled back to our "Station offices ███████████████and wrote reports on the ██ ███ ████████████████████████████████████ At each meeting, as we got to know each other better, Gary provided me with tantalizing tidbits ████████████████████████████ ██████████████ In the early meetings, I usually excused myself to go to the ladies' room during the meal and furiously scribbled down all the facts and figures and names he had given me on the little pad I kept in my purse. This is crazy, I thought more than once as I sat inside the bathroom stall, fishing around in my bag, but just as in paramilitary training, I was playing on the instructors' game board and I had no choice but to follow their rules if I ever wanted to become a case officer. Over time, I got better at retaining the flood of information, but it was a relief later when ████████████████████I could sit in hotel rooms with a real recruited asset and openly take notes without resorting to the ladies' room subterfuge.

While this exercise ██████████████████ was being played out over a course of weeks, we were simultaneously receiving training in ███ ███ █████████████████how to write an intelligence report and a slew of operational cables were all topics. Lectures in the auditorium, given by the resident instructor staff, were often supplemented by Agency officers visiting from Headquarters or the field who had relevant experience to impart. The best speakers were invariably surrounded by curious students later that evening ████ ████████████████████████ where if your schedule allowed and you didn't have any ops meetings or intel reports to write up, you could drop by for a beer, play Ping-Pong on a battered table, and socialize a bit. Visitors delighted in regaling their adoring audience with real-life war stories ████████████████████ ████████████████████████████████████

We were being inculcated into the Agency culture and through these stories we learned what we might face and what might or might not work once we got into the field.

Although the pressure to perform was intense, and the feeling of being constantly observed and judged could be oppressive, there was no doubt that learning some of these spy skills was fun ████████████████████████████████ ████████████████████████████████████ ████████████████████████████████████ ████████████████████████████████████ ████████████████████████████████████

████████████████ My friend David and I briefly considered using our new skills to clandestinely photograph two students who everyone knew were carrying on a torrid affair, even though one of them was seriously involved with yet another student in the same class. Max, a mild-mannered but obnoxious type, had apparently no idea that his "friend," Tim, was making passionate love to his girlfriend. We thought some well-timed photos would help set the record straight but finally decided to let Max find out the truth for himself.

Some lighthearted moments occurred ████████████████ ████████████████████████████████████ ████████████████████████████████████ ████████████████████████████████████

The cameraman laughed so hard the picture went out of focus.

Methodology and theory in the classroom was followed by plenty of on-the-road experience

██████████████████████ ███ ██████████████████
██
██

████████████████████ It was exacting, time-consuming work and we all spent hours in our cars with maps, watches, and piles of debris accumulated from our small purchases ███████████████████
██

████████████. I panicked when I realized that my meticulous plan ████ ████ had a fatal flaw; a ████ stop that I had included and was vital ████████████████ was closed. There were no other good choices nearby. The closest open establishment was a seedy top-less bar, and being a nice suburban girl, I didn't know how I would explain a visit there. I had no choice but to follow through, parking in front of the dark storefront and pantomiming shock and dismay at the store's closure. As I leaned into the windowpane, and cupped my hands around my eyes as if checking to see if there was anyone moving around in the store, I could see ██
████ I looked like an idiot. My evaluation on that particular exercise was "not satisfactory."

As the weeks turned into months we all sweated through countless evaluations of our writing, our planning abilities, our ████████████████ skills, and our ability to think on our feet and cope with increasing amounts of stress that was no less real for being artificially generated. Several students dropped out and went back to Headquarters to find another job in the Agency or left altogether. A few other students were asked to leave because of fatal flaws in judgment or attitude, such as making the same mistake twice, not demonstrating appropriate respect for the instructor cadre, cheating in any way, or simply not possessing the intangible "it" quality that makes someone into a case officer. This news naturally spread like wildfire among the students and while I found it terrifying, it only made me try harder because the prospect of working for the Agency, living abroad, and perhaps even having my own war stories to tell one day was simply too enticing. I didn't want to be asked to leave. One night, ███████ ████████████████████████████████████, I got out of my car and gathered my purse and notes. The June air was so heavily humid that my silk blouse stuck to my skin and my feet ached in my high heels (we had to dress up ████████████████ when appropriate ██████████████████████). I had at least three hours of work ahead of me to get all my report writing done; it was due to the instructors by 7 A.M. the next day. I paused to look up at the starry sky. I laughed at the absurdity of my situation, but at that moment, even when exhausted from the work I had done and still had to do, I had no doubts that I would pass the course.

During the final weeks of the ████████████ course, the students were divided into small teams ██████████████████████ ██████. Each team member needed to work closely with others to help solve operational problems and make sure that U.S. policymakers received the good intelligence they needed and deserved. Fortunately, my team was a strong one, its members all students I had become friendly with. The only exception was Gerry, a bespeckled, rather goofy-looking guy whom we all saw as the weak link. He never seemed to put two and two together and it was a mystery to us why he hadn't been booted out. We just rolled our eyes whenever he made another incredibly stupid suggestion and we tried to work around him the best we could. As the operational pace was ratcheted up even further during the weeks of the final exercise, our classroom, the Station, became a hive of activity at all hours. At 2 A.M. you could go to the room and no doubt find someone from the team finishing up a report ████████. Vicious summer thunderstorms cut out the power several times and rendered our ████████ useless, so on a few nights our classroom looked like a twisted tableau from a medieval monastery—we were bent over yellow legal pads writing out our reports in longhand while candles flickered in the middle of the table. We joked that the adverse conditions were preparing us for future assignments to Africa or parts of Asia.

The climax of the final exercise ████████████████████ ████████████████████████████████ was to test our skills in an environment where presumably we'd never been. We were supposed to ████████████████████████████████ pull together all the loose threads we left dangling █████████ in order to make the final week a success. Working both as a team and individually, we got to work ████████████████████ ████████ trying to figure out what surprises the instructors had in store for us. However, despite the instructors' best efforts to keep us under control, the months of pressure had taken their toll and ████████████████████████████████████we acted like eighth-graders on a class field trip. Coming down to the wire, we were giddy, feeling like we had completed a master's course in an eighth of the time. Although my team had no major screwups, our heretofore ironclad discipline broke down a little bit and we attended more than a few operational meetings with raging hangovers.

████████████████ the instructors met one final time to vote on whether to pass a student, fail him, or assign him probationary status. ████████████████████████████████████
██
██
██
████████████ As we finished up one of our last fried lunches in the mess hall and waited for the graduation ceremony, we heard that the instructors had voted out two more students and given three probationary status. The pain and humiliation of not graduating after completing the course would have been ter-

rible, and I was glad that everyone on our team, even Gerry, passed.

That evening ██████████████████████████████████ ███████████ our class graduated. This time I did not trade in my wineglass for water with a twist. ████████████████████████

████████, I had gone from an idealistic and intimidated █████ woman overwhelmed by my new surroundings, to an idealistic █████████ woman who had been challenged and had thrived. I had jumped out of airplanes, ███████████████ walked miles in pitch-black woods, knew how to write an intelligence report really fast, ████████████████████████████████████

██

████████ I was simultaneously exhausted and exhilarated. So far though, all these skills had been used █████████ ; calling on them in the real world would be the genuine test, but it was one that I welcomed. I was ready ███████████████

CHAPTER 2

███ Tour

I settled into my small wooden chair at an outdoor cafe in a crowded, bustling part of the ██████████████ and busied myself by pulling out a tour guide of ████████ and a map. It was the best time: early evening, the furnace blast from the summer day over, the jasmine just opening to perfume the air, and the sunset still streaking the sky pink and orange. I ordered a cold coffee in my halting ████████ —espresso and milk were shaken together in a drink with a frothy top ████████████ ████████████████████ —and settled in, ostensibly to study the map. I lit a cigarette, another gesture to fit in with the crowd because most ████████ smoke like chimneys, and tried to look relaxed. I was actually extremely keyed up and waiting for my target, a ██████ who the CIA thought might be associated with ████████████ highly dangerous terrorist group ██████ ██████. We had a vague description of him from another source and knew he often frequented this cafe in the evenings. My job was to ████████████████████ the target ████████████ ████████████ As a ██████ female with blond hair and blue eyes, I looked as nonthreatening and non-CIA as possible, and that was the whole idea. ██████████████████████████ ████████████████████████████ Sometimes when offi- cers are very "clean," that is, not overexposed to foreign intelli- gence services, they are capable of doing the most delicate work.

With my coffee nearly gone, and as I worked on my third cigarette, I had almost given up hope ███████████████████ ███████ when a man, one who matched the description given to me, sat down a few tables away, alone. I overheard him order ███ ████████████—a small plate of appetizers. He was maybe in his forties; his dark hair was streaked with gray and pulled back into a ponytail. His dress was rather sloppy and unremarkable. I tried not to let my hands tremble as I paid for my drink and slowly gathered up my things from the wobbly round table. As I did this, I plotted my path past the target, calculating how many angles I could get on him before I would be out in the busy pedestrian street outside of the cafe's boundaries. ████████████ ██ ██████████████ Swept into the throng of tourists enjoying the last bit of a summer's evening, I took a long, circuitous route to my parked car. Along the way, I stopped at many of the █████ brightly lit tourist shops, and bought little plates and a charm ███ ██████████████████ When I reached home later that night, I sighed with relief that my first real operational act as a case offi- cer had gone without incident.

I had been ██████████ on my first assignment for less than a month. I was constantly surprised at how much responsibility, for agents' lives and for significant sums of money, the CIA deemed a ███████ officer could handle. The Agency management put a lot of confidence in the Farm courses in paramilitary and operational training as a way to weed out the incompetent or unready. I was thrilled to have been chosen for the ███████████ assignment and spent days planning each aspect of the operation with colleagues. Hollywood gives the false impression that CIA operatives make decisions and act unilaterally; rogue operators appear to be the norm. While in the real CIA world there are moments of rash individuality, successful operations are always the result of a team effort. ██████████████████████ ████████████████████ I was delighted to be officially part of our team.

When I graduated from the Operations Course ████████ ████████ I had been picked up by ████████████████████ the Directorate of Operations (DO). In a furious horse-trading exercise, the various geographic divisions of the DO bid on the students deemed the best and the brightest at the Farm. In fact, each division routinely sent down several of its most senior officers to each class to proclaim the advantages of that division in a carefully choreographed dog-and-pony show. ████████████████ ██ ██████████████████████████ officers generally spent most of their careers in one region of the world, so getting in someplace where you actually wanted to live and serve was important. Students spent hours agonizing over their choices and attempted to game the system, to little avail. In the NFL draft–like atmosphere, few got what they really wanted. I was lucky. As a child, I had traveled widely in Europe with my family and felt comfortable and happy whenever I was there. My first trip was as a nine-year-old to Italy, where we rented a villa with another family in a little town north of Rome called Porto Santo Stefano. My strongest memories of that visit were tasting *gelato* for the first time and being impressed with the vastness of Saint Peter's Basilica in Rome. I had not yet studied ancient Rome in school, but what child's imagination would not be stirred by the idea of using the Coliseum to stage mock naval battles or to watch gladiators fight lions? From that summer on, I was absolutely hooked on travel. Fortunately, as a retired Air Force officer, my father and his dependents were entitled to fly "space A" (space available) on military aircraft crossing the Atlantic. My parents and I would show up at McGuire Air Force Base in New Jersey with bags packed, not really knowing where in Europe we would end up— the schedule was dictated by military needs, of course. Thus, we traveled to Italy, Germany, Ireland, Switzerland, and France. One time, we could not get space A, so we took the early 1970s version of discount airlines, the no-frills Laker Airways, to London. There we stayed at Doris Duke's magnificent town house near Marble Arch, which had been turned over to the U.S. military for officers' quarters after World War II. I wandered the vast building and imagined the opulent ballroom full of people. So though I briefly considered the Soviet and Eastern European Division (SE), I was relieved when the European Division (EUR) picked me up and promptly assigned ██████████. All that stood between me and my new career was ██████████ language training.

██████████. How are you? I am fine. I was not blessed with linguistic talent and learning a foreign language had always been hard, mind-numbing work for me. I seemed to need to hear a word fifty times for it to register. Every day on the Metro ride from my small apartment to the classroom in suburban Virginia, I reviewed vocabulary words on big stacks of white three-by-five cards. It was a painful process, further exacerbated by our teacher, ██████████ had been a resistance fighter ████ during World War II and was rightfully very proud of his service and ████ ancestry. Although good-spirited, he was not the most effective teacher and was convinced that his noble language could best be learned via memorizing obscure ████ proverbs. He would rattle off a saying ████. Glaring at me and my two classmates for our stupidity, he would finally deign to give us the translation. "It means: the goat's hair needs a fine-tooth comb!"

Of course. Finally, the Agency deemed me proficient enough to order off a ███████ restaurant menu and sent me to my first posting ████████████████ I felt like a racehorse at the gate.

████████████████████████████ was an incredibly vibrant and chaotic place. ████████████████ ████████████████████
███
███
███
███
███
███
███
███
███
███
███
███
███
███
███
███
███
███
███
███
██████████████████
     ██
███

My ▮▮▮ Chief, Dave, was idolized as a genuine DO cowboy. Despite family wealth (whispered to come from ▮▮▮▮▮ patents), a proper New England upbringing, and an Ivy League education, he could drink, smoke cigars, and curse like a sailor with the best of them. His operational exploits in Africa were legendary and he was now winding down his career with a posting to ▮▮▮ site of his first assignment years before. When I arrived ▮▮▮ I was given an appointment to see Dave and was ushered into his large and airy wood-paneled office. Dave was slouched in his leather chair with his feet up on his enormous desk; he chomped on an unlit cigar. I had been introduced to him ████████████ previously and was a little nervous, hoping to exceed the expectations of this lionized officer. He took the cigar out of his mouth long enough to say "Turn around," twirling his index finger in a downward spiral in case I didn't get the gist. I was confused. He wanted me to do what? I obediently turned around like a mannequin and waited for his next words. "Great, great. You'll do fine here." Dave had a twinkle in his eye and I didn't know how seriously to take him. After a few more words of welcome, I went back to my desk, trying to process what had just happened. Dave proved to be a very good boss who encouraged the best and engendered deep loyalty from his staff. He may have missed the memo about how to greet a ██████ female employee, but I decided not to let it bother me. Other female officers didn't shake off his sexist attitudes so easily and were offended by his remarks but I didn't want to waste time dwelling on it. He was not the first or the last male dinosaur at the CIA, and meanwhile there was work to be done and a reputation to earn.

When a junior officer 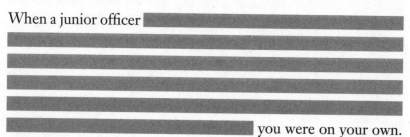 you were on your own. Just as law partners are expected to bring a certain amount of business to the table each year, so it was with CIA case officers. Consequently, there was a lot of "trolling," that is, looking for targets of interest under every rock and at every ██████ cocktail party. Working a social function effectively and efficiently to turn up potential recruitment targets became a necessary skill.

Without a doubt, the best officer I have ever seen work the room was my Deputy ███████Chief, Jim. Jim was tall, dark, and handsome and a legendary recruiter. While I was still learning the ropes ██████████, I found myself at a social function that felt like the bar in *Star Wars*; each introduction was to yet another weird character. I am of average height but I towered over most ██████ men of a certain age ████████████████████████████████ ██ ██

████████████████████████But it wasn't just the height issue; there seemed to be an unusually high proportion of oddly dressed partygoers and strange behavior in the crowd. Still, I did my best to mingle and pass out my calling cards, getting several in return. The next day in the office, a colleague and I compared notes on whom we had spoken to and whether to pursue further contact with any of them. Jim happened to walk by our desks and casually asked whom we had met the night before. We proudly passed him our little stacks of business cards and he rifled through them, dismissing each with "recruited already; don't bother; unreliable; recruited already; maybe." My colleague and I looked at each other and laughed. Jim had been to the party before we got there and canvassed the room thoroughly. We were choking in his dust. If we were to have any chance of finding someone of interest, we quickly learned to get to a function before Jim.

When I was finished with my ▬▬▬▬ duties for the day, I usually went ▬▬▬▬▬▬▬ a rabbit warren of rooms ▬▬▬▬ ▬▬ It was only then that I could write up my reports from any operational meetings of the night before or prepare for future meetings. The summer I arrived ▬▬▬▬▬▬▬▬▬ ▬▬▬▬▬ there were quite a few first-tour officers ▬▬▬▬▬ Looking back, we were like puppies: eager to please, enthusiastic about everything, but still needing to be housebroken. At times we were all impossibly arrogant, sure we had a recruitment just around the corner or nodding as if we actually knew what a senior officer was talking about in a complex operation ▬▬▬▬▬ became our training ground where we put into real practice all the lessons they had taught us at the Farm. With so much happening when I arrived, the sense of competition between the junior officers was keen, as was our common sense of purpose. We watched one another's successes and failures like hawks, calculating our own achievements against someone else's. We worked together, played together, and developed a tough facade that came in handy when dealing with the odd characters, in the office and out, who made up our universe.

One colleague who didn't quite fit the mold was Mark. A dapper Asian-American, Mark was a little older than the rest of us junior officers but was still on his first tour. He had enjoyed a successful career in finance before joining the Agency and completing the training. Mark was as ambitious as the rest of us, working long hours and pursuing the most promising targets for recruitment, and it was clear he was willing to do almost anything to endear himself to a target. One time he told us he had vacuumed the target's apartment at his request while the target collected the papers he wanted to give to Mark. I thought that was odd, but it got him what he wanted—information on which to base an intelligence report. However, there was a certain manic edge to his work that none of us could quite put our finger on. Within a year of his arrival, Mark had recruited a very good source and sent Headquarters dozens of reports ▓▓▓▓▓▓▓▓▓ ▓▓▓▓▓▓. After he recruited a few more targets, management touted him as the next big thing. Within months, however, they began to have serious doubts about the veracity of his cases. After Mark's tour was finished, I heard through the grapevine that a review of his reporting had shown that he had fabricated much of it, and I believe he was unceremoniously frog-marched out of Headquarters. For me it was yet another lesson in the tired but so true cliché that appearances can deceive.

Meanwhile, I was trying to make my mark as an operations officer and spent most evenings out and about, learning about my new environment ▓▓▓▓▓▓▓▓▓▓▓▓▓▓▓▓▓▓▓▓▓▓▓▓. It was a punishing schedule: a day full of ▓▓▓▓▓ work, followed by a few hours in the office to accomplish our "real" job reading incoming cables, writing up reports to send in to Headquarters, and operational planning, among other things. The evenings were devoted to meetings or social events. ▓▓▓▓▓▓▓▓▓▓ ▓▓▓▓▓▓▓▓▓▓▓▓▓▓▓▓▓▓▓▓ Many times I didn't get home until 12:30 A.M. or so, and had to be at the office by 8:30 A.M. ▓▓▓▓▓▓▓▓▓▓▓▓▓▓▓▓▓ ▓▓▓▓▓▓▓▓▓▓▓▓▓▓▓▓▓▓▓▓▓▓▓▓

████████████████████████████████ chronic sleep deprivation became a way of life for the junior officers.

As I worked ████████████████████████ I realized with a start that I might already have a potential ████████ star on my hands ████████████████████████████████. Nicholas was an excellent ████ ████ writer and highly intelligent, probably too much so for his own good ██ ████████ ████ ██ ██ ██ ██ ████████████ ████████████████████ After meeting with Nicholas several times ████████████████████████████████████ ████████████, I had a chance to evaluate what was wrong and try to figure out how to fix it. First of all, his enormous ego, already quite developed—since most ████ males from birth are led to believe by their mothers that they are precious beyond words—needed some ████ stroking. That was an easy fix. Second, like most humans he wanted someone to listen. So I listened to him talk about his personal problems and frustrations—everything from discussions over which school to send his child, to musing about buying a vacation house, to exasperations with both his wife and mistress. I would occasionally nod or make appropriate noises. Finally, and perhaps most important, he craved a challenge. If he felt he wasn't being pushed, he stopped caring. ████████████████ ████████████████████████—he was bored. So I began to use all the tools at my disposal to make his ██ meetings worth his while. I educated myself ████████████████████████████████ to sharpen and focus our questions, ████████████████████████████. Over several months, the intense care and feeding of Nicholas worked ████████████████████████████ ████████████████████████████ ████████████████████████████

After working with Nicholas ████████████████ as I was taking furious notes I looked down to see his hand resting on my thigh. "What are you doing?" I asked with scorn in my voice. This was a battle I didn't need to fight right now. Nicholas had always been an incorrigible flirt, and we had become good friends, but this time he had gone too far. He took his ever-present pipe from between his teeth and looked at me with big, brown, suddenly teenage-lovesick eyes. "You are so beautiful," he said, and leaned in for a kiss. What ensued was a scene out of a TV sitcom: I jumped up and Nicholas literally chased me around the room as I dodged and moved furniture between us. After what seemed like eternity, while I shouted "You are crazy, stop this!" we stopped to catch our breath and glare at each other over the round wooden dining table. "Nicholas, this is just not on. Bad idea. It'll only get you in trouble and stop us from working together at all." He chuckled and settled back down on the couch docile as a lapdog and declaring that nothing of the sort would happen again. Perhaps he felt his ▮▮▮▮ heritage demanded that he make a pass at a younger female, or was just curious about what would happen. Maybe it was just an insider's joke for him. I'll never know. I just remember feeling both furious and foolish and wondering how I could have handled it better or differently. When I returned to the office later that afternoon, I didn't tell anyone what had ▮▮▮

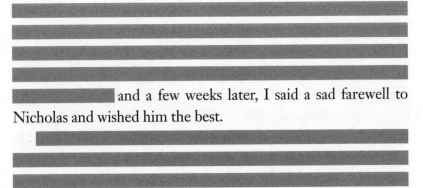

▮▮▮▮▮▮ and a few weeks later, I said a sad farewell to Nicholas and wished him the best.

████████████████████████████ It was like being in sales—for every hundred calls you made, perhaps ten would buy the encyclopedia set. I had been working on ████ a highly intelligent and well-connected ██████ who enjoyed the confidence of some of ██████ most elite political players, for some months. I had developed him first through meetings at his office, and later, during long lunches discussing U.S. ██████ relations. I had worked hard to show him that I was ██████████████████████████ ████████████ the person he should to talk to if he wanted to get his views to those who mattered in Washington. ████████████ ████████████████████████████

fought a bad case of nerves as I made my way to my meeting ████ ████.

We were sitting in a bustling tavern ██ ████████████████ ████████████████████████████. As the lunch crowd thinned and the waiter cleared the last of our ████████████ ████████████████████████████

didn't hide his high opinion of himself, often offering his ideas after taking long self-important drags on a Marlboro; however, his smarts and experience more than made up for his bravado. I took a small sip of ████████████████████ wine that somehow perfectly complements ██████ cuisine, and then a deep breath. "You know, ██████ your insights are brilliant and absolutely on the mark. They could really help Washington understand the changing political landscape ██████ ██████

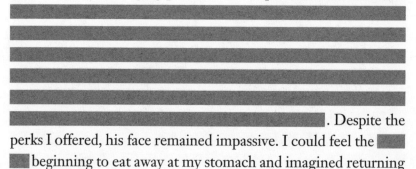

████████████████████████. Despite the perks I offered, his face remained impassive. I could feel the ████ ██ beginning to eat away at my stomach and imagined returning to the office empty-handed, my colleagues sympathetic but perhaps secretly a little pleased. When I finally paused for breath, he leaned toward me, his face so close I could see the stubble on his cheeks and the pores of his nose. After what seemed like an interminable silence, he exhaled smoke through his nostrils, smiled, and whispered in his heavy ▮▮▮▮ accent, "What took you so long?"

▮▮▮▮▮▮▮▮▮▮▮▮▮▮▮▮▮▮▮▮▮▮▮▮▮▮▮▮▮▮▮▮▮▮▮▮▮▮

▮▮▮▮▮▮▮▮▮▮ I felt some of the self-imposed pressure ease just a bit; I had proved to myself that I could do this bizarre but exhilarating job after all. However, I began to ask myself questions about what my work asked of me. ▮▮▮▮▮▮▮▮▮▮▮▮▮▮▮

▮▮▮▮▮▮▮▮▮▮▮▮▮▮▮▮▮▮▮▮▮▮▮▮▮▮▮▮▮▮▮▮▮▮▮▮▮▮

▮▮▮▮▮▮▮▮▮ I began to take stock of what my work really entailed, the ethics of it and how it affected the lives of my agents and their families. After observing many operational scenarios and seeing the effects of CIA activities play out in real life ▮▮▮▮▮▮▮ over many months, I came to some conclusions from which I have never wavered. In some cases, such as terrorists, Eastern Bloc officials (during the Cold War), or ▮▮▮▮▮▮▮▮▮▮▮▮ , individuals associated with the proliferation of weapons of mass destruction, there was no doubt that convincing them to provide the United States with privileged information was of the highest value to our national security. Other agents, ▮▮▮▮▮▮▮▮▮▮ ▮▮▮▮▮▮▮▮▮▮▮▮▮▮▮▮▮ did not contribute so sensationally to U.S. policy-making needs but they nevertheless played a vital role in keeping bilateral relationships on track. ▮▮▮▮▮▮▮▮▮ ▮▮▮▮▮▮▮▮▮▮▮▮▮ the good people of the State Department can only do so much to build and maintain a productive dialogue between the United States and another country. Sometimes events unfold so quickly that multiple channels, including sensitive ones from clandestine sources, are necessary to contain a crisis. I believed then, as I do today, that a strong intelligence service is essential to our country's security and it is sometimes the most effective means of providing U.S. policy-makers with the information necessary to make the right decisions to keep our nations strong. ▮▮▮▮▮▮▮▮▮▮▮▮ I felt a deep sense of personal obligation toward the agents ▮▮▮▮▮▮▮▮▮▮ handled. I made sure that my tradecraft practices were as solid as possible and always tried to deal with the agents with integrity, respect, and compassion. The CIA likes to point out that it couldn't do its job if it only recruited Boy Scouts, and operations officers often speak of their agents with bloodcurdling disdain. But while I came across some seriously flawed agents who were impossible to like or admire on any level, I treated them all decently; it was the least I could do, given their decision to help my country.

▮▮▮▮▮▮▮▮▮▮▮▮▮ John, ▮▮▮▮▮▮▮ had nothing but disgust for the CIA, and considered ▮▮▮ dirty rotten ▮
▮▮▮▮▮▮▮▮▮▮▮▮▮▮▮▮▮▮▮▮▮▮▮▮▮▮▮▮▮▮
John's opinion was shared by many, although not all, of his colleagues, who saw in the CIA the cowboy behavior that gave the United States a bad name and made their job ▮▮▮▮▮ ▮▮▮▮ that much harder. Their resentment was further fueled by the sense that the CIA officers tended to get ▮▮▮▮▮▮▮ more "perks." These feelings were strongly reciprocated by the CIA, who viewed State Department officers as feckless, ineffective

whiners who worked strictly bankers' hours. Although both sides contained elements of truth, more should have been done to educate young recruits at both the Agency and State about what the other side brought to the table. I thanked John for his information and promised to pass it along

While I accumulated these cultural experiences, I was increasingly baffled that many of my colleagues seemed determined to despise and its inhabitants, seeing only the frustrations and the shortcomings of life . They seemed to dwell on the many negatives to living abroad, raving

▮▮▮▮▮▮▮▮ about the impossible driving habits of ▮▮▮▮▮▮▮▮, the puzzling lack of street signs, bizarre store hours (someone drew up a matrix so you could tell what time your neighborhood pharmacy was open if it was Wednesday, summer, and in the afternoon), and the corrupt and nearly nonfunctioning nationally owned telephone service where you could wait for years to get a phone line. It was primarily, although not exclusively, the nonworking wives of ▮▮▮▮▮▮ officers who complained the most bitterly. While their husbands worked within a sort of small America, they were left alone and expected to navigate a foreign culture, get their children into school, negotiate with the landlord, fix the car, deal with the sullen shopkeepers, and then pleasantly socialize in the evenings to help advance their husbands' careers. Many families found solace at the "Hamburger Hut" on Saturday afternoons on the U.S. base ▮▮▮▮▮▮▮▮▮▮▮▮▮ ▮▮▮▮▮▮▮. Here, between bites of their burgers and fries, they groused with other Americans about living conditions and reminisced about how much better it was back in Smalltown, U.S.A. The PX was a mob scene on weekends as ▮▮▮▮▮▮ staff loaded their carts with American-made goods that were impossible to find at that time ▮▮▮▮▮: fabric softener sheets, Frosted Flakes, electronics, and the latest CDs from Sinead O'Connor and Madonna. ▮▮▮▮▮▮▮▮▮▮▮▮▮▮▮▮ I had nothing but contempt for this weak display of homesickness. I had not moved three thousand miles away from home to re-create it all over again. Most weekends, I zoomed onto the base only long enough to fill up my car with the cheap gas, and then drove off to explore the countryside in all its variety and magnificence.

▮▮▮▮▮▮▮▮▮▮▮▮▮▮▮▮▮▮▮▮▮▮▮▮▮▮

▮▮▮▮▮▮▮▮▮▮▮▮▮▮▮▮▮, I figured I was taking my boss's advice to heart ▮▮▮▮▮▮▮▮▮▮▮▮▮▮

Many of my weekend trips ▓▓▓▓▓▓▓▓▓▓▓▓▓▓▓▓▓▓▓▓▓▓▓

▓▓▓▓▓▓▓▓▓▓▓▓▓▓▓▓▓▓▓▓▓▓▓▓▓▓▓▓▓▓▓▓▓▓▓▓▓ had a secret
▓▓▓ agenda. I took several ▓▓▓▓▓ female ▓▓▓▓▓▓▓▓▓
▓▓▓▓▓▓▓▓▓▓▓ on these road trips and I learned more about
their desires and motivations in one weekend than in a slew of
dinner meetings in town. Inviting a male ▓▓▓▓▓▓▓▓ was trick-
ier, for the obvious reason of not wanting to send the wrong,
romantic signals. In those cases, I included a small group of
friends to block any assumptions that more than platonic friendship was involved, ▓▓▓▓▓▓▓▓▓▓▓▓▓▓▓▓▓▓▓▓▓▓▓▓▓
▓▓▓▓▓▓▓▓▓▓▓▓▓▓▓▓▓ I selfishly got to explore one
of the most interesting countries in Europe while doing my job.
It was a good thing that this was a built-in perk, because no
one joined the Agency to get rich. My hard-earned language
skills improved, encouraged by city-dwellers and villagers alike
who absolutely lit up when they saw a blond, blue-eyed woman
attempting to speak their language ▓▓▓▓▓▓▓▓▓▓▓▓▓▓▓

██

██████ my tour ████████ wound down. Professionally, it had been a success. I discovered that I loved my job and was getting better at it ████████████████████████

████████████████████████. My supervisors had consistently given me outstanding evaluations on my annual reviews. Personally, I had come to love ██████ and made good friends ████████
████████████████████, and I had traveled throughout the region as much as I could afford or justify. I began to think about my next tour when the cable from Headquarters arrived. I read, "We look forward to your return. Please report to ██████████ [essentially, the Chief of assignments for a division] to discuss your next assignment upon return from annual leave." My heart sank. This wasn't good. Usually an officer moved directly on to a second tour in the field if the first one had been successful, ██████
████████████████████████████████ and the Agency was not hiring enough new officers to fill the often boring but nonetheless critical support jobs at Headquarters. A new edict required first-tour officers to return to Washington at the completion of their assignments. This made for quite a bit of grumbling in the ranks; we had all joined the Agency anticipat-

ing spending the bulk of our careers overseas because not only was overseas work more professionally challenging, it was also the fastest way to get promoted. The last thing I wanted to do was return to Headquarters, but I had few alternatives. I had not acquired a "godfather" as some of my male peers had done. There were few senior female operations officers to act as mentors and the male officers seemed naturally to gravitate toward the young-buck officers who reminded them of themselves at an earlier, hungrier stage.

As I packed up to leave, my mind raced with plans. ▆▆▆▆▆
▆▆▆▆▆▆▆▆▆▆▆▆▆▆▆▆▆▆▆▆▆▆▆▆▆▆▆▆
▆▆▆▆▆▆▆▆▆▆▆▆▆▆▆▆▆▆▆▆▆▆▆▆▆▆▆▆
▆▆▆▆▆▆▆▆▆▆▆▆▆▆▆▆▆▆▆▆▆▆▆▆▆▆▆▆
▆▆▆▆▆▆▆▆▆▆▆▆▆▆▆▆▆▆▆▆▆▆▆▆▆▆▆▆
▆▆▆▆▆▆▆▆▆▆▆▆▆▆▆▆▆▆▆▆▆▆▆▆▆▆▆▆
▆▆▆▆▆▆▆▆▆▆▆▆▆▆▆ I had enjoyed an easygoing camaraderie with my colleagues at the Station, but realized that as much as I valued their company, it wasn't a prerequisite to my professional success or personal contentment. To my surprise, I realized that I had an entrepreneurial streak, and wanted to test it further. As I wrapped up breakable items in newspaper, I began to develop a plan ▆▆▆▆▆▆▆▆▆▆▆▆▆▆▆▆▆
▆▆▆▆▆▆▆▆▆▆▆▆▆▆

CHAPTER 3

When I checked back into Headquarters in Langley, Virginia ███
████████, I reacquainted myself with the vast building and its
endless, featureless white corridors. It had just been significantly
enlarged with a modern new addition, and connected to the
"old" Headquarters building by two long sunny hallways and a
soaring atrium anchored at one end by an enormous American
flag. Besides the faint glamour of the new building, Headquarters boasted a redesigned and spruced-up cafeteria, dry cleaning
services, a small gym, and an enlarged gift shop where you could
buy nearly anything from shot glasses to baseball caps embla-
zoned with the Agency seal—very popular with visitors. ████

Although my initial poly had not been painful, it is an experience that no one ever likes. This time, however, I approached the dreaded exam armed with a colleague's advice: treat it like a Catholic confession. That is, tell the examiner absolutely everything, every excruciating detail that you think might have relevance to the question posed. At a minimum, you'll bore the polygrapher to tears. I used this tactic, dredging up every possible incident that might negatively affect my responses and it worked like a charm; I was in and out of the claustrophobic exam room in a record three hours.

Like the unofficial Army motto, "Hurry up and wait," after blazing through all obligations

To my delight, I discovered that developmental relationships were easy to get started and maintain. Early on in my tour, I was invited to a large wedding in Eastern Europe. At the boisterous reception, where the bride's enormous white wedding dress skirt was pinned with gold coins, I chatted up a very senior military officer who worked in that country's intelligence service. The next day, another wedding guest and I were invited to have breakfast at his modest home with his family. Over a traditional breakfast of honey, yogurt, olives, and delicious chewy bread, I heard enough to convince me that the officer had information and access of interest to me. The hunt was on.

████████████████████████████I began to travel throughout Europe on various operational missions and to attend conferences to build my cover. I felt like I was back in school again, learning as much as I could, as quickly as possible, about my industry and venture capital. At the same time, I reveled in the freedom I had to pursue my own initiatives, and constantly sent cables back to Headquarters asking for "traces" (that is, information from Agency files, if available) on individuals of possible operational interest. Soon, though, something began to bother me: there was a distinct lack of direction or interest in the replies from Headquarters. I grew alarmed, thinking that Headquarters was unhappy with my performance. Was I going after the right targets? Was I aggressive enough? Was my tradecraft not up to snuff? I was prepared for a lag in response given my new circumstances, but I was puzzled. The Agency had sunk a tremendous amount of time and money into my training and I felt underutilized. I vowed not to become a diva, constantly pestering Headquarters with demands and queries, ███████████████who did not understand it was perceived with eye-rolling and resentment for the extra worked it caused ██████████████What was the matter? ██

█████████████████████████████We were knocking, but no one was home at Headquarters. █████████████████ ██████████████████gossiped about the malaise and lack of purpose we were experiencing from Agency leadership. Whispers about the Agency being "risk adverse" became increasingly louder. ███████████████████████████████████████ ██

A ██████████ friend of mine with many years of experience in

Africa and Europe mused sadly that the Agency had the capability to be used as a finely machined precision surgical tool but instead was about as subtle and delicate as a wooden club.

While I was trying to get some operations off the ground ████ ████████████ I searched for a respected senior female officer to help me. I wasn't looking for a formal mentoring relationship, just a model who could show me how to retain my femininity, perhaps have a family, and still be an outstanding operations officer in a male-dominated business. To my dismay, I found that few women had managed to "have it all" and still reach the top ranks of the operations cadre. I wondered how or even if it could be done. ████████████████ the Agency had ordered a classified "Glass Ceiling" study in 1991 to investigate complaints that female operations officers were not being promoted as quickly or given challenging assignments in comparison to their male colleagues. According to the study, in 1991 women made up 40 percent of the workforce but held only 9 percent of the Senior Intelligence Service (SIS) positions, that is, those above the rank of GS-15. In the DO, a traditional male bastion, the numbers were even worse: women made up 17 percent of the directorate but only accounted for 1 percent of the SIS ranks. The female operations officers didn't like the obvious inequities, but it seemed there was little we could do to improve the situation, other than keep trying to rise through the ranks and change the system from within. The dinosaurs were still running the show in the DO and most just thought women were not up to the job. As Melissa Boyle Mahle observes in her book *Denial and Deception: An Insider's View of the CIA from Iran-Contra to 9/11*, "there was a strong belief that women could not recruit agents, the core job requirement of the directorate. . . . Women were placed in assignments destined to be failures because of lack of management and peer support and lack of operational assignments in the field. Many women tried, but after a field assignment or two, assessed the career as a losing battle and moved elsewhere within the CIA or left the organization." ███████████ in 1992 a female officer initiated a class-action lawsuit. Typically resistant to any sort of change to the status quo, the CIA pushed back against the suit's organizers. Furthermore, Boyle Mahle notes, "there was widespread belief that those who complained about unequal treatment or harassment would create career advancement problems for themselves." After growing up with parents who never thought that my gender should inhibit anything I wished to pursue, as well as having been influenced by the 1972 Title IX amendment, which mandated that women's sports in schools should receive as much funding as men's, the fact of women's diminished status in the workplace was a revelation to me.

was skeptical about whether anything would really change. Although I had not faced any overt discrimination because of my gender up to that point ████████████, I felt that in general, most female officers didn't even know they were at bat when the ball was being pitched. That is, decisions about which good cases and operations would go to which officers were made behind closed management doors in field Stations and Headquarters. Many times, I believe, female officers were simply not even under consideration. There was a natural tendency for male CIA managers to see themselves reflected in the young, ambitious male officers in the

Station, and remember when they were starting out and hungry. Female officers were usually only considered as an afterthought.

CHAPTER 4

Love and the Island of Misfit Toys

Outside the dust kicked up from the windswept mesa and the air was bitterly cold. Eight of us sat around a beat-up government-issued table in a small dingy room with our coats draped across our shoulders. A large model of a nineteenth-century whaling ship perched inexplicably on a wooden sideboard. Our chairs were lumpy and uncomfortable and the harsh fluorescent lighting made us all look pale and tired. Still, I was thrilled to be on the compound of the highly secretive Los Alamos National Laboratory with our country's brightest nuclear experts. After its founding in 1943 to develop the world's first nuclear bomb, the laboratory was charged with ensuring the safety and reliability of the nation's nuclear stockpile. A couple of senior Agency officers and I had flown there to find out whether any of its latest unconventional research could be used to thwart our enemies' attempts to acquire nuclear weapons. While much of the technical discussion was incomprehensible to me—I was a liberal arts major, after all—I knew how operations worked, which was why I'd been included.

As one of the scientists laid out blueprints of his latest efforts on the table, we heard the steady report of hard metal pounding metal. Everyone stopped talking as the clanging was followed by a small, muffled explosion. We eyed each other nervously until the door creaked open and an elfin face peeked in, the wearer's expression sheepish. "Sorry. Under control now." The room let out a collective sigh. A few moments later, we all moved out to the area where the sound of the explosion had come from. As the door slid back again, I saw a huge dark warehouse space, piled high with gadgets, tools, and duct tape. It put me in mind of the laboratory of "Q," James Bond's gadget man, who could outfit 007 with such things as a sports car that could double as a submarine. "Would you like a tour?" asked one of the nuclear scientists. We were going to see some of the secret equipment that the Los Alamos group had worked on for months. *Finally*, I thought, I'm doing exactly what I joined the CIA to do.

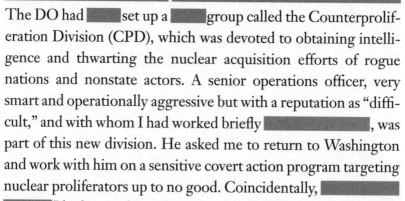

The DO had ▇▇ set up a ▇▇ group called the Counterproliferation Division (CPD), which was devoted to obtaining intelligence and thwarting the nuclear acquisition efforts of rogue nations and nonstate actors. A senior operations officer, very smart and operationally aggressive but with a reputation as "difficult," and with whom I had worked briefly ▇▇▇▇▇▇▇▇▇, was part of this new division. He asked me to return to Washington and work with him on a sensitive covert action program targeting nuclear proliferators up to no good. Coincidentally, ▇▇▇▇▇▇ ▇▇▇▇▇ I had recently read a magazine article about the activities of a nonprofit group, The Center for Nonproliferation Studies, based in Monterey, California, and I thought that their work was meaningful and intriguing. The profiles of the Center's stars made them sound a little like case officers, and they traveled widely trying to save the world from nuclear annihilation. I had entertained the notion of sending my résumé to the Center just to see what might happen. Although I had no training in nuclear studies, I was hopeful that I might have other skills they would find useful. I also considered staying in Europe, which I loved, to find work in journalism that would utilize much of the skills I already had. The cable that came out of the blue to ask me to join CPD changed all those calculations in an instant. Besides terrorism, I thought, the most vital issue in U.S. national security was the threat of nuclear proliferation. Here was an opportunity to stay under the CIA's umbrella, with a career I loved, but currently found disappointing. The thought of working on counterproliferation operations revived my interest in the Agency's work.

It is shocking to realize that prior to 1996 there wasn't a single U.S. government entity devoted to the growing proliferation threat. The 1995 sarin gas attack in the Tokyo subway highlighted this gap in our national security apparatus. In response, the CIA created CPD under the command of Deputy Director of Operations Jim Pavitt, since retired. Pavitt, a career operations officer, was a popular choice in the Agency. Usually well dressed in a blue blazer and a perky *pochette*, and with a slightly manic side to his character, he quickly set up a division whose mandate was to gather intelligence in countries like North Korea, Libya, Iran, and Syria that were suspected of harboring dreams of becoming a nuclear state. Prior to the conception of CPD, the issue of counterproliferation was confined to two or, at the most, three officers in each individual geographic division. That is, EUR had a counterproliferation focal point, NE (Near East) had another, and so on. There was no overarching structure or communication, much less a comprehensive U.S.

counterproliferation strategy. I thought that the creation of CPD was an opportunity to make the CIA relevant again.

To get CPD operations off the ground, Pavitt handpicked a dozen or so officers. Many of these men and women were undeniably brilliant and experienced, but many were eccentric and didn't fit in well in the traditional divisions, which were based on geographical, not topical, boundaries. As a result, CPD quickly became known as the "island of misfit toys" for the diverse and sometimes flaky nature of its early staffers. The older divisions eyed it with deep suspicion and distrust. Because counterproliferation was a transnational issue, we didn't own any "real estate" as the Near East or European divisions did and so every operation in another division's region had to be done with its cooperation and consent. Naturally, this led to savage bureaucratic turf battles. Field Stations around the globe gave the new kid on the block short shrift and many times didn't even bother to answer CPD's cables from Headquarters. In the post-9/11 world, with its huge paradigm shift in how we ranked our national security priorities, real money started to pour into CPD and the division suddenly became more popular. Once it became clear to the powerful Chiefs of Station that the only way they were going to get more money for their operations was to generate and support counterproliferation operations, they became much more compliant and friendly toward CPD.

One day I got on the elevator with a grandmotherly woman perfectly dressed in a Chanel suit and a beauty-parlor coiffure and wheeling an elaborate baby carriage. I peeked around the top expecting to find a blissfully sleeping child, and instead saw two cream-colored pugs, perfectly dressed in Burberry plaid coats and collars. Their deep brown eyes stared at me impassively █████████████ ███████████████

████████████████████████████████████

[REDACTED]

Joe and I were immediately consumed by our respective responsibilities; [REDACTED] I was happily back in full-throttle operations, traveling so much that I sometimes had to check the hotel's notepad by the bed first thing in the morning to remind myself where I was. [REDACTED]

[REDACTED] Unlike the string of lackluster and feckless DCIs that followed William Casey, George Tenet actually appeared to covet the job. The others after Casey had made little attempt to hide their view that the DCI job was a stepping-stone to something bigger. Tenet's immediate predecessor, John Deutsch, had been a disaster for the Agency. Gossips noted that when he deigned to walk the halls of Headquarters, he did so with a security detail in tow—as if the inhabitants of the asylum would jump out of their cages and tackle him. So Tenet's penchant for suddenly showing up in your office unannounced, unlit stogie in hand, to ask, "How's it going?" was a refreshing change. On many occasions he could be found pushing his tray down the cafeteria line along with the rest of the lunchtime troops, and that simple act alone earned him huge respect and admiration from the professional cadre. More important, he talked about the CIA taking risks again, about personal accountability and rebuilding a demoralized DO that had been gutted by mid-1990s budget cuts. He oversaw the revamping of the Agency's recruitment efforts to bring in more and diverse intelligence officers and streamline the process so they wouldn't wait years for their security clearances and a job offer in those early years of his tenure. I, along with most of the Agency's employees, came to respect his leadership and focus on operations.

As I settled into my new job, I noticed an obvious shift in power from the field to Headquarters. Vastly superior communications that provided faster, more secure, and sometimes real-time connections allowed Headquarters to give more input as an operation was unfolding rather than relying on the field Station to tell them what had happened after the fact. Second, shifting emphasis to the transnational issues of counterterrorism and counterproliferation operations meant that sometimes only Headquarters saw the whole picture and the field Station just had a small piece of the action. Chiefs of Station still zealously guarded their prerogatives and turf, but out of necessity, they had to cooperate more with other field and Headquarters operational elements. When the counterterrorism center (CTC) had first opened in the mid-1980s, it exemplified a major change in how to approach operations. For the first time, operations officers and analysts sat side by side, comparing notes and contributing to the whole; the idea was that the integration of these two elements would produce faster and better-sourced intelligence. Prior to the creation of the giant bullpen that became CTC, Headquarters was literally a building divided into halves. One side was devoted to operations, and the other to analysis of intelligence, and you knew when you left the end of the operations corridor and stepped over into the usually quieter and more sedate analytical half. Having analysts aware of the sources and operations to bring in the information was thought to have a deleterious effect on the quality of intelligence they produced and strict protocols between the two sides were in place and observed.

As CTC broke down this model, CPD took the integration

concept and advanced it considerably by attracting officers and experts from throughout the intelligence community to work on the complex problems of counterproliferation together. In addition, CPD did much to create and nurture an entirely new cadre of operations officers called "targeteers." These professionals were a hybrid: they had been given operational training, but tended to be more analytical in their thinking. Their responsibilities were just as the job title suggests—providing focused and coherent targeting to the officers in the field. By culling through thousands of open-source databases and also using classified operational reports, they really could help you find the needle in the haystack. In an increasingly complex world, and with so much information available on the Internet, their assistance in keeping an operation on track proved to be vital.

I found that I thrived amid the patriotic zeal and a renewed sense of mission. During this time,  This effort was enormous and required a cast of sometimes bizarre agents called upon to play a specific role in hopes of luring our target closer to our objective.

Actually, it was just these sorts of sudden detours and re-verses that made operations fascinating for me ▓▓▓▓▓. Being able to think on your feet and acknowledge that Murphy's Law lurked everywhere was critical to success. Being prepared with plan B was always a good idea, as was strictly adhering to security practices. The small group working on this project spent hun-dreds of man-hours planning and traveling to far-flung places to brief senior management on a need-to-know basis about what we were doing. Part of the equation was the constant care and feed-ing of agents, ▓▓▓▓▓▓▓▓, so that they could continue to con-tribute to the operation. Everything from negotiations about pay to tax form discrepancies to suspicious wives to errant children to serious illnesses became our responsibility. Being a case officer is a little like being a mother and you can easily become the focus of the ire and frustration leaking from other things in the agent's life. Because of the inherently secretive nature of the relationship between agent and case officer, it somehow breaks down normal social inhibitions about discussing sensitive subjects. And per-haps because I was female, I heard way too much in the way of intimate details of my agents' lives. Solving their problems, or at least helping them feel better about them, is essential to keeping the ultimate success of the operation. So, although it's not taught in training, you quickly find out that as a case officer you've become part confessor, part psychologist, and part financial adviser. It certainly keeps the job interesting.

Sometimes a case officer just needs to be the agent's friend. Romney, an agent who played a key role in one aspect of our operation, was a bit of an outsider in his straitlaced community.

He had divorced his wife of decades and his five children were furious with him. He was still vigorous in his seventies and was contemplating getting a European mail-order bride to staunch his loneliness. After several days of intense meetings to debrief him on his latest trip abroad and plan for next steps, he invited us to his childhood home several hours away. My supervisor, Bill, and I declined his offer to fly with him in his small plane, not needing that much adventure, but arrived via car at his lakeside homestead in nearly desolate countryside untouched by modern development. His father had built the home at the turn of the twentieth century, and when Romney turned the door handle to let us in, we stepped into a perfectly preserved time capsule of the 1930s. The house had been restored, or at least kept in the exact condition it was when Romney was a boy. From the wood-burning stove, to the shelf of decaying children's books circa 1925, to the June 1932 calendar nailed to the wall, it was astounding. I stopped to marvel at the wood tombstone-style radio around which I am sure they listened to Roosevelt's "fireside chats" during the Depression. Romney enthusiastically pointed out all the small home's features, and I couldn't tell if he knew the whole thing was a museum piece or he thought it was normal. Watching his bounce and animation as he showed us around the house and the expansive property, I silently dubbed him the "world's oldest Boy Scout." After this strange visit, Romney became easier to work with, although years later, after I was off the project I heard that he had completely disregarded some stern warnings from Bill about his business dealings and was promptly investigated by the FBI.

██████ space at Headquarters was always at a premium. The Chief and Deputy, along with a few others in senior division management, got the obligatory corner offices in the new Headquarters building with real windows. The rest of the division had to beg and scramble for whatever empty space became available. Most of us were delegated to the vast subterranean vaults that had been divided into shoulder-high cubicles. The great perk of being a manager meant you had an office with a real door, so you could at least make your doctor appointments in private. Since there were no windows, CPD employees checked the weather on their computer to see if they needed to take an umbrella with them on their way out the door in the evening. Despite the substandard, crowded working conditions and the continuous complaints of recycled, bacteria-laden air—one employee's cold meant two others would have it the next day—morale in CPD was high as the division grew at an astounding pace and began to coalesce as a respected operational entity within the CIA.

With such an ambitious mandate and strong support from management, CPD ops officers quickly developed several cunning operations designed to infiltrate procurement networks and wreak havoc. With our high esprit de corps, there was plenty of good-natured competition to see who could come up with the most creative and effective operations. I shared my quarters, dubbed the "secret squirrel den"—complete with the rare and much-coveted windows—with a small group of people devoted to tracking and bringing down the A. Q. Khan nuclear proliferation network. Khan, a Pakistani, was a one-man proliferator. For decades he had made a personal fortune by selling high-tech nuclear components to Libya and North Korea, among others. Operations against this elusive and cagey target ▓▓▓▓▓▓▓ culminated in October 2003 with the dramatic seizure of uranium enrichment gas-centrifuge components bound for Libya's secret nuclear research facilities. Muammar Qadaffi's public announcement that Libya was abandoning work on its nuclear program in December 2003 was one of CPD's most brilliant successes to date and the result of years of unrelenting work by dedicated CIA professionals. It showcased what worked best about the Agency when it had a clear mission, management support, and the right mix of experts and policy-makers willing to take risks.

As I worked with our small team on our sensitive operations, I traveled often and sometimes at a moment's notice. ████████ ██ ████████ I traveled domestically and abroad using a variety of aliases, confident that my tradecraft skills and solid cover would keep me out of the worst trouble. ████████████████████ ██.

I drew on my business experiences and personal situation to create a credible and airtight cover for living in Washington and traveling widely. When I was in Washington rather than on the road, I drove every day to Headquarters, always taking different routes and remaining acutely aware of my surroundings. I had no fear that the Russian or other intelligence services could discover my true identity and follow me to Headquarters one morning, but old habits die hard. Besides, it just made sense to remain vigilant ████████████████████████████████████ ████████████████████████████████. Lessons learned at the Farm—that most people readily talk about themselves if someone asks the right questions—remained valid.

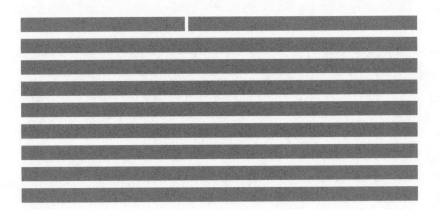

CHAPTER 5

Motherhood

The hospital staff had clearly made a grievous error, a terrible mistake; there had to be some protocol in place, some regulation on the books that would not permit them to discharge me with two mewing newborns, barely weighing five and four pounds each. I was now responsible for two babies who weighed less than a bag of flour. The twins had been born five weeks prematurely, which, for twin births, was normal, and, given advanced neonatal care, was fully within the safety zone. Still, my anxiety skyrocketed as I contemplated taking these incredibly tiny babies home just three days after their birth. Their "sucking reflex" was not yet fully developed, meaning they would have trouble taking nourishment, but the nursing staff paid little heed to my mounting questions and concerns. Undeterred, they filled a plastic bag with extra-small knitted caps, some diapers, and lots of literature on the importance of putting an infant to sleep on her back, and packed us into our car with the spanking new baby seats. By the time Joe drove all of us up to our house ten minutes later, I was in a full-blown panic. I have never been as scared and overwhelmed in my life as when I contemplated what seemed to me an insurmountable task of caring for and raising the two bundled-up babies. I was literally shaking as I unbuckled my sleeping son from his seat and carried him inside; I had no idea that the challenge I would face over the next year would make my ▓▓▓▓▓▓ ▓▓▓▓▓▓▓▓▓ look like a day at the beach.

Like most couples, before we married, Joe and I briefly discussed having children. The first time, we were in Paris, walking along the Seine late at night. The Hale-Bopp comet was directly overhead, on one of its closest approaches to earth, with its fierce brightness and long silvery tail making a spectacle in the sky. I knew that Joe had two teenage children, Jody (or Joseph C. Wilson V) and Sabrina, from an earlier marriage. I braced myself in case he said he didn't want any more children and was perfectly satisfied with the two wonderful ones he already had. I, on the other hand, wanted at least one child. I had no overt maternal instincts and had virtually no experience with babies or small children, but I just knew that it was a life experience I wanted, if at all possible. As a friend of mine said after having his son, "Babies relieve you of toxic self-absorption." To my relief, Joe quickly agreed to have a child together and it felt as if all my dreams were coming true. The next day, on a lark, I visited a French astrologer, Rosine, who had been warmly recommended by a mutual friend. I had never been to an astrologer or palm reader, and carried a healthy skepticism about her alleged ability to see into the future. As Rosine pored over the colorful chart she had prepared for my visit, she pointed out a small symbol and announced I would have twins. "No, that's not me, that's because of the person I'm involved with—he has twins." "Oh no," Rosine said. "His twins are here," she said, pointing to another exotic symbol on the circular chart, "yours are here." I shrugged, and when the session was over, I paid and walked out of her chic

Right Bank apartment.  I called Joe from the doctor's office. "Honey, the doctor says he hears two heartbeats—we're having twins." Joe let out a delighted yell.

I reveled in the last weeks of a smooth and happy pregnancy, with little to do but read for pleasure or watch old movies at night with Joe. I had worked nonstop since graduating from college at twenty-one, and I enjoyed the break from my ever-serious job. But by December 1999 when my doctor ordered me to modified bed rest, I was happy to comply. I had put on so much weight that just climbing one level of stairs had me gasping for breath. Finally, early on the morning of January 11, 2000, Joe drove me to the hospital and within an hour of checking in, I was whisked into the delivery room with what appeared to me to be a cast of thousands, ready to assist. With a ridiculous amount of ease and relatively little pain, Trevor Rolph Wilson was born at 10:28 A.M., and Samantha Diana Finnell Wilson followed at 10:58. Joe had barely returned from parking the car. Despite their small size, they were perfect and the doctors gave them both a "10" on the Apgar scale, used to score the health of newborns. Trevor had a little fluid in his lungs and was taken to the neonatal intensive care unit (NICU) for closer observation. Samantha, although tinier, was put into her clear plastic bin, along with at least a dozen other newborns, in the regular nursery. I was wheeled back to my room, and promptly ordered lunch.

Elatedly, Joe and I called my parents and friends with the good news. Soon he had to leave for a business meeting and I knew my parents wouldn't arrive for a few more hours, so I planned to enjoy a nap. After pushing aside the tray of bland hospital food and settling in for a rest, I thought of my friends' tales of painful forty-eight-hour labor, emergency C-sections, births that went awry at the last moment, and other horror stories that pregnant women pass among themselves. I was smug. I had sailed through one of the defining moments of a woman's life with ease and looked forward to having my new babies brought into me later that afternoon. I should have known that the euphoria was too good to last.

Late that night, I awoke from a fitful sleep shivering so much with the chills that my teeth were chattering. I thought it might be the onset of an infection and I called the nurse. The Nurse Ratched who came to my door was clearly in no mood for coddling or nurturing a new mother. "It's just your hormones readjusting," she said as she pivoted on her heels and walked out again. I was discharged from the hospital the next day, but the the babies were still there. Trevor was in the NICU, and at five pounds he looked like a pink giant compared to the real preemies weighing two pounds. It was heartbreaking to see these tiny, vulnerable infants alone in their plastic chambers, hooked up to IV lines and beeping monitors. According to the maternity ward doctors, Trevor and Samantha could be discharged on Thursday, just two days after they were born. But because Joe and I felt that they weren't ready to come home yet, I pleaded with the staff to keep them one more day. I was sternly told that insurance would not pay for the extra day—the expense would have to come out of our pocket. I agreed immediately. I thought with envy of the 1960s, when my mother and every other woman in America stayed in the hospital for a week after delivery, complications or not. After years of proving I was every bit as tough as a man, I was suddenly longing for pampering and acknowledgment that motherhood was something quite different.

From the moment the babies came home, I was anxious, fretful, and increasingly obsessive. Learning how to nurse didn't help matters. As any new mother can attest, breastfeeding is *not* the most natural thing in the world and to learn how to do it correctly is difficult and frustrating. Despite the stack of books beside my bed and the pile of colorful brochures from the hospital crammed with helpful advice and pictures of nursing positions, it was hard. However, I, like new mothers everywhere in America, felt enormous pressure to breastfeed, especially given the arguments, from pediatricians to the ubiquitous La Leche League, on the significant nutritional, cognitive, and emotional advantages of doing so. You feel that if you give your infant formula, you'd probably let them suck on lead paint chips and put the car seat in backward. It simply isn't done if you want to be considered a caring mother. In my case, our learning curve was further exacerbated by my twins' underdeveloped sucking reflex and the fact that their tiny stomachs could only hold an ounce or two of milk at a time. I was constantly nursing; putting one baby down just to pick up the other. Although my mother and father were staying with us and were incredibly loving and helpful, Joe and I decided to hire a nurse for the first week or so, until we all felt more comfortable with the babies' care and feeding schedules. Elsa was a tall, imposing red-haired woman from Denmark, and her air of authority and no-nonsense manner inspired confidence in me. She commanded us to keep a log of all the feedings and diaper changes so the babies would not become unintentionally dehydrated and we could monitor their progress to ensure they were growing and putting on weight. Of course I meekly agreed, and I obediently kept a notebook by my bed for weeks, noting every ounce consumed, every diaper changed, and every anomaly.

After about two weeks, our pediatrician recommended that we supplement my breast milk with formula to make sure that they were properly nourished. Because the babies still didn't suck very well, we were told not to use bottles, but instead a large dental syringe that essentially squirted the formula into their mouths. It felt a little like feeding a baby bird. Switching between breast and syringe feedings when they took only a few ounces each time and capturing each detail in a notebook soon took its toll. I was exhausted ████████████████████ ████████████████████████████████████ Every baby book out there recommends that the mother sleep when the baby sleeps. If only I could have! Somewhere along the way, I had passed the threshold where I could no longer sleep, even when I desperately wanted or needed to. In this new state of hyperconsciousness, I gave away the high-tech baby monitors I had received as a shower gift. I didn't need to hear every amplified sigh and cry of the babies in their nursery just down the hall because I never slept. I heard everything just fine; I was so high-strung, I swear that I could hear their fingernails grow. It was agony.

As the days turned into weeks, I became increasingly anxious, worried, and unable to cope with the slightest problem. I obsessed over every little health or developmental issue of the twins. Anything to do with their safety put me into near panic—I was on "high alert" all the time and could not shut down or relax. When the babies were about a month old, we hired a wonderful nanny, Monique. Monique is from Haiti and she has a warm and loving embrace. One day, shortly after Monique arrived (we had taught her how to feed the babies with the dental syringe), she found me sobbing uncontrollably in my room; I had been gripped by a sudden fear that Samantha's occasional tremors were the sign of a much more serious neurological condition. A deeply religious woman, Monique held me and promised God would make sure everything would turn out fine. Samantha's shaking turned out to be her premature nervous system developing, but at the time I was beyond reason. I was self-aware enough to see that I found no joy in my babies. The pictures of an adoring mother cuddling her infant with looks of sheer contentment seemed alien. I went through all the motions, but each day I detected a little more distance between myself and reality. I felt hollow inside and was scared to death that someone would discover that I was a terrible mother. I vowed not to let anyone know that I was falling apart piece by piece, but I didn't know how long I could keep up the charade. Sometimes my obsessive actions bubbled to the surface, as when I stood in my walk-in closet making sure all the hangers had exactly the same space between them. After completing that task I moved on to the issue of type. Should I separate the wooden hangers from the padded hangers? Put them all together? Toss them out and use only the pink plastic ones? The questions completely bewildered me, as did the lack of consistency among the skirt hangers, but there wasn't time to buy new ones. Just as I was working out these weighty decisions, I heard a cry from the nursery and had to hurry off. I knew this was not healthy behavior, but I felt powerless to stop it.

In stark contrast to my increasing anxieties and bewilderment was Joe's supreme confidence and delight in the twins. He had baby experience and it showed when he scooped up both of them in his arms and deftly swaddled them in blankets to put them in the crib. I was jealous of his obvious joy and poise with the babies, even when they were screaming.

When his first set of twins had been born, there had been enormous and nearly fatal medical complications with their mother. As a consequence, the babies spent much of their early months with their grandparents in California when Joe returned to Washington for work. Five years later, when Joe and his first wife separated, he knew that he and his children would be separated for years, with only annual summer visits of a few weeks between California and Africa. This caused him great pain. So, it's not surprising that Joe felt blessed that he had another opportunity to get it right and watch his children grow up without being six thousand miles away on another continent.

As I retreated further into myself, not telling anyone of my rising panic, I had more experiences that I could not understand. One day when the babies were a few weeks old, I walked outside to get the mail. Perfectly normal activity, nothing out of the ordinary. Except that on the way to the mailbox, my heart starting beating as though I had just finished a marathon and such a sense of dread came over me that I thought I would have to drop on all fours. Getting the mail seemed impossible. I was frozen on the sidewalk, not knowing what the hell was happening to me. I finally turned back to the house—without the mail—scared to death. I found out later that I had what is commonly called a panic attack. I could no longer trust myself at all—it felt like my body and mind were both betraying me. Around this same time, I also began to hear phantom cries from the babies. Even when I was "resting"—lying on my bed while the babies were napping—I heard them cry. I would race to the nursery only to find them slumbering far more peacefully than I had for weeks and weeks.

I knew this was not normal, but my abilities to cope, problem solve, and adjust to new situations, abilities that had served me so well ▮▮▮▮▮▮▮▮ were beyond my reach now. Finally, I began hunting through the stacks of baby books to try to figure out what was going on inside of me. A few of the books mentioned the "baby blues," a condition experienced by most new mothers in the first weeks after the birth of a baby. It was characterized by crying, "feeling low," and mood swings. The books said it would last a little bit and then go away. I was well beyond that now. I never cried, I was just afraid. The stacks of pamphlets from the hospital were useless as well, with lots of information on the baby's well-being, nothing on that of the mother's. What was going on?

About two months later, Joe's good cheer and patience evaporated, replaced by frustration and anger at my nonresponsiveness and utterly changed personality. "What the hell is the matter with you? You have two beautiful babies, Monique here to help you ▮▮▮▮▮▮▮▮▮▮▮▮ What do you want?" I had nothing to say because I didn't know myself what was happening. The day before, I had been to my doctor for the regular postpartum checkup. As the doctor worked through his checklist, I answered the best I could. He never looked up when he asked, "And how are you feeling?" I wanted to scream that nothing was right, but I was struck dumb. What was really happening just seemed too terrible, too dark, too humiliating to share with anyone. I mumbled "fine" and shuffled out of his office and back home. After Joe's outburst, I realized that I needed help. A few days later I returned to the doctor's office for a minor infection and finally summoned the courage to say, "I don't feel very well." This time, a different doctor, a female, looked up from her clipboard, cocked her head to the side, and took a hard look at me. She left the office and came back with a slip of paper with a name and number on it. "Call Sharmine," she said. "She's a patient of mine that might be able to help you." In my fog of misery I didn't think to ask any more questions; I was just grateful that I had someone to talk to. As soon as I got home, I called Sharmine and for the next hour I sat on the floor of my bedroom closet (hangers perfect) and talked to a complete stranger about my panic, anxieties, and utter despair that I would ever feel well or enthusiastic about life again. Sharmine was compassionate, direct, and best of all, seemed to know how I was feeling. "It sounds like you have postpartum depression and you need to seek professional help." It was literally the first time I had heard the term "postpartum depression" and I was shocked to the core. Throughout birthing classes at the hospital, countless baby books, a doula, and many loving friends, no one—at least that I recalled—ever mentioned the possibility of postpartum depression.

Unfortunately, the nightmare continued. The next day, I called my insurance provider and croaked out that I wanted a psychiatrist who had experience dealing with postpartum depression. From the customer service representative's response, you would have thought I asked for doctors with three arms. They had no such listings, but I did get several names of local psychiatrists who were on our insurance plan. When I called each one, none could see me for at least six weeks. I was in so much pain that they might as well have said it was six years for the next appointment. I got increasingly desperate as I neared the end of the list and began to divulge that I "really am not doing well at all"—a huge admission for me. One doctor asked if I had thoughts of hurting my babies. When I said no, I was apparently knocked down the priority list and was told the next available appointment was five weeks hence. When I called up Sharmine to report that I had been unable to get an appointment sooner, she kindly intervened and arranged for me to see her psychiatrist—off my insurance plan, naturally. Still, I was so relieved that I would get some help soon because every day felt that I had slipped further away.

The only psychiatrists I had ever seen were during my Agency interview process and I had no idea what to expect. The female psychiatrist was a beautiful black woman, dressed in a chic suit. As she settled into the soft leather chair in her perfectly decorated office, I stared at the orchid on the window shelf. She wanted to talk. I wanted a magic pill to feel better. I felt absurd; was I going to say that I was ████████████████ on maternity leave and that through some weird twist of fate I was now losing my mind? Of course not. Some secrets are just too precious. However, I gave her a thorough description of what I had been living through over the last few months and walked out of her office with a prescription for antidepressant and antianxiety medicines. I felt that the slip of paper was gold—my ticket out of the terrifying landscape of my mind.

The nasty secret of antidepressants is that they usually take three to four weeks to "kick in." I wanted immediate relief and the confidence that I could climb out of the deep, dark well I felt I lived in, but day after day I took the tiny pink pill and not much seemed to happen. The antianxiety medication I took at night gave me hellish nightmares and made me feel like a zombie during the day. I quickly tossed them out. I talked with Joe about postpartum depression and what I was doing to treat it. Initially, he seemed reluctant to accept or understand what I was saying;

despite my "flattened" personality, I had done a pretty good job of keeping the most terrifying episodes from him. Finally, I had a breakthrough. I explained that if I had a broken leg, he obviously wouldn't make me hobble around the kitchen to make dinner. This postpartum depression business was just as serious an injury, and although we couldn't see it, it still needed to be treated. With that, Joe was completely on board and supportive, making sure I took the little pink pill every day and arranging for a night nurse to come in once a week so that I could get a full night's rest. He wanted his wife back, too.

Slowly, imperceptibly, over weeks, I began to improve. There were good days and days as dark as the worst times, but the trend was definitely in the right direction. I never woke up one day feeling completely healed, but as the weeks turned into months the anxiety, obsessiveness, and strange behavior began to slowly abate. At five months, the babies started to sleep through the night—a blessed event for any new parent. The fog in my mind was beginning to clear. Each day and night still seemed much longer than twenty-four hours, but I was mending. As the twins developed, I began to enjoy them as I should have from the beginning. Each milestone—sitting up, taking solid food, reaching for objects, pulling themselves up on the furniture to cruise around the room—was reason for delight. When they were about nine months old, I felt strong enough to throw away all the pills.

At Samantha and Trevor's first birthday party on January 11, 2001, I put their miniature cupcakes down in front of them and helped them blow out their single candles. It felt like the first time in a year that I had taken a breath. I had survived the most frightening experience of my life and my babies were thriving. The cliché is true: what doesn't kill you can make you stronger. Intact and on the other side, ▮▮▮▮▮▮▮▮▮▮▮▮ ▮▮▮▮▮ ▮▮. I realized I was enjoying being a stay-at-home mother, but I knew it was not something I wanted to do indefinitely. Before going back to work, however, I was determined to see if there was some way I could help other women experiencing postpartum depression (PPD). If I, a highly educated ███████████ who had demonstrated significant coping skills on the job with a loving family and financial resources, could suffer from PPD, many others out there were going through the same nightmare without the support infrastructure I had.

I began to do some research on PPD and discovered that nearly 15 to 20 percent of new mothers fall prey to this easily diagnosed and treatable mental disorder. Although that percentage is probably underestimated because of new mothers' reluctance to ask for mental help, the numbers still come out to about four hundred thousand women a year in the United States alone. PPD symptoms left untreated can develop into chronic lifelong depression, and the negative consequences for the mother, children, and family are profound. As I spoke to more women and experts in the field, I found that a lack of early diagnosis of PPD is generally the culprit. The pediatrician, who sees the new mother the most in the early months, is more concerned with the health of the infant. The mother's doctor, the obstetrician/gynecologist, usually has a full waiting room and does not specialize in mental disorders. Ironically, there is an easy and fast screening tool for PPD to identify depression in new mothers. Developed in 1987 it is called the Edinburgh Scale and it poses ten questions about the mother's mental well-being. It has been validated and numerous research studies have confirmed it to reliably detect depression. If every new mother were given the test at the regular six-week postpartum checkup as part of a standardized protocol, I believe the incidence of crippling PPD could be significantly decreased.

Looking to channel my restored energy into something worthwhile ██████████████████████ ███████████, I became involved in a local nonprofit foundation devoted to educating new mothers about and reducing the occurrences of PPD. Several times per month I volunteered with a peer support group designed to help women through their PPD experiences. I think that by nature women are good problem solvers. It was very rewarding when a wreck of a mother left weeks or months later a whole and happy person. Some returned later to the group to volunteer as well. I had never done anything like it, and I found great satisfaction in talking and helping other women get through what I knew felt like an enormous obstacle. Although I would not wish PPD on my worst enemy, I had grown in ways I had not anticipated a year earlier and I liked developing this side of my character—quite different from working to keep weapons of mass destruction out of the hands of terrorists or rogue states. This harrowing experience, during which all the touchstones of my life before motherhood were lost, ultimately provided me with a more developed sense of compassion and a drive to help others in ways that I never had before. ▮▮ ▮▮▮▮▮▮ I was a changed woman ▮▮▮▮▮▮▮▮ ▮▮▮▮▮ .

CHAPTER 6

Mother and Part-Time Spy

███████ ███████ ███████

███████████████████████████████ waiting for an assignment.
The truth was, I had somewhat ambivalent feelings about ██████

███

███

███

██████████████████████████ on the work front, I had no
idea what I was facing. Would I be able to find traction again in
my career as an operations officer after my extended leave?
Could I actually do ████ job on a less-than-full-time basis? ██████
██████████████████████████████████ I looked around the
large, airy office and waited. The new Chief, Richard, a debonair,
fastidiously dressed man, had furnished the room with character-
istic elegance. An ornate and beautiful Persian rug covered the
floor and various mementos, undoubtedly gifts from assets and
other intelligence services around the world, were displayed on
the sleek mahogany desk and bookcases. I exchanged some brief

polite chitchat with Richard and one of his top lieutenants, an experienced and capable administrative type who knew where all the bodies were buried and actually knew how the budget worked. Finally, Richard asked me where I would prefer to work ▮▮▮▮▮▮▮▮▮▮▮▮▮▮▮▮▮▮▮▮▮▮▮▮▮▮▮▮▮▮▮▮▮▮▮▮▮▮▮ ▮▮▮▮▮▮▮▮▮▮▮▮▮▮▮▮▮▮▮▮▮▮▮▮. That I was given a choice in the matter was both surprising and flattering, since most assignments in the pseudomilitary culture of the CIA were usually made by fiat. Fortunately for me, the answer to his question was ▮▮▮▮▮▮▮▮▮▮▮▮▮▮▮▮▮▮▮▮▮▮▮▮▮▮▮▮▮▮▮▮▮▮▮▮▮▮▮ ▮▮▮▮▮▮▮▮▮▮▮▮▮▮▮▮▮▮▮▮▮▮▮▮▮▮▮▮▮▮▮▮▮▮▮▮▮▮▮ ▮▮▮▮▮▮▮▮▮▮▮▮▮▮▮▮▮▮▮▮▮▮▮. I couldn't wait to get going—back into operations.

Decision made, I left his office and headed directly downstairs to the subterranean level of the new Headquarters building. My desk was in a vast windowless vault, where a hundred-plus desks were divided by flimsy fabric-covered partitions. There were papers and binders everywhere, stacked high on tables and the floor and in the "hallways" between long rows of partitions. The joke was that the biggest threat to some offices was paper lice. A peek into the small office of the Division's counterintelligence Chief, one of the few around the perimeter of the large room with a coveted door, was particularly alarming. Mountains of paper were everywhere—on the floor, on the desk, on the small couch, and on the bookcases. A coffee cup balanced precariously on a small hill of files on the desk. It was chaos. The officer, who with his full white beard looked a little like Santa Claus, claimed that he could find any piece of paper he wanted, but given his important responsibilities—to ensure that CPD operations were kept safe from outside threats—I didn't share his confidence that his filing methods were effective. Looking back out over the vault, I saw several balloons decorating a small open area where someone must have thrown a party, but never cleaned up. Suspended from the ceiling here and there were the flags of Iran, Iraq, North Korea, and other rogue nations. This was my new home.

I found my new supervisor, a bookish man with blond hair and wire-rimmed glasses who had served in several Middle Eastern posts, and introduced myself. He greeted me warmly and then took me to meet my new colleagues in their cubicles. As I chatted with my new coworkers, I began to realize with some dismay that only I and two others were "real" operations officers—that is, certified and trained at the Farm. Almost none of the others had ever sat down with an asset in the field or written a raw intelligence report. Yet this small, inexperienced group was charged with tracking ▮▮ WMD research and procurement efforts and developing operations from scratch that could open a desperately needed window into ▮▮ suspected WMD programs. The wholesale gutting of the operations cadre in the mid-1990s was now showing its insidious effects. The task ahead of us was humbling, but the group was small, junior, and anemic.

I got settled in my cubicle; rearranged the placement of the computer screen; the green phone, used for "secure" conversations; and the black phone, used for "clear" calls, and tacked up a calendar. I tried to look busy and efficient but I had no computer access. One of the most persistent administrative problems throughout the Agency was that no matter what grade you were, it took the computer folks a week or so to get a secure computer; without it, you were dead in the water. I read some of the files left on my desk. After about fifteen minutes of quiet reading, I realized that no one was tugging at my skirt for attention. I didn't have to comfort a crying toddler while trying to amuse the other one. I didn't need to read at lightning speed to get through the paragraph before I had to run and make sure that strange noise I heard wasn't trouble. No one was going to bother me at all. I could even get a second cup of coffee if I liked.

I opened the top file off the stack of large, old, and dusty orange folders on the desk. They were stuffed with crinkled, onion-skin paper, the kind used to make carbon copies in the 1970s. Some only had a few pieces of paper inside; others had two or three volumes. They were the files of ███████ that could possibly help us understand what was going on in Saddam Hussein's weapons programs in Iraq. As I flipped through what little we had, my heart sank. It was obvious that ████████ would need to move quickly, creatively, and aggressively if we were to expand our asset base and provide U.S. policy-makers with any credible intelligence. ████████████████████████████████████

██

██

██

██

██████████████████████

Fortunately for me, developing ingenious ways to reach targets was just the sort of operational work I loved. Once the target was identified, the next problem was always reaching him or her. Did he frequent a club? Who were his relatives? Did he always walk his dog along a particular street in the evenings? It was only after establishing contact that one could begin to discover what made the target tick and set up the right conditions for the ultimate objective, recruitment. ████████████████earlier ████████ ████████my Station had grown increasingly frustrated by our inability to access a powerful but deeply corrupt politician who we believed was linked to terrorists. Through some research, we discovered that he had had an affair with his mousy secretary and had broken it off against her wishes. Our thinking was that if we could reach her and convince her to work with us, she might provide us with some valuable information, or perhaps even direct access to his office. Through some basic detective work, I discovered she took an aerobics class three times a week at a local exercise studio. The next thing I knew, I was sweating next to her, gaining her trust. It ultimately led to her recruitment. *That's* what made operations interesting.

I dug in, and over the next few months, my branch worked hard to convince CIA Stations worldwide to take a closer look at the ████████ on their radar screens. Were there businessmen in their respective countries dealing in high-tech goods that could be used in ████████ weapons programs? Did they have any ████ ████████████ working on areas of potential applicability to WMD? Perhaps there was a close relative of a senior official ████ ████████████ living abroad? Our branch was starting at nearly zero, and it was worth looking in every corner in the hopes of generating some productive operations and intelligence we could use. ████████████████████████████ the responses from CIA Stations on the ████ target were mostly halfhearted or, worse yet, no acknowledgment at all. There were other, more compelling targets and our little CPD ████branch had to fight to be heard above the din of other, competing interests for time and resources.

Our other focus was energizing various friendly liaison services to join forces against the ████████ target. Liaison—Agency shorthand for a foreign intelligence service—was on the uptick. Traditionally, the CIA looked at liaison relationships as a necessary evil, especially under the Cold War rubric. You worked with liaison somewhat grudgingly, providing them with specialized training they wanted or needed, and tossed them the occasional technical goody ████████████████████████████████ ██ ██ ████████████████████ for all the daily care and feeding that liaison relationships demanded. Unilateral operations by the CIA were still greatly preferred and trusted, but the rise of the counterterrorism and counterproliferation Divisions changed that long-held equation profoundly. The reach of both Divisions was transnational, spilling over borders and regions and CIA Divisions. Furthermore, CTC and CPD were after generally mutually compatible targets as their foreign interlocutors. As a consequence, in recent years the Agency's liaison activities have expanded considerably and are now considered to be a force multiplier against the bad guys. ████████████████████ ██████████████████

Our digging and pleading finally yielded a possible gem—a young ████████ woman from a middle-class ████████ family doing highly technical ████████ work in a European country. Her expertise was in an area of keen interest for CPD, and further increasing her value was the discovery that her ████████ adviser ████████████████ was a highly respected and well-placed scientist suspected of working for ████████ covert weapons program. After briefing liaison on our find ████████ ██████████████████████████ we developed an operation that would lead to her recruitment. My job was to orchestrate a meeting between her ████████ in such a way that she would never suspect she was being pursued by the CIA. After a flurry of cables ██████████████████████████ we decided that he would pose as a ████████ man, who had read a paper of hers published in an obscure academic journal. ████████ was familiar with the target's esoteric field of study and could genuinely talk the talk. Probably a bit lonely in a foreign country, the target fell hard for the ████ flattery and perhaps, too, his ability to discuss her area of arcane study with some degree of sophistication and competency. Over a series of dinners ████████ ████████████████████████████████████ ████████████████████████████████████ ████████████████████████████████████

████, he explained, everything had to be kept completely confidential and she agreed. The idea was that her "assignments" would become increasingly sensitive and we could begin to explore what she knew about what her ▮▮▮▮▮ adviser ▮▮▮▮▮ ▮▮ was working on. An operation almost never unfolds without problems to solve—it's just a question of size—and one of our biggest headaches turned out to be her visa. It was due to expire within a few months and renewing it was not automatic. In fact, in normal circumstances she would have been expeditiously returned ▮▮▮▮▮ And if she were to return home, our operation would go cold. Consequently, I spent many hours pleading with my ▮▮▮▮▮▮▮▮▮▮▮▮▮▮▮▮ to "fix" the visa problem so our promising operation could continue without compromise or end prematurely. After weeks of foot-dragging and promising to take care of the problem, liaison finally delivered.

Of particular interest ▮▮▮▮▮ were Iraq's worldwide procurement networks. Although the Iraqis had a well-educated scientific cadre, their country did not have the indigenous capacity to produce the basic materials necessary to make nuclear, chemical, or biological weapons. As a result, Iraqi officials or their proxies constantly shopped in Europe or Asia for everything from glass-lined vats for cooking biowarfare batches to specialized accelerometers. U.S.-manufactured equipment was generally considered more desirable but also more difficult to obtain due to tight sanctions. Of course the Iraqis knew they were under close observation from intelligence services and, in response, they constantly changed the company names or those of the officials of their suspect supplier companies. They were playing the shell game on a very high level and many CIA officers were devoted to keeping track of who was who. As helpful as the information we gleaned was, ▮▮▮▮▮▮▮▮▮▮▮▮▮▮▮▮ many perpetrators managed to keep one step ahead of us. Adding to the difficulty and frustration was our discovery that many procurement entities did 95 percent of their business in legitimate sales; it was the other 5 percent that was in illegal goods. We tracked thousands of worldwide transactions, each of which went through multiple countries with each receiver changing the "end user" to obscure its final destination at some laboratory in Baghdad. The other adage in tracking prey, either terrorists or WMD procurers, is "follow the money." But the Iraqis had devised ingenious financing methods that obscured the true source or destination of funds, and they were frustratingly effective. Sometimes when we were hot on the trail of a transaction linked to a WMD purchase and ready to move in, the once-hot tip would vanish into thin air. Fortunately our branch had several young, devoted, and talented targeting officers who every day combed through hundreds of pages of intelligence, putting together complex charts of locations, sellers, and buyers. Our operations were invariably better because of these dedicated officers.

Writing these pages in 2007, four years after the invasion of Iraq, and the evidence of the manipulations of intelligence and failures of the intelligence community prior to the war, it is easy to surrender to a revisionist idea that all the WMD evidence against Iraq was fabricated. While it is true that powerful ideologues encouraged a war to prove their own geopolitical theories, and critical failures of judgment were made throughout the intelligence community in the spring and summer of 2002, Iraq, under its cruel dictator Saddam Hussein, was clearly a rogue nation that flouted international treaties and norms in its quest for regional superiority. The U.S. intelligence community was not the only actor that found Iraq's provocations alarming. The Center for Nonproliferation Studies (www.cns.miis.edu), a nonpartisan, nongovernmental research organization devoted to training the next generation of nonproliferation experts, was also concerned. Here's what some of their research revealed about the state of Iraq's WMD programs in 2001:

Nuclear

- With sufficient black-market uranium or plutonium, Iraq probably could fabricate a nuclear weapon.
- If undetected and unobstructed, could produce weapons-grade fissile material within several years.
- Engaged in clandestine procurement of special nuclear weapon-related equipment.
- Retains large and experienced pool of nuclear scientists and technicians.
- Retains nuclear weapons design, and may retain related components and software.
- Repeatedly violated its obligations under the NPT, which Iraq ratified on 10/29/69.
- Repeatedly violated its obligations under the United Nations Security Council (UNSC) Resolution 687, which mandates destruction of Iraq's nuclear weapon capabilities.
- Until halted by Coalition air attacks and UNSCOM disarmament efforts, Iraq had an extensive nuclear weapon development program that began in 1972, involved 10,000 personnel, and had a multiyear budget totaling approximately $10 billion.
- In 1990, Iraq also launched a crash program to divert reactor fuel under IAEA safeguards to produce nuclear weapons.
- Considered two delivery options for nuclear weapons: either using unmodified Al-Hussein ballistic missile with 300km range, or producing Al-Hussein derivative with 650km range.
- In 1987, Iraq reportedly field-tested a radiological bomb.

Biological Warfare

- May retain stockpile of biological weapon (BW) munitions, including over 150 R-400 aerial bombs, and 25 or more special chemical/biological Al-Hussein ballistic missile warheads.

- May retain biological weapon sprayers for Mirage F-1 aircraft.
- May retain mobile production facility with capacity to produce "dry" biological agents (i.e., with long shelf life and optimized for dissemination).
- Has not accounted for 17 metric tons of BW growth media.
- May possess smallpox virus; tested camelpox prior to Gulf War.
- Maintains technical expertise and equipment to résumé production of *Bacillus anthracis* spores (anthrax), botulinum toxin, aflatoxin, and *Clostridium perfringens* (gas gangrene).
- Prepared BW munitions for missile and aircraft delivery in 1990–1991 Gulf War; this included loading Al-Hussein ballistic missile warheads and R-400 aerial bombs with *Bacillis anthracis*.
- Conducted research on BW dissemination using unmanned aerial vehicles.
- Repeatedly violated its obligations under UNSC Resolution 687, which mandates destruction of Iraq's biological weapon capabilities.

Chemical

- May retain stockpile of chemical weapon (CW) munitions, including 25 or more special chemical/biological Al-Hussein ballistic missile warheads, 2,000 aerial bombs, 15,000–25,000 rockets, and 15,000 artillery shells.
- Believed to possess sufficient precursor chemicals to produce hundreds of tons of mustard gas, VX, and other nerve agents.
- Reconstructing former dual-use CW production facilities that were destroyed by U.S. bombing.
- Retains sufficient technical expertise to revive CW programs within months.
- Repeatedly used CW against Iraqi Kurds in 1988 and against Iran in 1983–1988 during the Iran-Iraq war.
- An extensive CW arsenal—including 38,537 munitions, 690

tons of CW agents, and over 3,000 tons of CW precursor chemicals—has been destroyed by UNSCOM.
- Repeatedly violated its obligations under UNSC Resolution 687, which mandates destruction of Iraq's chemical weapon capabilities.
- Not a signatory of the Chemical Weapons Convention.

Ballistic Missile

- May retain several Al-Hussein (modified Scud-B) missiles with 650km range and 500kg payload.
- May retain components for dozens of Scud-B and Al-Hussein missiles, as well as indigenously produced Scud missile engines.
- Maintains clandestine procurement network to import missile components.
- Reconstructing missile production facilities destroyed in 1998 by U.S. bombing.
- May possess several hundred tons of propellant for Scud missiles.
- If undetected and unobstructed, could resume production of Al-Hussein missiles; could develop 3,000km-range missiles within 5 years; could develop ICBM within 15 years.
- Launched 331 Scud-B missiles at Iran during the Iran-Iraq war, and 189 Al-Hussein missiles at Iranian cities during the 1988 "War of the Cities."
- Developing Ababil-100 with 150km range and 300kg payload, flight-testing Al-Samoud with 140km range and 300kg payload, and producing Ababil-50 with 50km range and 95kg payload.

Given Saddam Hussein's unpredictability and ruthlessness, even toward innocent Iraqis, these cruel laundry lists seemed ominous.

Long before the Iraq war became such a highly politicized,

divisive issue in the United States, those of us who followed pro-liferation issues for a living saw that Iraq was dangerous and erratic. Many of the CIA liaison partners around the world were picking up evidence that Iraq was seeking to procure items that could be used in their suspected WMD programs. It was a huge puzzle with only a few pieces that fit together correctly. Worse, none of us knew what the completed puzzle would look like. A consistently frustrating hurdle in the CIA's quest to get a more detailed picture of Iraq's capabilities was the abundance of "dual-use" items sought by Iraq. These were designated high-tech pieces of equipment from various manufacturing disciplines that could be used in WMD assembly or for legitimate purposes. An export license was required to ship the goods, but because of the dual nature, Iraq—or other rogue states—could subvert the process to their own advantage. The tracking and registration problem deteriorated further when a questionable item was shipped to several countries before its final destination. Each stop brought its own bureaucratic haze and a dilution of the export controls. But the Iraqis were persistent and knew how to game the international export control regime well. And it infuri-ated their CIA trackers.

In CPD's Iraq branch, the job ███████████████ was to fig-ure out how to mount the operations that would produce credi-ble intelligence on suspected Iraqi WMD programs. It was the responsibility of the DI analysts, housed in WINPAC (Weapons Intelligence, Nonproliferation, and Arms Control), a huge group of about seven hundred people, to sift through the "raw" intelligence and put the pieces together. Given the sophistication of the Iraqi denial-and-deception campaigns, it was not an easy task. But we were intelligence professionals, and we sure as hell were going to try.

As I settled back into a working routine, I struggled with the challenges every working mother faces finding a balance between the incessant demands of home and office. On the one hand, I recognized and understood that I needed to be available to travel worldwide on a moment's notice to smooth out a liaison relationship or debrief a promising ███████████████████ ████████████████████████████. On the other hand, I also wanted time to enjoy being a mother to my twins. I didn't have children only to turn their upbringing over to someone else. This dynamic was fraught with stress, of course, but sometimes I just had to laugh at my ludicrous situation. When I had to deal with pressing operational issues I had no choice but to bring the toddlers into my office on a Saturday. Making decisions on how much money to offer a potential asset while handing crayons to my daughter who sat under my desk was strange indeed, but not without humor. I found that if I gave Samantha Magic Markers and paper, and Trevor some special snacks, I could buy myself about thirty minutes to draft some cables out to the field. ██████████████████ overseas, most of my female colleagues agreed that we all needed a "wife"—or someone to take care of life's administrative essentials while we concentrated on the job. Now *I* was the wife but still on the job. Before I left on a trip to the Middle East to meet with a friendly liaison service, I wrapped little silly gifts for the children to open after I was gone. I left notes with my mother, who was staying with us to help while I traveled, to read to the children. Hopeful that my children would understand that Mommy was coming home soon, I switched gears as soon as I got into the taxi to the airport, mentally reviewing the points I wanted to make with my foreign counterparts. It was an unusual life by others' standards, perhaps, but we were happy and it worked for us.

That summer, once the twins were in bed and Joe and I had a few minutes to talk before collapsing in bed ourselves, we discussed our future plans. We liked the idea of going overseas once the children approached kindergarten age. I would go back to work full-time, perhaps with a good management position ▮▮▮▮ ▮▮▮▮▮▮▮▮▮. Joe, who had retired from the State Department in 1998 after twenty-three years of service, had started an international consulting business that was thriving. He thought he could easily relocate his business overseas as well. The future looked bright.

CHAPTER 7

Trip to Niger

██████████████████████████████ I settled six ranking intelligence officers from the Middle East into a well-appointed conference room in the older section of the Headquarters building. The officers were in Washington to discuss operational issues of mutual interest and enhance the already deep cooperation between our two services. After providing introductions to the opening briefer and reviewing the agenda one last time, I promised to return later that morning to begin their session with CPD staffers. Calm and content, their only concern was whether they could smoke. My day was jammed with meetings so I hurried out of the room. ████████████████████████

██████████████████ our humble ████████████████ Branch" had acquired a weightier and more imposing name ████████████ This change in nomenclature alone was not unusual; task forces pop up like mushrooms at the CIA, and it usually just means that management wants to put greater emphasis on a given issue. Unfortunately, these task forces never seem to be dismantled when the crisis or issue is resolved; they linger on life support for years, victims of bureaucratic inertia. Our branch was happy enough to be made into a task force—we needed all the help we could get to figure out what was going on inside ███████████ WMD programs. In addition, there was talk of moving across the hall to a more spacious and freshly refurbished space, which pleased everyone who was tired of our rather cramped current quarters. ███████████████████████████ however, there was an unmistakable quickening in the pace and tempo; ██████████ ██████████████████████████and we were all eager to protect and serve our great country. ██████████████████████ ██ ██ ██ ██ ██ ██████████

████████ our small group quickly and radically expanded to accommodate the wave of experts in the nuclear, biological, chemical, and missile fields who were pouring into the CIA from other parts of the intelligence community. I enjoyed having these accomplished officers so close at hand and I came to rely increasingly on their technical knowledge and ability to translate complicated terms and issues into language that I, a simple ops officer, could actually understand. It began to feel like we were getting some traction in our quest to upgrade our intelligence on ████████ WMD. We began to appreciate even more our increased numbers because the workload began to expand considerably. Leads from all around the world poured over the transom daily. Some had obviously been fabricated by people who were trying to sell the CIA a thin gruel of information for money. Others were not so clear-cut and required more thorough follow-up. A precious few appeared valuable from the beginning. The trick was sorting through the mess, prioritizing, and figuring out where to apply our limited resources to a growing problem.

Somewhat typical of what ███ might take in on an average day ████████████████ was a "walk-in" ████████████ who had told us he'd been to a secure ██████ site ████████████ that may have been used as a biological weapons laboratory. ███ ████████████████ he was able to describe the scene in gruesome detail: prisoners tied to their beds, given a mysterious shot, bodies convulsing, blood streaming from ears and nostrils. This story got everyone's attention, of course, but the veracity of these sources and their reports had to be confirmed. The nuances and slight differences the intelligence community made in source descriptions was critical. Over the years, source descriptions in intelligence reports had become so vague that it was extremely difficult for a consumer of the report to understand how much faith was placed in a source. Source descriptions were later updated so that it was easier to assess their veracity, but for too long, finished intelligence reports were not the top-notch, crisp products they should have been. In the case of our walk-in and the possible biological warfare testing site he described in unnerving detail, we sent a very good Army reserve officer to comprehensively debrief the source. Armed with pages of satellite maps and significant biological weapons expertise, the officer spent days with ████████████████, trying to pin down the location of the site on a map of greater Baghdad. Eventually, that initially promising lead, like so many, came to a disappointing nothing. However, to confirm that the lead was cold, the CIA spent hundreds of man-hours and thousands of dollars. At that time, ██████ still did not have a full appreciation for the Machiavellian work of Ahmed Chalabi, an Iraqi who left his country in 1956. Despised by the CIA for his deceitfulness and lionized by the Pentagon for his ability to predict a democratic Iraq (with him as its head), Chalabi probably sent dozens of tantalizing but ultimately false leads into the CIA net. Given what was at stake, we had no choice but to follow them all.

Soon, I was asked to serve as ▓▓▓ Chief of Operations ▓▓▓▓ ▓▓▓▓▓▓▓▓▓▓▓▓▓▓▓▓▓ That CPD management would choose a part-time mother for such a critical leadership role surprised and thrilled me. Maybe the dinosaurs were dying off after all. I had never been given so much management responsibility and was committed to helping my team perform as well as possible. Many mornings I answered questions as I took off my coat, with a line already forming outside my door. My responsibilities covered a broad spectrum. I coordinated our approaches to ▓▓ scientists worldwide, scheduled polygraph exams to test the authenticity of some of the outlandish claims we heard, and continuously conferred with our targeting and reports officers as well as our resident experts. I also brought the WINPAC analysts into operations as needed and generally tried to encourage my officers to approach their work with imagination and creativity. I personally hated being micromanaged, and tried hard to give my employees a sense of empowerment and confidence that I would support them in their efforts.

One dreary day in February 2002, a young and capable officer rushed into my office. Normally somewhat reserved and calm, ▇▇▇▇ looked unusually animated and alarmed. She hurriedly told me that "someone from the vice president's office" had called on her green secure line. Apparently, the caller, a staffer, said they were intrigued by an intelligence report that the Italian ▇▇▇▇▇▇▇▇▇▇▇▇ government had passed to the U.S. government ▇▇▇▇▇▇▇. It alleged that in 1999 Iraq had sought yellowcake uranium, the raw material used for the uranium enrichment process, from the impoverished West African country of Niger. The vice president, ▇▇▇ had been told, was "interested and wanted more information." If the report was true at all, I knew that it would be damning evidence indeed that Iraq was seeking to restart its nuclear program. I was momentarily nonplussed that someone from the vice president's office had reached down into the junior working levels of the Agency to discuss or find an answer to an intelligence report. In my experience, I had never known that to happen. There were strict protocols and procedures for funneling intelligence to policy-makers or fielding their questions. Whole offices within the Agency were set up and devoted to doing just that. A call to a random desk officer might get the policy-maker a quick answer in the heat of the moment, but it was also a recipe for trouble. Handing a senior policy-maker "raw" intelligence that had not been properly vetted, placed into context, or appropriately caveated by intelligence professionals usually led to misinterpretation—at a minimum.

However, I quickly shook off my surprise and turned to solving the problem presented to us. The president and vice president have long been the Agency's most important customers by a wide margin. So, when the vice president's office calls with questions, it is embedded within the Agency's DNA to respond as quickly and thoroughly as possible with answers. At that time, I was not aware of the unprecedented number of visits that the vice president had made to our Headquarters to meet with analysts and look for any available evidence to support the Iraq WMD claims the administration was beginning to make. According to the *Washington Post*, Vice President Dick Cheney and his senior aide, I. Lewis "Scooter" Libby, visited the CIA on "multiple" occasions prior to the war to talk to Agency analysts working on Iraq WMD issues and ask them about possible links between Iraq and the terrorist network Al Qaeda. When these visits first became publicly known in June 2003, just as the Iraq insurgency was in its infancy, senior intelligence officials acknowledged that these heretofore unknown visits by the vice president had created "an environment in which some analysts felt they were being pressured to make their assessments fit with the Bush administration's policy objectives." The senior intelligence officials added that "while visits to CIA Headquarters by a vice president are not unprecedented, they are unusual."

However, in February 2002, I was still blissfully ignorant of any special visits or pressure from the administration vis-à-vis Iraq. I just wanted to get some answers. Thinking through the options available, the first and most obvious choice would be to contact our ██████████████ office in Niger and ask them to investigate these allegations using local sources available on the ground. Unfortunately, the severe budget cuts of the mid-1990s had been particularly devastating for the Africa Division and many of our offices on the continent were closed, including the one in Niamey, Niger. ████████████████████████ ██████████████████████████████. Where else to go and who could do it for us? A midlevel reports officer who had joined the discussion in the hallway enthusiastically suggested: "What about talking to Joe about it?" He knew of Joe's history and role in the first Gulf War, his extensive experience in Africa, and also that in 1999 the CIA had sent Joe on a sensitive mission to Africa on uranium issues. Of course, none of us imagined the firestorm this sincere suggestion would ignite. At that moment, the only thought that flashed through my mind was that if Joe were out of the country for an extended period of time I would be left to wrestle two squirmy toddlers into bed each evening. Joe and I had often said it was best not to be outnumbered by the twins. So I was far from keen on the idea, but we needed to respond to the vice president's office with something other than a lame and obviously unacceptable "We don't know, sorry." The reports officer and I walked over to the office of the ▮▮ Chief to discuss our available plans of action. Bob, our boss, listened carefully and then suggested we put together a meeting with Joe and the appropriate Agency and State officers. He finished with, "When you see Joe tonight could you please ask him if he would be willing to come into Headquarters next week to figure out what we're going to do? Oh, and send a Lotus note to Scott [our acting Division Chief] and let him know what we're thinking." I hurried back to my desk and drafted a quick e-mail to Scott to explain the situation and added that "my husband has good relations with both the PM [prime minister] and the former Minister of Mines (not to mention lots of French contacts), both of whom could possibly shed light on this sort of activity." Although the acting Division Chief had actually been in CPD—in another senior position—when Joe had gone to Africa in 1999, I was gently reminding him of Joe's credentials to support why my boss thought he should come into Headquarters in the first place. Months later, those words would be ripped out of that e-mail and cited as proof that I had recommended Joe for the trip. But at the time, I simply hit the "send" button and moved on to the other tasks that were demanding my attention.

That night, between cleaning up dinner dishes, picking toys

up off the floor, and corralling our twins into the bath, I told Joe that my office had received a report from a foreign intelligence service, which I did not name. ████████████████████ ████████████████ I said that we were working on getting the vice president's office some answers as quickly as possible and passed on the request from my boss that he come into Headquarters to discuss the matter further. "Of course," Joe said without hesitation. So, the next week, I showed Joe into my cramped little office and introduced him to some of my colleagues and escorted him into the scheduled meeting with Iraq/Niger experts from CPD, the DI, and State. We entered the windowless conference room and I introduced Joe to the ten or so participants. I was secretly proud that Joe might be able to assist in the Agency's work. After a minute or so, I went back to my desk to attend to what seemed like a hundred other operational crises. When the meeting broke, Joe poked his head in my office to say that the group had asked him to consider going to Niger to discuss the report. "Okay, sure. When do you go?" It looked like I would be outnumbered by the twins after all.

Three weeks later, in early March, Joe left on an evening flight from Washington to Niamey, Niger, via Paris. Joe undertook the mission pro bono—the Agency only paid his travel expenses of a few thousand dollars. Joe was happy to go. He figured that if the vice president had asked a serious and legitimate question, it deserved a serious answer and he would try to help find it. I stayed home, working on operational issues ████ at my CIA office, taking care of the kids, and trying to get back from work at a decent hour. When Joe returned home nine days later, the twins and I rushed out to the taxi to greet him. Tired and stiff after his journey, he put down his bags in the hallway, gave the children a big bear hug, and delighted them with some trinkets and colorful fabrics he'd purchased at the Niamey souk. I was so happy he was home safely. Before long, the doorbell rang and two clean-cut CIA officers, one of whom was the Reports Officer who had suggested sending Joe to Niger in the first place, stood on the doorstep, clearly eager to debrief Joe so they could immediately write up an intelligence report on his trip. There is a standard procedure for distributing intelligence reports to all the government departments that have intelligence components, such as the State Department's Bureau of Intelligence and Research (INR), the National Security Agency (NSA), the Pentagon, and the overseas military commands. All of us had every reason to believe that their finished report would indeed be sent to the vice president's office as part of the established protocol. I ushered the officers in, took their coats and their orders for Chinese food, and left the three of them alone in the living room. They broke off the session when the takeout arrived, and the four of us sat at our dining room table talking about general topics, laughing over Peking duck and spicy beef with broccoli. I wish I had saved the fortune cookies from that night. While I tidied up, the officers reviewed their notes with Joe and thanked him for his time and efforts before hurrying out the door. There was, of course, no inkling of the scandal that Joe's trip would ignite. Both of us felt that we were doing our jobs and serving our country. It was the right thing to do.

CHAPTER 8

Shock and Awe

A day or two after Joe returned from Niger, ▮▮▮▮ the Reports Officer, as a simple courtesy, showed me a copy of the finished intel report on the supposed yellowcake transaction between Niger and Iraq. It was a couple of pages long and fairly straightforward, in the typical bland style of such reports. Much of it was devoted to Niger's strict, private, and governmental controls on mining consortia to ensure that no yellowcake went missing between the uranium mines and the marketplace. I read the piece, made no changes, thanked the Reports Officer for showing it to me, and handed it back to him. It was duly circulated, including, we all assumed, to the Office of the Vice President. It raised no particular comment or waves. I did not know it at the time, but analysts closely following this issue would have seen reports submitted by U.S. Ambassador to Niger Barbro Owens-Kirkpatrick, a career foreign service officer, and Army four-star general Carlton Fulford just weeks prior to Joe's visit that also concluded the yellowcake sale claim was bogus. Joe's report corroborated and reinforced what was already known. ▮▮▮▮▮▮

█████████████████████████████████On the personal front, Joe and I returned to our routines—I went to work every day at CIA Headquarters, and Joe went to his office in downtown Washington. For a few months at least, it all seemed very normal.

In the late summer of 2002, I went on a whirlwind tour of several Middle Eastern countries to collect intelligence on the presumed cache of Iraqi WMD. I distinctly remember thinking how much the atmosphere reminded me of Barbara Tuchman's classic work on the beginnings of World War I, *The Guns of August*. Each move by the Great Powers led inexorably to the loss of hundreds of thousands of lives and untold destruction.

Overseas trips are expensive, even on government rates, but some things simply cannot be done except face-to-face. A thirty-minute visit in person can accomplish as much as a month's worth of cables in resolving a persistent problem and working out conflicting approaches to an operational impasse. Personal contact, despite its cost, is much more efficient and productive than the formal cables that can take forever to coordinate through the various Headquarters offices. Every office that could claim turf on an issue wants to add or subtract something from the message—whether necessary or not—and it is not unusual for directives given in Headquarters cables to be overtaken by events on the ground. Sometimes, we spoke with an overseas office on secure satellite phones, but the sound quality was always distorted and delayed by an echo of up to five seconds or so, making a genuine discussion nearly impossible.

One of my traveling companions was also a new mother who worked "part-time" as I did. But like me, she worked far longer hours, driven by a combination of guilt and concern for how she would be perceived by colleagues. As we waited to board the long flight overseas (secretly enjoying a few quiet, undisturbed moments of peace with fashion magazines), we marveled at how much the Agency had changed from the rigid and paternalistic organization that it had once been. ▓▓▓▓▓▓▓ On its inception in 1947, it was a stronghold of the "old boys school" but had become a more modern and flexible organization as it realized it had to compete successfully with corporate America for talented and dedicated workers.

Our first stop was with a longtime U.S. ally ▓▓▓▓▓▓▓▓▓ ▓▓▓▓▓▓▓▓▓▓▓▓▓▓. As we were ushered into a conference room, I glanced up at the ceiling and saw what appeared to be a huge aluminum stove hood, like what one would see in a restaurant kitchen. It was a bit disconcerting. As we sat down and turned from social chitchat to the serious business at hand, someone switched on the hood fan. A low droning hum filled the room. That was the signal for nearly all our gracious hosts ▓▓▓ to light up their cigarettes, which they did in unison. The smoke drifted neatly into the ventilation hood, keeping the room relatively clear. Apparently, our interlocutors thought better when smoking, because the meeting was considered a success by both sides. ▓▓▓▓▓▓▓▓▓▓▓▓▓▓▓▓▓▓▓▓▓▓▓▓.

We traveled next to another stalwart Middle Eastern ally for discussions with both the foreign service and our ▓▓▓▓▓ staff ▓▓▓▓▓▓▓. I was saddened to see that the embassy, where I had been years before on business, was now a virtual fortress. Barbed wire, concrete barriers, bulletproof glass, and a solid show of Marines surrounded the sprawling complex that made up the American presence in this ancient city—all an inevitable consequence of terrorist threats and a drastically changed world climate toward Americans. It was a reasonable and prudent reaction to keep American officials safe, but I lamented how it distanced them, both physically and emotionally, from their foreign hosts.

Despite our group's best efforts to select our food carefully and stay away from unbottled water, on the day of our departure, gastric disaster struck. As we were checking out of our hotel, I noticed that one of my colleagues, David, looked a little green, and in almost the next moment, I realized why. As I waited at the hotel desk to sign my credit card, I broke out in a cold sweat and suddenly felt so light-headed that I wanted to rest my head on the counter. Only my pride and the knowledge that we had to make our next flight kept me from crumbling into a little ball on the ground. Nearly all foreign travel carries the risk of stomach upheaval, but while it is an inconvenience as a tourist, it is a catastrophe when on business. We soldiered on, each of us feeling varying degrees of wretched. The long wait in the crowded and stuffy airport didn't help matters, nor did the one-hour delay on the tarmac in 100-degree heat. When we finally reached our next destination, after a wild ride in a taxi from the airport to the hotel, we each went to our respective rooms to collapse, turn on CNN International, and hope the misery would soon pass.

In the grand tradition of "if it's Tuesday, it must be Belgium," forty-eight hours later, we traveled on to yet another country. In August, temperatures routinely topped 120 degrees. At those temperatures, the "dry" aspect of the heat made no difference at all—it was just stinking hot. The first morning, I felt well enough to consider a short dip in the sparkling sea just behind the hotel before starting the workday. I noticed the little marker on the bedside table, helpfully pointing in the direction of Mecca, should I decide to do morning prayers. Instead, I quickly put on my bathing suit, covered myself with a long robe, and went out the sliding door to the sandy beach. The water was warm and delightful, but it had a strange texture—and then I noticed the oil refineries several miles away. I could just make them out in the early morning light. Not the most refreshing swim I've ever had.

When we arrived ▮▮▮▮▮▮▮▮▮▮▮▮ for our meetings, the ▮▮▮▮▮▮▮▮ Station Chief greeted us warmly and after meetings with his staff, he offered to take us on a tour of the surrounding countryside. The demarcation between civilization and the desert was striking. Leaving the modern city filled with high-rise buildings and designer boutiques, we abruptly entered the desert with nothing on the horizon for miles. ▆▆▆▆▆▆▆▆▆▆ The Station Chief was an engaging tour guide, pointing out landmarks in blowing sand ▆▆▆▆▆▆▆▆▆▆▆▆▆▆▆▆▆

▆ After several hours of this, we pulled up at a few desolate buildings that suddenly materialized out of the sand dunes. He promised us the most delicious local sandwich we would have on our trip. We tumbled out of the Jeep, whose windshield thermometer had topped out at 122 degrees, and walked into the even hotter shack where the locals, sweat streaming down their faces, put together our lunch order. Munching on the sandwiches made with onion, some unknown meat, and a soft bread wrapping, which were indeed tasty, we continued on our tour. ▆

▆▆▆▆▆▆▆▆▆▆▆▆▆▆▆▆▆ War was going to happen. We didn't know when, but it was all but a certainty. The sense of urgency I felt to find and provide good intelligence on Iraqi WMD ratcheted up yet another notch.

▆▆▆▆▆▆▆▆▆▆▆▆▆▆▆▆▆

▆▆▆▆▆▆▆▆▆▆▆ Our final stop was a Middle Eastern city that can be compared to Las Vegas on steroids. After completing operational discussions with our staff, we had a half day free before our flight home the next day. Since it was a Saturday, we didn't feel guilty taking the advice of one of our local officers to visit a nearby beach club, ████████████████████ ██ ████████████████████████████████████ As we stepped out of the air-conditioned taxi, the wave of humidity immediately steamed up our sunglasses. It really was like walking into a sauna. When our vision cleared, we saw an enormous luxury hotel on a small, man-made island about 450 yards from the pounding surf. It was like a mirage in the desert. We watched in amazement as stately cream-colored Rolls-Royces drove slowly over the causeway to and from the glass-sided high-rise. The suites-only hotel starts at eight hundred dollars a night. At those prices, we were content to stay at a more reasonably priced beach resort and just relax a little for the day. Modern and beautifully appointed, if somewhat garish in design, the club offered a refuge from the strict tenets of Islam practiced just outside its door; alcohol flowed freely, women of all nationalities dressed in nothing but string bikinis were lying around the enormous and elaborate pool and the floating bar. The contrast between the women on the streets of the city ███████ who if not wearing the *abaya*, which covers the body from shoulders to feet, at least wore the *hejab* headscarf to cover their hair, and the women around the pool in crocheted bikinis could not have been more striking. And they say Americans are schizophrenic and hypocritical about sexuality.

The next morning, I lingered in the airport gift shop before boarding my flight home. I leafed through a copy of *Vogue*. It and every other woman's fashion magazine on the rack had been reviewed for any offensive images and each wayward belly button, breast, or revealing glimpse of skin had been carefully blacked out by the country's censors. I put back the defaced copy of *Vogue* and thought about the countries of northern Europe where naked women on billboards selling shower soap don't rate a second glance. ████████████████████████████████

██
██
██
██
██
██
██
██
██
██████████████████████

████████████████████████████████ The clouds of war continued to build that autumn in a flurry of official statements and actions. In a speech in early October 2002, President George Bush, said with typical brio, "[t]he regime has the scientists and facilities to build nuclear weapons and is seeking the materials required to do so." Several days later, he asserted that Saddam Hussein "is moving ever closer to developing a nuclear weapon." On October 7, right before Congress voted on the Iraq war resolution, President Bush gave another speech and declared: "Knowing these realities, America must not ignore the threat gathering against us. Facing clear evidence of peril, we cannot wait for the final proof—the smoking gun—that could come in the form of a mushroom cloud." Other senior administration officials echoed that striking phrase in the following months. On October 11, the White House declared a major victory when both houses of Congress voted to authorize President Bush to attack Iraq if Saddam Hussein refused to comply with United Nations resolutions and give up weapons of mass destruction.

In November, the Pentagon issued a "stop-loss" order for the National Reserves. This meant that personnel who could otherwise leave the military when their volunteer commitments expired were obliged to remain to the end of their deployments and up to another ninety days after they came home. I began getting calls from Pentagon officials asking ███ my office to coordinate closely with theirs on issues dealing with Iraqi infrastructure that would probably be destroyed in the initial hours of an attack. ██ While they never said it explicitly, it was clear that the opening battle plan included taking out all communication units to isolate Iraq from the rest of the world. If possible, the pace in our office intensified further. On November 8, 2002, the U.N. Security Council unanimously adopted Resolution 1441, which demanded that Iraq give the United Nations inspectors the unconditional right to search anywhere throughout the country for banned weapons. Furthermore, Iraq was required to make an "accurate, full, and complete" declaration of its nuclear, chemical, biological, and ballistic weapons and related materials used in civilian industries within thirty days. In a CBS Radio News interview, then defense secretary Donald Rumsfeld declared, "There will be no World War III starting with Iraq," and rejected concerns that a war would be a quagmire. "The idea that it's going to be a long, long, long battle of some kind I think is belied by the fact of what happened in 1990. . . . Five days or five weeks or five months, but it certainly isn't going to last any longer than that." On November 14, Secretary Rumsfeld added that Iraq could give weapons of mass destruction to Al Qaeda in "a week, or a month," resulting in the deaths of up to one hundred thousand people. He continued, "Now, transport yourself forward a year, two years, or a week, or a month, and if Saddam Hussein were to take his weapons of mass destruction and transfer them, either use them himself, or transfer them to the Al Qaeda, and somehow the Al Qaeda were to engage in an attack on the United States, or an attack on U.S. forces overseas, with a weapon of mass destruction you're not talking about 300, or 3,000 people potentially being killed, but 30,000, or 100,000 . . . human beings." Congress, just like the general public, was being bombarded with dreadful scenarios of what would happen if the perceived imminent threat from Iraq was not stopped in its tracks. In a declassified letter to the Senate dated October 2002 (which appeared in the *New York Times* eight months *after* the war began), Tenet outlined links between Al Qaeda and Iraq:

- Our understanding of the relationship between Iraq and Al Qaeda is evolving and is based on sources of varying reliability. Some of the information we have received comes from detainees, including some of high rank.
- We have solid reporting of senior level contacts between Iraq and Al Qaeda going back a decade.
- Credible information indicates that Iraq and Al Qaeda have discussed safe haven and reciprocal non-aggression.
- Since Operation Enduring Freedom, we have solid evidence of the presence in Iraq of Al Qaeda members, including some that have been in Baghdad.
- We have credible reporting that Al Qaeda leaders sought contacts in Iraq who could help them acquire W.M.D. capabilities. The reporting also stated that Iraq has provided training to Al Qaeda members in the areas of poisons and gases and making conventional bombs.
- Iraq's increasing support to extremist Palestinians coupled with growing indications of relationship with Al Qaeda. Suggest that Baghdad's links to terrorists will increase, even absent U.S. military action.

During this frenetic time, interagency policy disputes on the WMD evidence began to filter down to our offices. There was always a mild background hum among the WINPAC analysts themselves and between WINPAC and the rest of the intelligence community. On the operations side, we usually paid relatively little attention to these debates because our energies were so focused on finding and running secure sources to produce raw intelligence in the first place. This was expected, as part of a healthy exchange of differing views. We knew most of the analysts—who were relatively young—to be competent and honest professionals who would quit on the spot rather than stand accused of bias or making a judgment with anything other than all the available facts.

But one particular tug of war became so contentious that everyone took notice. A full-throated battle erupted between the Department of Energy, the intelligence section of the State Department, and the CIA over the purpose of the aluminum tubes that Iraq had begun to order back in mid-2001. The Department of Energy claimed that the tubes were used for rocket casings and were closely modeled on an Italian military design for a rocket called Medusa 81. This was the State Department's opinion as well. But one Agency analyst, a former worker at Oak Ridge National Laboratory, clung ferociously to his belief that they were for centrifuge rotors. Centrifuges are precisely engineered metal cylinders that are used in isotope separation to enrich uranium. At [redacted], in my office, we tended to see it strictly as a debate between experts. Our job was to find the tubes and figure out the manufacturers, the suppliers, the maze of international procurement agents, and the tubes' ultimate destination; it was someone else's job to determine their purpose. Over a year later, in August 2003, a front-page article in the *Washington Post* headlined "Depiction of Threat Outgrew Evidence" and written by Barton Gellman and Walter Pincus gave one of the best and most thorough overviews of the aluminum tube controversy. Although I was privy only to the Agency's perspective on the debate, the dynamics described in the article were accurate. The administration's belief that Iraq had purchased the tubes to restart its suspected nuclear centrifuge program was a key pillar of the case for war. The crime and the colossal failure of the intelligence community—and the CIA in particular—was that these deep disagreements were relegated to footnotes in tiny type at the bottom of the National Intelligence Estimate (NIE). The NIE was hastily ordered by Congress in October 2002 (just prior to the vote to authorize use of force against Iraq) and pulled together by the CIA in an unprecedented few weeks. Even more damning is the intellectual sloppiness of a document known as the "President's Summary," which distills the NIE down to one page. The summary warned President Bush and senior administration officials that "serious doubts existed about the intended use of the tubes." There it was in black and white for the president and his closest advisers to read, but that inconvenient fact did not fit well into their war planning. In March 2006, the *National Journal* reported that "in mid-September 2002, two weeks before Bush received the October 2002 President's Summary, Tenet informed him that both State and Energy had doubts about the aluminum tubes and that even some within the CIA weren't certain that the tubes were meant for nuclear weapons." A warning from the CIA Director to the president, followed by a fleeting footnote in the NIE, is simply not adequate pushback when building a case for something as serious as war. The CIA failed to demonstrate convincingly to the administration that there was a serious and sustained debate over this issue. Through a deeply troubling cascade of errors of professional judgment, lax congressional oversight, cynical political manipulation, and a sense of the inevitability of war, the American public was encouraged to believe that the aluminum tubes were proof positive that Saddam had reconstituted his nuclear program.

• • •

In the fall of 2002, Joe had growing misgivings over the war's purpose, proposed execution, and possible unintended consequences. He was particularly incensed by neocons such as Defense Policy Board member Ken Adelman, who blithely predicted the whole venture would be a "cakewalk" and that the invasion would start democracy blossoming throughout the Middle East. Joe was also hearing from his former State Department colleagues that little to no attention was being given to postwar planning. Joe followed the debate closely, read extensively, and discussed every development in the story with others knowledgeable about the region, and by late 2002, his thoughts of how to approach the Iraq problem had begun to crystallize. It is important to note that when he went to Niger in March 2002, he did not have fixed opinions about U.S. foreign policy toward Iraq. He had gone to Niger because the CIA asked him to and because he wanted to be a good citizen. He had no other agenda, despite what many others on the Right said later.

In October, Joe wrote "How Saddam Thinks" for the *San Jose Mercury News*. In it, he championed "an aggressive UN-sanctioned campaign to disarm Iraq—bolstered by a militarily supported inspection process—that would combine the best of the US and UN approaches, a robust disarmament policy with the international legitimacy that the United States seeks." He appeared on CNN's *Paula Zahn Show*, ABC's *Nightline*, and PBS's *NOW with Bill Moyers* to further explain his thinking. His was one of the lone voices in the United States cautioning that a war with Iraq might not be as easy, nor bring about the positive results from the right, as the administration was promising the public. As the acting ambassador to Iraq in the lead-up to the first Gulf War, the last American diplomat to meet with Saddam Hussein, and his many years of diplomatic service in Africa and the Middle East, Joe had a unique perspective on the issue. He was not antiwar per se; he was, as he said repeatedly, "anti-stupid war." He thought it was critical that the country conduct a thoughtful debate on sending our troops into combat— especially if it was to be a war of our choosing. The most impor- tant act a nation undertakes is ordering its young men and women to kill and be killed in its name, and making sure that we had good national security reasons for doing so was the best way to honor those in military service. In his opinion, Iraq did not present a clear and imminent threat and, even if it did, the Bush administration still needed to offer a satisfactory exit strategy. Without either, Joe didn't think the invasion, conquest, and occupation of Iraq was a valid policy option. I admired Joe for his nuanced and thoughtful stance on the pending war, but we had little time at home to have any in-depth or far-reaching conver- sations about it. Our hurried calls or yellow Post-its to each other were usually about whose turn it was to pick up the kids from a birthday party or what we needed from the grocery store, as it is with every overscheduled married couple with children. However, I began to sense a silent disapproval from some of my colleagues, who saw Joe as perhaps idealistic or at a minimum, uninformed and naïve about the threat Iraq posed.

On January 28, 2003, the president delivered his State of the Union address. Joe watched the speech from the studios of a Canadian network who wanted him to comment afterward in French; I watched from home. The State of the Union is arguably the president's most important speech of the year, and even more so on the eve of possible war. I remember trying not to wince as the president promoted his disingenuously named "Clear Skies" initiative and called for extending what I thought were reckless tax cuts in a time of mounting deficits. It wasn't until at least two-thirds through his speech that he began discussing his reasons for going to war with Iraq. I suddenly heard "the British government has learned that Saddam Hussein recently sought significant quantities of uranium from Africa." What? Had I heard him correctly? Hadn't Joe's report on his trip to Niger nearly a year ago, distributed throughout the intelligence community, including presumably the vice president's office, proved the emptiness of these charges? When Joe got home later that night, we briefly discussed what we thought the president's claim could have meant. It seemed so odd. The next day, Joe called a former colleague at State to see what he could find out. This colleague told Joe that the president must have been referring to a country other than Niger. That seemed plausible to Joe. After all, three other countries in Africa (Gabon, where Joe had also been ambassador, South Africa, and Namibia) also mined uranium in commercial quantities. Several years later, the assistant secretary of state for African affairs told Joe, "You don't think that if we had seen the State of the Union address before it was delivered, that we would have allowed that phrase to remain in it, do you?"

Someone shouted, "He's on!" I quickly engaged the security screen on my computer and got up from my desk and went to the television to watch Secretary of State Colin Powell address the United Nations. It was February 5, 2003, just three weeks after Bush's State of the Union address. There had been much speculation among my colleagues about what evidence Powell would use to justify the decision to go to war. Despite feverishly pursuing intelligence on Iraq's nuclear and other WMD capabilities for some time, we all knew that much of the evidence was circumstantial and patchy and our collective frustration was mounting. I had heard that the secretary himself had spent long nights at Headquarters in the previous weeks to review the speech and its sources with senior CIA and State officials. I assumed Powell's presentation would be, in a sense, a Kabuki-like performance, in which the secretary of state's sterling reputation would persuade the world of the righteousness of a decision the administration had already made. Still, I had enormous respect for the secretary—I had heard him speak in the Agency's bubble-shaped auditorium and had been quite impressed with his eloquence and natural charisma.

Several of us clustered in the open office space and watched the TV monitor suspended from the ceiling. George Tenet could not be missed sitting just over Powell's right shoulder, looking tired, but wearing a jaunty sky-blue tie. His presence telegraphed the unmistakable message that the CIA was in agreement with all that Powell said. Powell gave a bravura performance in his smooth baritone voice. He held up a vial of white powder, referring to it as anthrax, and noting the horrors that even a minuscule amount could unleash; played audiotapes of Iraqi military officers discussing how to avoid an upcoming U.N. inspection as proof of Iraq's policy of evasion and deception; and showed grainy black-and-white satellite images of supposed weapons facilities, decontamination trucks, and bunkers. He shaped what appeared to be a compelling, airtight case against Saddam Hussein.

It was a powerful presentation, but I knew key parts of it were wrong. As I listened, particularly shocking to me were the passages about Iraq's alleged mobile biological weapons labs. The secretary had clearly drawn his description of the labs from a deeply flawed defector source, a former Iraqi military officer code-named CURVEBALL. CURVEBALL, a drunk, was living in Germany at the time. His reporting could never be verified, and the German service ▮▮▮▮▮ would not allow any CIA officer to meet with him, despite our repeated requests. Although an official "burn notice" (i.e., notification to the intelligence community that a source was fabricating or somehow unreliable) did not go out until June 2004, it was widely known that CURVEBALL was not a credible source and that there were serious problems with his reporting. My colleagues and I later learned that we were not the only ones stunned by Powell's speech. In the *Los Angeles Times* article of November 20, 2005, a German ▓▓▓▓▓ official spoke publicly about CURVEBALL for the first time. "We were shocked," he said. "Mein Gott! We had always told them [the CIA] it was not proven." The Germans also said that CURVEBALL's information was often vague, mostly secondhand, and impossible to confirm—and they had been handling him for the last six years. But there was Secretary Powell, before millions on TV, warning that Iraq's trucks could brew enough weapons-grade microbes "in a single month to kill thousands upon thousands of people." Tyler Drumheller, then Chief of CIA's European Division and responsible for the CURVEBALL case, was also shocked. He retired in 2005 and in 2006 wrote *On the Brink: An Insider's Account of How the White House Compromised American Intelligence.* Drumheller writes that he telephoned Tenet late in the night before Powell's speech and warned him (not for the first time) about CURVEBALL, saying "there are some problems with the German reporting." His office had carefully removed the most egregious and unsubstantiated parts of CURVEBALL's claims. Tenet's distracted answer was "Yeah, yeah, yeah, don't worry about it. We are exhausted. I have to go." As Drumheller points out, only a small section of the overall speech was devoted to CURVEBALL, but "it was crucial, because it hinted not only at intent, but also at actual capability." He writes, "Someone, somewhere, remembered the CURVEBALL reporting and resurrected it. WINPAC analysts first started discussing it with CIA management in August 2002, right before the National Intelligence Estimate came out. It now appears that CURVEBALL's reporting fit in well with information obtained from Ahmed Chalabi's Iraqi National Congress (INC), which at the time, was still receiving a $350,000 stipend from the Department of Defense."

Powell's presentation was probably the single most important factor in selling the upcoming war to the American public. It wasn't until September 2005 in an interview with ABC News that Powell expressed his deep regrets about it, describing it as a "blot" on his record. He added that he had "never seen evidence to suggest" a connection between the September 11, 2001, terror attacks in the United States and the Saddam regime. "I'm the one who presented it on behalf of the United States to the world, and [it] will always be a part of my record. It was painful. It's painful now."

When the program ended and we all drifted back to our desks, I was deeply upset, my head was spinning. I was experiencing what I can only call cognitive dissonance: "a psychological phenomenon which refers to the discomfort felt at a discrepancy between what you already know or believe, and new information or interpretation." I had been tracking Iraqi WMD efforts carefully for some time ███████████████ and the facts I knew simply did not match up with what Powell had just presented. It wasn't that the evidence he was citing had no factual basis, but our intelligence had so many caveats and questions that his conclusions seemed, at a minimum, much too optimistic and almost glib. It seemed he had used only the most sensational and tantalizing bits as evidence, without any of those appropriate caveats or cautions. ██████████████████████████ As an intelligence professional, I was well aware that there is never enough evidence, the intelligence is never good enough, and there can be agonizing doubts when making decisions based on what little is known for sure. That is simply the nature of the secretive world of intelligence. What we had struggled so hard to obtain was much too thin, and not nearly robust enough to start a war over. ██

████████████████

Back at my desk, I tried to focus and reengage in the work at hand. But I could not get Powell's speech out of my head. ████████ ██████████████████████████████████. I told myself that there were many individuals, way above my pay grade, who had broader access to the intelligence and perhaps higher clearances and therefore had a better, more informed knowledge about the genuine state of the Iraqis' suspected weapons programs and intent to use it. Perhaps someone had managed to recruit a source deep inside Saddam's innermost circle who was providing alarming evidence of his plans. The idea that my government, which I had served loyally for years, might be exaggerating a case for war was impossible to comprehend. Nothing made sense.

Let me be clear: I am no starry-eyed idealist. I know that sometimes war is a necessary final option when all other attempts at diplomacy and other foreign policy tools have failed. My father fought in World War II in the South Pacific and my brother received wounds in the Vietnam War that he carries to this day. I am proud of their military service and believe in a strong show and projection of U.S. military strength. But, up to the moment I heard Powell's speech, I realized that my focus had been on the micro aspects of preparing for war; my all-consuming tasks were getting the operations in place to produce needed intelligence and making sure that the sources and officers worldwide working feverishly on this issue continued to be safe and productive. I had never taken the time to step back and look at the bigger picture that was developing and the huge forces at work that were shaping public opinion. I don't recall anyone ever talking about being "for" or "against" the war. It simply wasn't done and it wouldn't have been appropriate. However, the Agency was much like the rest of the country, which felt increasingly polarized since the divisive 2000 election. When I joined the Agency, no one mentioned their political affiliation. However, with the passage of time, politics began to creep into the environment and one tended to have a general idea of where one's colleagues stood on the Bush administration. I also sensed among certain colleagues an unmistakable excitement at going to war; whether it also contained strains of perceived glory and imperial dreams, I cannot say. Everyone was working at a fast pace, sensing that time was growing short. As war became inevitable, I worried incessantly about U.S. troop protection. I thought, as I believe most of my colleagues did, that Iraq may have been harboring WMD caches throughout the country that we had failed to find. So, my primary concern was that the CIA would fail our troops because we could not get a clear picture of what our troops would face if they invaded the country.

The long-expected "shock and awe" invasion of Iraq began March 20, 2003. Like most others in the CIA, I watched the bombardment of government buildings and the destruction of Iraqi infrastructure in the little CNN picture at the corner of my computer screen. In my office, it felt like our work was over and our reason for being had been overtaken by reality. I felt we had failed miserably; it was a disaster in the making. I thought there was a pretty good chance that our troops could encounter some sort of WMD offensive. Time and again Saddam had demonstrated his ruthlessness when he felt his regime was threatened, and in the pictures on my screen it was being decimated by the overwhelming firepower of the U.S. military. In those opening days of assault, I felt like I was holding my breath, waiting to hear that Saddam had unleashed a nuclear weapon we had not found or used deadly chemicals on the battlefield against U.S. troops. As we watched the war unfold, Joe and I both felt hopeless.

Back again at Headquarters, I threw myself once more into the business of finding and getting intelligence on Iraq WMD. ▇▇▇▇

Shock and Awe | 133

CHAPTER 9

Exposed

Over the first six months of 2003, the question of how the Niger claim got into the State of the Union speech continued to concern members of Congress. Joe spoke to senators and House and Senate Intelligence Committee staffers and made it clear to former State Department colleagues and to former senior officials close to the White House that the administration needed to "come clean" on the yellowcake-uranium claim. Intrepid journalists, Nicholas Kristof and Walter Pincus among them, were doggedly pursuing the story but the administration continued to stonewall them and very little made it into print. As Joe struggled with what he should do, Tom Foley, former Speaker of the House and one of Joe's mentors through the years, counseled patience. He quoted former president Lyndon Johnson saying, "if you sit quietly with your rifle in your hand, eventually all of your enemies will pass by." For a while, it looked like the queries from Joe and others would go unanswered and the whole issue would simply vanish.

In March 2003, International Atomic Energy Agency Director General Dr. Mohamed ElBaradei told the U.N. Security

Council that the claim related to Niger was based upon forged documents. In early May, at a retreat for Democratic senators, Joe participated in a panel discussion with *New York Times* columnist Nicholas Kristof and he used the occasion to share with the senators the story of his trip. Afterward, Kristof asked Joe if he, Kristof, could write an article on the issue. Joe agreed, with the condition that he not be cited by name and they settled on the thin veneer of "retired former ambassador." Joe's motive was not to hide from our government, but to avoid drawing attention to himself. In retrospect, if anything, he underestimated the potential for those in the administration, and their allies, to change the subject from the lies in the president's address to lies about us.

Then, sometime in early June, a journalist called Joe to warn him that he would probably be identified by name in an upcoming news account of the controversy. This was a huge leap from the generic appellation journalists had used for Joe so far in writing their stories, that of "a former U.S. ambassador." Closely following this development, on June 8, then national security adviser Condoleezza Rice appeared on *Meet the Press*. She dismissed questions about whether the White House knew about the inaccuracy of the Niger claim with ". . . maybe somebody in the bowels of the Agency knew something about this, but nobody in my circles." That statement was simply not true. And it was the final straw for Joe. He was angry that his government was lying.

We decided to take a family vacation in late June to Hilton Head Island with my parents and my brother and sister-in-law. We all drove from Washington, D.C., to South Carolina, my brother Bob and Joe zooming ahead of the rest of our caravan in Joe's sports car with the top down. For the entire twelve-hour drive, Bob was a captive audience, as he and Joe talked about this troubling disconnect and dishonesty at the highest levels of government. Thinking out loud and using his Vietnam veteran brother-in-law as a needed foil, Joe went through his options but came to no conclusions on what, if anything, he should do. A few days later, while he was sitting on the beach attempting to relax but actually brooding, Joe's ever-present cell phone rang. We learned that the London *Independent* newspaper had published a piece headlined "Retired American Diplomat Accuses British Ministers of Being Liars." The headline sounded sensational, but it had nothing to do with the content of the article. However, it was clear that things were beginning to spin out of control. At that point, Joe thought the best course of action was to write an article himself, laying out the facts as he knew them.

As soon as we returned home from vacation, Joe sat down and pounded out an article that he had been composing in his head for some time. On July 6, the *New York Times* published Joe's op-ed, "What I Did Not Find in Africa," 1,500 words that refuted the administration's claims that Iraq had sought uranium from Niger. Joe showed me what he had written before sending it to the newspaper, and I thought it was accurate and straightforward and that publishing it was the right thing to do. Joe had not signed a nondisclosure agreement with the Agency when he went to Niger and he felt that the public was better served by facts than by continued silence. At no time did Joe or I ever consider that my cover and work at the CIA would be compromised by his submission of the op-ed. I had worked at the CIA without any threats to my cover ▮▮▮▮▮▮ and Joe had every reason and the bona fides to write the article, quite apart from my career. Minutes after the piece was posted on the *Times*'s Web site late that Saturday night, a producer for the popular Sunday talk show *Meet the Press* invited Joe on the show the next day to discuss his article. As I straightened Joe's tie prior to his big-time TV appearance and made sure his hair went just right, I was more outwardly nervous than he was. He acted as if he did this sort of thing every day. In his fifteen-minute segment on the show, Joe answered the questions put to him by Andrea Mitchell, who was sitting in for Tim Russert, clearly and calmly. I thought he hit a home run and marveled at how cool he remained under pressure. The next day, we experienced short-lived jubilation when a highly respected *Washington Post* journalist relayed to us that a White House spokesman had acknowledged that "the sixteen words did not rise to the level of inclusion in a presidential speech." Joe felt his work was done; he had made his point. He refused any further interview requests and headed off to the golf course, where cell phones were not allowed.

Two days after the op-ed appeared, however, it was clear that a hornet's nest had been disturbed. A business acquaintance of Joe's saw columnist Robert Novak on the street in downtown Washington. The acquaintance recognized Novak from his frequent TV appearances and asked if he would mind walking together a block or two, since they were going in the same direction. The acquaintance brought up the uranium controversy—which was everywhere in the news. They chatted a bit and the acquaintance asked Novak what he thought about Joe—without saying that he knew him. Novak turned to this complete stranger and blurted out that "Wilson's an asshole. The CIA sent him. His wife, Valerie, works for the CIA." They parted company a block or so later. The acquaintance headed straight to Joe's office and relayed the strange conversation. Joe immediately called the head of CNN, Eason Jordan, then one of Novak's employers, to complain. A few days and several missed calls later, Novak and Joe finally spoke. Novak apologized for his "asshole" comment and then brazenly asked Joe to confirm what he had already heard from an Agency source: that I worked for the CIA. Joe told him he didn't answer questions about his wife and then called me with this unsettling news. I was uneasy knowing that a journalist had my name and knew my true employer, and quickly informed my supervisors in CPD, who assured me that "it would be taken care of."

The following weekend, I took the children to Chicago to visit their godmother and my dear friend of many years, Janet. In between the dolphin show at Shedd Aquarium, riding the giant Ferris wheel on Navy Pier, and enjoying a boat ride on sparkling Lake Michigan, Joe and I talked constantly by cell phone, trying to figure out what could be next. I had a deep sense of foreboding. I shared some of my fears with my mother, who was also in Chicago with my father. What would Novak do with my name? Who else would he tell? How had he even gotten my name and my position in the first place? How would the Agency management react to the fact that a journalist now knew where I worked? How exactly was this going to affect my career? As my mother helped me bathe one of the twins in the hotel tub, she listened carefully to my ramblings. Then, with that clear-eyed, innocent optimism that only mothers seem to have on demand, she said, "Well, what can happen, really? Joe just told the truth of what he knew." Yes, but something still didn't feel right.

Ironically, that same weekend, the White House had decided that the CIA alone should take the full brunt of the blame for the "sixteen words" in the president's State of the Union address. According to the *Washington Post* on July 12, the president "defended the use of the allegation by saying the January 28 speech was cleared by the intelligence services." Shortly thereafter, Tenet said the information "did not rise to the level of certainty which should be required for presidential speeches and the CIA should have ensured that it was removed." Senator Pat Roberts, then chairman of the Senate Select Committee on Intelligence, didn't waste any time or words placing blame. "So far, I am very disturbed by what appears to be extremely sloppy handling of the issue from the outset by the CIA," Roberts said in a statement.

He added that it was Tenet's job to have told the president directly about his concerns about the material in his speech as Bush's senior intelligence adviser and not have left that job to his subordinates. "What now concerns me most, however, is what appears to be a campaign of press leaks by the CIA in an effort to discredit the president," Roberts said. With so much moving behind the scenes, that following Monday would prove that my dark premonitions in Chicago were on the mark.

Our bedroom was just beginning to show the first hints of morning light on July 14 when Joe marched in, dropped the newspaper on the bed, and said in a tight voice, "Well, the SOB did it." He set a steaming mug of coffee on my bedside table and left the room. What? I struggled to wake up. I sat up, switched on the lamp, and opened the *Washington Post* to the op-ed page; I didn't know what I would find, but I knew it wouldn't be good. Robert Novak had written in his column that "Wilson never worked for the CIA, but his wife, Valerie Plame, is an Agency operative on weapons of mass destruction." The words were right there on the page, in black and white, but I could not take them in. I felt like I had been sucker-punched, hard, in the gut. Although we had known for several days that he had my name and knew where I worked, we never believed for a moment he would actually print it or that the Agency would allow it. It was surreal.

I dropped the paper to the floor and tried to think clearly, but my mind was racing in a hundred directions at once. There was so much to consider, so many people to worry about. 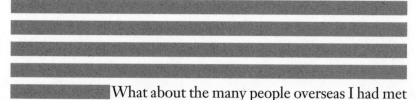What about the many people overseas I had met under completely innocent circumstances? They too could come under a cloud of suspicion if their governments learned of our contact. I tried to calculate the level of risk and weirdly sought to remember if Novak's column ran overseas, as though that would make it better if it didn't appear outside the United States. The next instantaneous thought was for my family's security. There are many disturbed people out there who hate the CIA or anyone associated with it. I didn't want to deal with a stranger on my doorstep or worse. Furthermore, Al Qaeda now had an identified CIA operative to put into their target mix.

I thought of my three-year-old twins and a ferocious maternal protectiveness welled up in me. I put on my robe and checked in on them in their cribs, each clutching their favorite stuffed animal, sleeping deeply. As I walked downstairs to the kitchen in a fog, I pondered the fate of my ▮▮▮▮▮▮▮ career with the CIA as a covert operations officer. The questions I had in my head in Chicago came flooding back in a roar. How exactly did Novak get my name? Why did he think fingering me was newsworthy? Joe's trip to Niger was obviously no boondoggle. And why did Novak use my maiden name—*Plame*—when I had used *Wilson* since I married in 1998? I could barely breathe.

I got dressed, fixed the twins' breakfast, mediated their little squabbles, greeted the nanny on her arrival and gave her the day's instructions, hunted for the car keys, and tried to get out the door by 8 A.M. all in a zombie-like state. I don't remember Joe and me saying much at all to each other that morning. What was there to discuss at that moment anyway? At one point, I called the Acting Chief of CPD, already in his office, and talked briefly. There wasn't much he or I could do at that point. Of all days, that morning I was scheduled to begin a weeklong "management and leadership" course. I had not taken any training classes for the last two years because work had simply been too busy. The Agency is a big advocate of continuing education as a prerequisite for promotional advancement, so I signed up for the course in what we all thought would be a relatively slow and quiet period. As I sat in Washington's terminally congested traffic en route to a CIA classroom in an outbuilding somewhere in the Virginia suburbs, I felt a new emotion begin to bubble up— anger. ███████████████████████████████ ██████████████████████████ I had served my country loyally ██████ ██████████. I had played by all the rules. I had tried to always act professionally and competently. Was it all about to be thrown away in a moment? And if so, why? And what about all my friends and family who didn't know I really worked for the CIA? Would they hate me for lying to them ███████████?

As I sat in the classroom with forty or so other officers drawn from all over the Agency and heard the instructor drone on about CIA core values, mission, and its desire to improve its managerial cadre, I put on my best "interested and engaged" look, but my thoughts were far away. I went over the last few months to piece together how and why I was being pulled into the public square. As I sat in the classroom with my mind racing, back at our home our neighbor spotted Joe on the back deck, where he was smoking a cigar and trying to make sense of what had just happened. The neighbor held up his newspaper and shouted, "Hey, what's this about your wife?" I think that it was one of the rare times that Joe was at a loss for words.

During our lunch break, when most of us ate at our desks, a woman gestured wildly to me to come over to her table. In the training class, we went by first names and last initial, but she had figured out who I was. "Did you know your name was in Novak's column today saying you worked for the CIA?" she hissed over her bag lunch conspiratorially, eyes wide. I thanked her for her concern, and told her that, yes, I knew. The next day, July 15, I received a message that the Agency's Executive Director (ExDir for short) was trying to reach me. Buzzy Krongard, a wealthy investment banker, had joined the Agency in 2001 as its number three, essentially the Chief operating officer. When I called Krongard back, he told me not to worry about the Novak article. "It's just the flavor of the week and it'll die down soon." The conversation lasted about two minutes. I thanked him and hung up, wishing I shared his confidence. There was no indication that the Agency, at that time, thought that what had just happened might be illegal. Nor was there any hint of what action, if any, the Agency intended to take. I guess I was just expected to go on as if nothing out of the ordinary had happened. Months later, Joe confessed to me he had suggested to a friend of his that Buzzy make the call, so that I would not feel so out in the cold.

A few days later, I ran into another neighbor, a lovely, gregarious woman who was always kind to us, inviting my children over to swim in her lap pool on hot summer days. Standing on the sidewalk with watering can in hand, Vicky told me that when she read Novak's column, she said out loud, "That can't be!" and ran to show her husband, unable to believe that their neighbor and mother of twins was actually a spy. She was solicitous, and obviously didn't want to pry too much into what I was really doing at the CIA, but I felt a great sense of mortification all the same. I think I managed a few head bobs and a weak smile and tried to end the exchange as quickly as possible and rush back inside my house. I was deeply uncomfortable.

Slowly, the media were beginning to understand the implications of leaking my name. David Corn, the Washington bureau Chief of the *Nation* magazine, was the first journalist to point out that if I was in fact what Novak had asserted it was not just a political dirty trick to say so, but possibly illegal. In his July 16, 2003,

Nation blog he noted, "This is not only a possible breach of national security; it is a potential violation of law. Under the Intelligence Identities Protection Act of 1982, it is a crime for anyone who has access to classified information to disclose intentionally information identifying a covert agent. The punishment for such an offense is a fine of up to $50,000 and/or up to ten years in prison. Journalists are protected from prosecution, unless they engage in a 'pattern of activities' to name agents in order to impair US intelligence activities. So Novak need not worry." But despite its national security implications and the possible crime, neither Corn nor anybody else in the media thought there would an investigation into the leak. The Agency had not yet commented publicly, and Corn closed his blog with, ". . . sometimes in the nation's capital, controversies fizzle and fade, sometimes they intensify and spread. Will these Administration officials get away with a smear that may have harmed national security? If Bush has his way, they will."

But despite the summer doldrums and a general slowdown in hard news, articles and stories on Joe's piece and my CIA connection continued to spill out in dribs and drabs. On July 18, a friend of Joe's sent him an e-mail with the first really nasty op-ed, which Caspar Weinberger, former secretary of defense under Reagan, wrote for the *Wall Street Journal*. It was titled "The Anatomy of a Campaign," and in it Weinberger wrote, "Completely frustrated by their inability to belittle, sneer at, or just plain falsify about the victory of our troops in Iraq, opponents of the president are now reduced to using bits and pieces of non-evidence to contend that we did not have to replace the brutal regime of Saddam Hussein." He went on to call Joe "a very minor former ambassador" and "self-serving" in his *Journal* op-ed but Weinberger completely missed the larger point of Joe's charge—that for a blunder of the proportion of the uranium claim to appear in the State of the Union speech, the president had been poorly served by his staff. That's rich, I thought. Weinberger had been indicted on charges stemming from the Iran-Contra affair and likely only avoided prison time because of a presidential pardon.

In the late afternoon of July 21, I got home from work and walked into our den to greet Joe. He clicked off the phone just as I came into the room and he had a look on his face that I had never seen before. He said he had just been talking with journalist and *Hardball* host Chris Matthews, who had told him that he had just spoken with the powerful presidential adviser Karl Rove. "Matthews told me that Rove told him that 'Wilson's wife is fair game,'" Joe said. Things were getting stranger all the time. Later that night, *Newsday*, a Long Island newspaper, posted an article on its Web site by their Washington reporters Timothy Phelps and Knut Royce. "Intelligence officials confirmed to *Newsday* Monday that Valerie Plame, wife of retired Ambassador Joseph Wilson, works at the agency on weapons of mass destruction issues in an undercover capacity—as least she was undercover until last week when she was named by columnist Novak." Not only was it very rare for the Agency to validate that an officer was undercover, no matter what the circumstances, but no one from the Agency had told me that my undercover status would be confirmed. It would have been nice to at least get a heads-up from someone at work.

When I returned to Headquarters the week after my training course, my colleagues were generally low-key about what had happened. Some made some supportive comments, others said nothing. Most of them knew me as Valerie Wilson, not Valerie Plame, and may not have made the connection between me and the woman fingered in Novak's column. In fact, as late as 2005, when I was working in another CPD office, one of the Agency psychologists, with whom I had worked closely on various cases ▓▓▓▓▓▓▓ came into my office with a sheepish look on her face. She had just been on assignment in a Gulf country, and working out on the treadmill in the hotel gym, she saw my face flashed up on the TV screen with my name. She told me she was so shocked that she fell off the treadmill and got tangled up in her iPod cord. Despite our long working relationship, she confessed that she had never put the "outed Valerie Plame" and me together.

In mid-August 2003 I was suddenly summoned to the office of CPD's Chief. I was to accompany him to brief Jim Pavitt, the DDO, on the background and current status regarding the disclosure of my name. While I was waiting for Mark to finish up with his last appointment so we could go up to the seventh floor together, I was called into the adjoining office of our Deputy Chief, who had been Acting Division Chief when Joe had gone to Niger. Scott, a kind and hardworking man, asked me how I was faring. He said he thought the situation was quite unfair and that obviously, I was not guilty of any nepotism. "In fact," he said staring straight at me, "if we had asked you to take our message to Joe about coming in to Headquarters to discuss possible options relating to the yellowcake allegation and you refused for some reason, you would have been derelict in your duty." He left no doubt that he thought I had done the right thing.

I was still absorbing Scott's comment, when Mark came in to take me to Pavitt's office. DDO Pavitt greeted us warmly; he had a good working relationship with Mark, and he knew me, too, from the various sensitive programs I had worked on. ████████ ████████████████████████. He invited us to sit at the small round conference table in his spacious office looking out on the late summer green of the trees. As is his manner, Jim did most of the talking in a fast, staccato tone. He summarized what had happened so far and asked if "Buzzy" had reached me. He finally asked me if Joe or I knew Karl Rove. I said not really, but he and his family attended the same church that we did in northwest Washington. "Really?" Jim drew back, white eyebrows practically at his hairline. I noted that although I knew who Rove was, I doubted he knew what I looked like. However, I promised Jim that the next time we were in line for Communion, I would pass him the wafer plate and whisper softly, "My name's Fair Game, what's yours?" Jim concluded the ten-minute session with the standard "Is there anything we can do for you?" query. ▮▮▮▮▮▮▮

▮▮▮▮▮▮▮▮▮▮▮▮▮▮▮▮▮▮▮▮▮▮▮▮▮▮▮▮▮▮▮▮▮▮

▮▮▮▮▮▮▮ Before I left, I mentioned that I had not been told that the Agency would confirm my undercover status to the public. Jim seemed perplexed. "We did that? I'll look into it." And that was the last meeting I would ever have in my CIA career with senior Agency management.

As August droned on, the smear campaign began against Joe. It ran the gamut from charging me with nepotism to accusing Joe of sloppy and inconclusive reporting. He became preoccupied and agitated and anxious to "do something." I wondered what exactly we could "do." I saw it as a waiting game—we could only react if and when the other shoe dropped—although I had no notion whatsoever of what the "shoe" would be. The tension between us came to a head one hot and humid Sunday morning, just before we left the house to go to a luncheon at Tom Foley's home on Capitol Hill. Joe had known and respected Foley and his wife, Heather, since the mid-1980s, when he served on Foley's staff as a Congressional Fellow. Frustrated and mad, I yelled at Joe that I thought he was wrong to want to approach the leak with some sort of preemptive strike—and furthermore, I wasn't going to the lunch. So there. Joe countered, at equal volume, that I was indeed going to the lunch and furthermore, we should tell Tom our respective viewpoints and have him decide. I thought that seemed reasonable, so I finished dressing and got into the car without saying another word.

After a lovely lunch with a dozen or so of Tom and Heather's friends, which they have collected from every walk of life and corner of the globe, we settled onto the white couches in the Foleys' art-filled living room. When most of the guests had left and Tom, a first-class raconteur, had finished up his last story, I charged ahead and told Tom that Joe and I disagreed over what we should do and we wanted his advice. Tom leaned in as we each made our case. I felt that we should sit tight until something happened, official in nature or not. Doing something now was premature. Joe wanted to be more proactive and stir the pot somehow to precipitate movement. When Tom heard our appeals, he leaned back into the cushions, arms behind his head, and stretched out his long legs. "Well, Valerie's right, Joe. You have to wait for your pitch." I wallowed in the glow of victory, but it faded quickly when I realized that we had no idea of what might be coming next. So, we decided to say or do nothing for the time being. Joe ultimately got his way, however. In late August, invited to a town meeting in Seattle by Congressman Jay Inslee, Joe answered a question from the audience with "Wouldn't it be fun to see Karl Rove frog-marched out of the White House in handcuffs?" The audience cheered wildly over this vision, but I thought he had gone too far and mentally cringed when I heard what he'd said. Husbands. What can you do? It was clear that our critics were monitoring our every move and word to turn them to their advantage. We were still on a steep learning curve.

Meanwhile, my close circle of girlfriends from college were burning up the Internet exchanging notes on *what had happened* to Valerie. I found out that most of them had set up an automatic Google search that would shoot them an e-mail whenever my name appeared in the media. To a person, each and every one of them remained loyal and supportive as the affair unfolded. Not one of them reproached me for telling them lies about my work ▇▇▇▇▇▇▇ but offered me their outrage at what had transpired. They understood that I could not tell them the truth of my employment, but some did mention that they now understood my constant ▇▇▇▇▇ travels. I was overcome with relief and felt blessed that our friendships, thanks to their understanding, would endure. Many times, others would ask me, how could my closest friends *not* have known? The truth is our talks had always been about boyfriends, husbands, vacations, then babies, shared interests, and clothes. These sorts of things may seem small or insignificant, but actually cement friendships. Talking in detail about our careers just wasn't of much interest to any of us.

Back at CIA Headquarters that summer, our ▇▇▇ once bustling office fell eerily quiet. There was tension, but the frantic activity of the months leading up to the invasion of Iraq fell dramatically. It was oddly deflating. We had watched quietly and proudly as our troops captured Baghdad and the surrounding region in a short period of time. But almost immediately, the city was engulfed in chaos and looting. In mid-April, the National Library was burned to the ground and thousands of priceless artifacts were stolen from the Iraqi National Museum. According to press accounts, at least 170,000 items, representing one of the finest collections of antiquities in the world, were plundered. To add to the dismay, some U.S. troops stood by and watched while others guarded the oil ministry. It was all deeply disturbing. When asked about the debacle, Defense Secretary Rumsfeld replied, "Freedom's untidy and free people are free to make mistakes and commit crimes and do bad things," adding, "stuff happens." I recall a conversation I had at that time with a conservative-minded colleague. I had seen the wild pillaging as a bad omen for future stability in Baghdad; if U.S. troops could not—or would not—stop people from carrying a load of TVs out of the stores, how could they bring order to the city? It seemed to me that a sense of security was critical to fashioning Iraq into a democratic model, especially in those early days. My colleague said with absolute certainty that the number of artifacts stolen from the museum was much smaller than reported. He dismissed the TV reports as overblown and manufactured stories from an obviously liberal-biased media that was looking only for negative stories to send back to the United States. Neither one of us managed to persuade the other. Then again, the favorite TV news channel in most Agency offices was Fox—so of course the other networks appeared more liberal by comparison. In any case, despite the use of "embedded" journalists in the armed forces, getting a handle on the real state of affairs on the ground was incredibly difficult.

Just a few weeks later, reports started to come out of Iraq that several nuclear facilities had also been looted and materials suitable to build a so-called "dirty [i.e., radioactive] bomb" had been taken from the carelessly guarded sites. What an irony it would be if the U.S. invasion had allowed nuclear material to fall into the hands of terrorists. The IAEA raised the alarm and urgently requested that coalition forces provide increased security for the nuclear facilities. The State Department's response was casual and denied that much looting had taken place at all.

In April and again in May, our spirits in the office had been briefly buoyed when coalition forces in northern Iraq discovered two curious flatbed trailers; the immediate suspicion was that they were part of a possible Iraqi mobile biological weapon production system. One trailer had all its equipment intact. Maybe this was it! The beginning of CIA's validation of WMD caches scattered throughout the country. But, just as we were absorbing the discovery and possible implications, along came the dismaying news that the trucks and their equipment could have just as easily been used for hydrogen production—to fill large and innocuous weather balloons. There was a period of confusion as the analysts tried to figure out what they had. Experts were dispatched to northern Iraq to investigate the find on-site. However, daily evidence seemed to mount that the trailers had a non-bioweapons use. Still, some WINPAC analysts clung stubbornly to the belief that this find was significant and proved Iraqi bioweapons intent. As the reports on the flatbed trucks filtered back to the Washington intel community, a dispute as bitter as the earlier one over aluminum tubes erupted. In June 2003 the *New York Times* reported that the State Department's intelligence division strongly disagreed with the official CIA assessment that the trucks were used to make biological weapons. The president used the find as proof of Iraq's biological weapons program. "In an interview with Polish television on May 30, Mr. Bush cited the trailers as evidence that the United States had 'found the weapons of mass destruction' it was looking for. Secretary of State Colin L. Powell echoed that assessment in a public statement the next day, saying that the accuracy of prewar assessments linking Iraqi trailers to a biological weapons program had been borne out by the discovery." Unfortunately, their statements just didn't match with reality, as much as they might have wished otherwise. The CIA ultimately had to conclude that the flatbed trucks were harmless. The "Comprehensive Report of the Special Advisor to the DCI on Iraq's WMD," issued by the Agency in September 2004, dryly noted that "Iraq Survey Group (ISG) has found no evidence to support the view that the equipment had a clandestine role in the production of BW agents; and ISG judges the equipment's configuration makes its use as a fermentor impractical for the following reasons. . . ."

As the summer went on our anxieties gradually shifted from

fears that our troops would be subjected to a surprise WMD attack (which would have made the "intelligence failure" of 9/11 pale by comparison) to bewilderment over why we weren't finding any WMD caches at all. I began to have a sinking feeling in my stomach that Saddam had pulled off one of the greatest intelligence deceptions of all time: he had made the world believe he had significant stashes of WMD that he would use, if threatened, when in fact, he had nothing. Apparently, even his top generals believed in the WMD myth. Half a year later on January 28, 2004, in his appearance before the Senate Armed Services Committee, outgoing Iraq Survey Group Director David Kay said that even the Iraqi Republican Guard generals had believed Iraq had weapons of mass destruction. From his testimony:

SEN. JEFF SESSIONS (R.-ALA.): I believe at one point you noted that even his own military officers believed they had them [WMD]. In other words, they would think—

DAVID KAY: that someone else had them.

SESSIONS: Could you explain that?

KAY: Well, in interviewing the Republican Guard generals and Special Republican Guard generals and asking about their capabilities and having them, the assurance was they didn't personally have them and hadn't seen them, but the units on their right or left had them. And as you worked the way around the circle of those defending Baghdad, which is the immediate area of concern, you have got this very strange phenomena of no, I don't have them, I haven't seen them, but look to my right and left. That was an intentional ambiguity.

In retrospect, it appears that Saddam Hussein wanted it both ways; to convince certain audiences that Iraq had WMD, while simultaneously working to convince others that it had abandoned all its illegal programs. The May/June 2006 issue of *Foreign Affairs* probably got closest to the truth when it noted that

> Ali Hassan al-Majid, known as "Chemical Ali" for his use of chemical weapons on Kurdish civilians in 1987, was convinced Iraq no longer possessed WMD but claims that many within Iraq's ruling circle never stopped believing that the weapons still existed. Even at the highest echelons of the regime, when it came to WMD there was always some element of doubt about the truth. According to Chemical Ali, Saddam was asked about the weapons during a meeting with members of the Revolutionary Command Council. He replied that Iraq did not have WMD but flatly rejected a suggestion that the regime remove all doubts to the contrary, going on to explain that such a declaration might encourage the Israelis to attack.

That summer of 2003, however, there was just confusion at CIA Headquarters as we tried to figure out what the hell had happened to the vaunted Iraqi WMD program. Why aren't we finding anything? What is going on out there? How could we have been so wrong? Six months later, some tried to make the case publicly that Iraq had managed to transport all of their WMD and any evidence that it had existed to safe haven in Syria before the war began. In an interview with the *Telegraph* around the time of his Senate testimony, Dr. David Kay said that he had uncovered evidence that unspecified materials had been moved to Syria shortly before the 2003 war. "We are not talking about a large stockpile of weapons," he said. "But we know from some of the interrogations of former Iraqi officials that a lot of material went to Syria before the war, including some components of

Saddam's WMD programme. Precisely what went to Syria, and what has happened to it, is a major issue that needs to be resolved."

As the challenging task of securing and stabilizing Iraq began in earnest, the drive and energy drained out completely from █████ my team at Headquarters and morale was low. My office mates began to █████ look for new jobs elsewhere in the DO. █████

███████████████████████████████████████ And it was the stories they told us when they returned from their stints that helped us sort out the sometimes disjointed media portrayal of the U.S. occupation in Baghdad. ██████████████████

█████████████████████ the situation was volatile and making every-

one very nervous. ▓▓▓▓▓▓▓▓▓▓▓▓▓▓▓▓▓▓▓▓▓▓▓▓▓
▓▓▓▓▓▓▓▓▓▓▓▓▓▓▓▓▓▓▓▓▓▓▓▓▓▓▓▓▓▓▓ One offi-
cer made sure the night's aerial bombardment from the nascent
insurgency, which they could hear clearly even though it was a
mile or so away, was over before calling his wife. "She would
have just been worried sick the whole time," he told me. ▓▓▓▓▓

▓▓▓▓▓▓▓▓▓▓▓▓▓▓▓▓▓▓▓▓▓▓▓▓▓▓▓▓▓▓▓▓▓▓▓▓▓▓

▓▓▓▓▓▓▓▓▓▓▓▓▓▓▓▓▓▓▓▓▓▓▓▓▓▓▓ According to
James Risen's *State of War*, the AARDWOLF (a situation report
written by the senior intelligence officer on the ground), "written one day after a deadly bombing of the United Nation's
offices in Baghdad that killed the UN's top official in the country,
was so grim that it immediately caused a stir within the CIA
and the Bush administration, and even prompted a tart rebuttal
from [L. Paul] Bremer [administrator of the Coalition Pro-
visional Authority]." It continued, "the new and bold insurgency . . . would discredit and isolate the U.S.-led coalition, and
warned that insurgents and terrorists had the capability to carry
out many more attacks against 'soft targets.' The insurgency was
increasingly dangerous and threatened to erase the early progress made by the Americans and could actually overwhelm occupation forces." ▓▓▓▓▓▓▓▓▓▓▓▓▓▓▓▓▓▓▓▓▓▓▓▓

▓▓▓▓▓▓▓▓▓▓▓▓▓▓▓▓▓▓▓▓▓▓▓▓▓▓▓▓▓▓▓▓▓▓▓▓▓▓

▓▓▓▓▓▓▓▓▓▓▓▓▓▓▓▓▓▓▓▓▓▓▓▓▓▓▓▓▓▓▓

On Saturday, September 27, Joe and I were invited to a farewell
party for a well-liked French journalist returning to Paris after
his stint in Washington. As I milled around the living room of
the narrow town house in Georgetown, I kept an eye out for Joe,
since I didn't see anyone else I knew. The hundred-year-old
house had uneven wooden floors that sloped to one side and gave
me the vague sense of being on a gently rolling ship. The small,

hot rooms were packed with guests, most of them from the European media clique in town. I noticed that many of the German guests had on those small dark-framed glasses they seem to favor. I forced myself to practice my social French with a fellow guest but I was bored. The weeks since the leak of my name in July had been a blend of surrealism and paralysis. A critical part of who I was—an undercover Agency operative—was no longer in place and everything felt disjointed to me. Happily, that night no one recognized me and I still felt like I had some semblance of privacy. But I was uneasy all the time, not knowing what would happen next. It felt like a dangerous waiting game, but we didn't know what we were waiting for. At least the French serve interesting appetizers, I thought, as I eyed the plate of exotic cheeses and delicious little bite-sized charcuteries.

It wouldn't be a Washington party unless the majority of the guests carried cell phones or the ubiquitous BlackBerries—especially vital to journalists. As I was reaching for another hors d'oeuvre, several phones suddenly went off around me and I moved away to find a more peaceful space. I pulled my phone from my purse and checked it quickly—no call from the babysitter, so I figured Joe and I could stay a little while longer. After a few minutes, Joe found me in the crowd and told me he had heard that the Justice Department might be investigating the leak, but he didn't have any more information. I didn't understand exactly what that meant, but I knew it was a change from the status quo. Joe wanted to stay a few more minutes so I told him I would wait for him on the front porch. I bummed a cigarette from another guest—something I hadn't done for years—and slipped outside. I took a deep breath of the cool autumn air and enjoyed the quiet moment. I needed the quick smoke to focus my thoughts and calm down a bit, and didn't feel guilty about it for a moment. Something was about to happen and I needed all the clear thinking I could muster.

CHAPTER 10

The Only Washington Scandal Without Sex

The next morning, Sunday, September 28, 2003, the article on the front page of the *Washington Post* was headlined: "Bush Administration Is Subject of Inquiry—CIA Agent's Identity Was Leaked to Media," and reported that the CIA had referred the leak to the Justice Department. Apparently, the Agency thought there was enough evidence to warrant an official investigation. Even more damaging to the White House, the article quoted a senior administration official as saying "Clearly, it [the leak] was meant purely and simply for revenge." Whatever shreds of privacy or normalcy our lives had until that moment were ripped away. Political dirty tricks have been around since Washington was founded. But this time, besides going after their opponent's family, the perpetrators may have committed a crime against national security.

For Joe and me, the article validated what we had suspected all along—that the leak was in retaliation for his having angered the administration and frustrated their attempts to portray the war and the run-up to it strictly on their own terms. It was intended to undercut Joe's credibility by claiming that I had sent him to Niger in an act of nepotism. There were unmistakable whiffs of "she had to get her hapless husband a job" and therefore "who can believe what he reported, anyway?" in the accusation.

"Leak of Agent's Name Causes Exposure of CIA Front Firm," "Justice to Begin Leak Interviews Within Days," "If the Secret's Spilled, Calling Leaker to Account Isn't Easy," "CIA-Disclosure Flap Intensifies" were just some of the headlines that greeted me each day. I found it mentally impossible to go from living a covert cover ████████ to openly acknowledging my CIA status. It was profoundly unsettling. Our wide circle of friends and family here and overseas who might have missed the ripple of comments when my name was initially published in Robert Novak's column in July could not miss the news now. Our phone rang incessantly—it rang when I left the house in the morning and was ringing when I came home at night. When I checked our voice mail, the recorded female voice usually said "there are fifteen unheard messages in your mailbox." When I checked my personal e-mail after putting the children to bed, there were at least twenty unread notes from friends and family. Friends from high school, long-lost sorority sisters, distant cousins, all seemed to find my e-mail address—or, in this age of six degrees of separation, found someone who knew my e-mail address—and reached out to me. It felt a little like *This Is Your Life* as the parade of anyone who ever knew me went by.

If any of my close friends were angry with me over my ████████ deception ████████████, they did not express it to me. They responded with "It's okay, Val, we understand. What can we do?" In my world, which had just been turned upside down, their fierce loyalty was a small but critical solace. As those first days blurred together, I found sympathetic understanding in the most unlikely places. One morning, when I dropped the children off at our neighborhood nursery school, several mothers, Washington "insiders" themselves or married to one, came up to my car and offered their support. "How could they do this to you? Don't they get what you were doing? It wasn't like you were a card-carrying member of the ACLU, after all. You were working at the CIA on WMD!"

Later that week, an older female colleague of mine hustled into my office waving that day's *New York Times*. She handed me the paper folded to a profile of me titled, "The Employee," and whistled low. "They got everything in here except your bra size." I gingerly picked up the paper, feeling something akin to nausea. True enough, the enterprising reporter had dug up information on my family, my education, and myriad other personal information that I found amazing and mortifying. Fortunately, the one piece of my identity that hadn't reached the papers yet was my image. Because public photographs of me were not yet available—they wouldn't get to my high school yearbook pictures for a while—I at least could still shop at Safeway dressed in yoga pants and a T-shirt without enduring whispers and glances.

For someone who had lived under cover, assuming it as a part of my life and protecting it zealously ████████████████, this instantaneous shift to being a public persona brought great anxiety, manifested both emotionally and physically. It didn't matter that most of the press attention was positive; all of it seemed intrusive, and I didn't want any part of it. I didn't care if I was called a "beautiful blonde" or not (I suppose that was better than an "ugly blonde"—I *do* have an ego). I developed a noticeable tic under my left eye and what would become chronic erratic digestive problems. I became wary, jumpy, frightened—all out of character for me. I slept poorly but was afraid to take any sleeping pills. Unlike most people, stress decreased my appetite and I lost weight off my already slim frame. I took up smoking a few furtive cigarettes a day for the fleeting moments of peace they seemed to offer. As the media maelstrom increased to hurricane strength I felt like all I heard was the rushing wind. Friends and acquaintances kindly offered their advice on how to cope with the incredible stress. It got to the point where I thought if one more person suggested that I take up yoga I would run screaming from the room. All the asanas and deep breathing exercises in the world weren't going to get me through this. I was going to have to find and tap some unknown reservoirs of strength and resolve if I didn't want to end up a damaged, bitter character. When Joe and I collapsed into our bed one night, we managed to joke that this must be the only Washington scandal ever without sex—we were just too exhausted.

On the professional front, my colleagues at the CIA tried to respect my privacy and offer their support sotto voce, when they could. From the day my name appeared until the fall, when the Justice Department investigation was announced and the issue became so politically charged, most of my coworkers saw the leak in strictly national security rather than partisan terms, and they expressed their vehement desire to find and punish whoever had done the dastardly deed. They realized that it could have easily been their names and lives plastered across the newspapers. For many, however, the sudden rush of media attention on one of their own was like hearing someone had died. They didn't know what to say, and therefore, said nothing. As strong political sentiments started to become attached to the different sides of the case, I didn't know whether to interpret their silence as hostility or discomfort. For the most part, I just tried to keep my head down and do the job.

In the midst of all this, I left the position I held for a little over two years ██████████████████ and assumed a new job—██████████████████████ for the Counterproliferation Division. Long before the leak, the acting Chief of CPD, Scott, asked me to consider this assignment. ████████ is one of those necessary, bureaucratic, ticket-punching jobs that helps one move up the ranks. It is worlds away from conducting exciting operations, but it allows the officer to see "how the sausage gets made" and a stint in the post usually leads to a more desirable position ████████ is responsible for all the job assignments, both domestic and overseas, throughout the division as well as making sure the division employees get the right training and are on the right career path. When I was first asked, I politely demurred. Who wants a line job when there were so many good operational positions out there? When Scott asked again that week, talking about how much *his* tenure as ████████ had benefited him years before and vaguely speaking of a good foreign assignment as a follow-on, I realized that my answer had to be "Yes, sir" and it was. I came in on a Saturday to clean my small office and threw out boxes of papers and junk that my predecessor had accumulated. I hung my name on the door and started my new job.

No sooner had I begun to get my arms around a branch that desperately needed staff, leadership, and serious organization if it was going to be effective at all, than the FBI paid me a visit. The Justice Department was wasting no time in getting started in its investigation. Two young, conservatively dressed women flashed their ID badges, sat down on my ratty office sofa, which I had attempted to dress up with some colorful throw pillows, and dove right into questioning. The women were friendly, and asked me the expected questions about my work at the CIA, my cover, and how Joe's trip to Niger came about. I told them everything I could remember. The interview was over in half an hour and after shaking hands all around again, they left, leaving behind their cards should I need to contact them. I sighed, and went back to figuring out CPD's arcane and secretive job assignment process, which I had identified as my first improvement project.

One of the most positive and appealing aspects of my new position was the opportunity to come into contact with freshly recruited Career Trainees. The Agency hires many qualified people each year for an amazing array of jobs, but less than one hundred are put into the elite CT program, from where they will go on to work in different facets of operations. According to an Agency spokeswoman, the CIA received 135,000 résumés in 2006, up from the about 60,000 in 2001. Many of the CTs—most in their late twenties—were inspired by the idea of public service in the aftermath of 9/11. They left lucrative and exciting careers to start at the Agency on salaries averaging forty-five thousand dollars per year—which doesn't go very far in expensive Washington, D.C.

and so many other idealistic, smart, and talented young people. As I reviewed their impressive résumés, looking to place them in a three-month interim assignment in CPD, I thought that if I were applying to the CIA today, my simple bachelor's degree from a state university probably would not make the cut. True to Tenet's vision, which he had laid out when he arrived as DCI, the Agency was finally finding and hiring much more ethnically diverse employees with a broad range of native and acquired language skills. Still, the Agency, like most federal agencies, is well behind the curve when it comes to hiring Arabic speakers. A July 2001 *Atlantic* article by former CIA officer Reuel Marc Gerecht caused a stir in the office when he wrote that "a former senior Near East Division operative says, 'The CIA probably doesn't have a single truly qualified Arabic-speaking officer of Middle Eastern background who can play a believable Muslim fundamentalist who would volunteer to spend years of his life with shitty food and no women in the mountains of Afghanistan. For Christ's sake, most case officers live in the suburbs of Virginia. We don't do that kind of thing.' A younger case officer boils the problem down even further: 'Operations that include diarrhea as a way of life don't happen.' "

The optimism and lack of cynicism of these young recruits, in stark contrast to many of us older officers, were a balm to my frazzled state. They had joined the Agency for all the right reasons and they gave me some hope that it would be in good hands as they rose through the ranks.

In mid-October, I requested half a day off from work so that I could accompany Joe to a luncheon given by the Fertel Foundation and the Nation Institute where he was to be honored with the first Ron Ridenhour Award as "Truth Teller of the Year." Ron Ridenhour was the Vietnam veteran who in 1969 had described the details of the My Lai Massacre in letters to Congress, President Nixon, and the Pentagon. His perseverance attracted the attention of *New York Times* reporter Seymour Hersh, who broke the story. Ridenhour went on to become an investigative reporter and died suddenly in 1998. Although I was anxious about being out in public, I certainly wanted to be at Joe's side when he accepted his special award. The sponsors agreed to keep the press and photographers out of the luncheon and it turned out to be one of the most emotional events of my life. The room was full of patriotic Americans from all walks of life who were committed to telling the truth and fighting for our democracy— and it was humbling to be in their company. I thought of George Orwell's famous quote, "In a time of universal deceit, truth telling becomes a revolutionary act." I was so proud of Joe and what he stood for. When Joe gave his remarks, he started to acknowledge me, our loss of privacy, and apologize for what the government had done, when he stopped suddenly, blinking back tears. I had never seen him like this—Joe is always an unruffled and articulate public speaker, but he was clearly struggling with the moment. Our connection, from the instant we saw each other seven years before at the reception, to all we had lived through since, was stronger than ever. Seeing his moist eyes, I felt my own eyes well up. "Oh good Lord," I thought. "We're both going to break down here." Fortunately, we both regained our composure, but it was truly a moment in time for us.

In early October 2003, the Senate Select Committee on Intelligence (SSCI) announced that it would hold hearings on the leak and the prewar intelligence on Iraq. The SSCI is a very powerful investigative body. Established in 1975 in the wake of Watergate, SSCI is mandated to oversee the work of the entire U.S. intelligence community. The committee was conducting interviews and preparing a public report that Joe and I hoped would, at a minimum, reveal how the administration had cherry-picked intelligence to justify going to war with Iraq. I also hoped it would show that the decision to go to war was premature; the intelligence community simply did not have the hard evidence from current, reliable human sources to match the confident rhetoric coming from the White House and its supporters.

On a picture-perfect fall day, clear and crisp, when I would have loved to have been walking along the picturesque C&O canal, which meanders alongside the Potomac River from Georgetown deep into the hills of western Maryland, I was in a rather sterile Senate office building on Capitol Hill, waiting to testify before the committee. A few days before, the CIA lawyers had called to tell me that the SSCI staff had requested that I appear before them to speak about the Niger episode. I was told that a CIA attorney would accompany me, but they made it very clear that he was there to protect the CIA's interests—not mine. I took one last look in my compact cosmetic mirror, tucked it back into my purse, straightened my posture, and strode into the small hearing room, trying to exude confidence. Although somewhat nervous, I wasn't frightened. I knew that neither Joe nor I had done anything wrong and I would simply tell the truth, just as I had done with the FBI agents.

When I entered the room, I was somewhat surprised to see that there were no senators present. Four relatively young staffers—two Democrats, two Republicans—all of whom looked as if they'd just stepped out of a J. Crew catalog came in, but they did not come over to shake hands or introduce themselves. They gave a general nod in my direction, which I took for a greeting and invitation to sit down. They situated themselves behind a grand horseshoe-shaped table. The CIA lawyer, who'd barely said six words to me in the car ride from Headquarters—"beautiful day, isn't it?"—settled in next to me and took out a notepad and pen. His job, I supposed, was to stop the proceedings if they dipped into an area more classified than what had been agreed on. "Just answer their questions to the best of your ability," he muttered. I took a deep breath as the hearing opened, "Please state your name and your responsibilities at the CIA."

The questions started simply enough: give us a brief description of your career; tell us about your work at the time of Joe's trip to Niger; how did you hear about the report alleging a sale of yellowcake uranium from Niger to Iraq? As the hearing progressed, the questions took on a slightly more aggressive tone. It was obvious to me that the staffers knew very little about how CIA cover actually worked, yet they acted as if they were veterans of the intelligence community. "Didn't you think your cover would be blown when your husband, Ambassador Wilson, wrote his op-ed piece for the *New York Times*?" I explained politely that

The Only Washington Scandal Without Sex | 167

my cover had been intact ▓▓▓▓▓▓▓▓▓▓▓▓▓▓▓▓▓▓▓▓ The fact that my husband's credentials made him a perfect candidate to travel to Niger on behalf of the CIA and to speak publicly about the war had nothing to do with my own (former) covert status. "Why did you suggest your husband for the trip to Niger?" This obviously leading question came from a Republican staffer who had been particularly pointed in his earlier queries. His increasing hostility concerned me, but I had no idea then of how the Republicans were seeking to shape my testimony. In my desire to be as accurate and truthful as possible, I answered, stupidly, "I don't believe that I recommended my husband, but I can't recall who suggested him for the trip." This was true. Given the incredible pace and scope of my work during that prewar period and the subsequent passage of time, I simply did not recall the sequence of events leading to the trip. I had completely forgotten that it was a Junior Reports Officer who had first suggested to me that CPD consider talking to Joe about the alleged transaction. I had forgotten that Penny received the call from the vice president's office that had set Joe's trip in motion. I had also forgotten that we went to our Branch Supervisor and it was *he*—not me—who requested that I ask Joe to come into Headquarters to discuss "options." No lawyer had prepared me for my SSCI interview; I did not review the events with Joe or any of my colleagues prior to my appearance because I did not think it was proper to "compare memories."

The fact was, however, that I neither suggested Joe nor recommended him. There was no ulterior motive; I did not have the authority to send Joe to Niger or anywhere else, even if I had wanted to. "What did you do when the two CIA officers came to your home to debrief Ambassador Wilson upon his return from Niger?" This I remembered clearly: I ordered Chinese food for delivery and stayed out of their way—precisely to avoid any appearance of a conflict of interest. The staffers busily jotted down notes and looked very serious.

After about forty-five minutes, I left the hearing room with the CIA lawyer in tow, calm in the knowledge that I had answered all of their questions fully, truthfully, and to the best of my ability. Still, a little voice in my head was saying it felt like a setup. In retrospect, it was clear they weren't seeking information, but simply confirming their already closed conclusions. But in my naïveté, my heart actually felt light because I believed in our democratic institutions. I believed that the truth would prevail, but I would soon find out that in Washington, the truth is not always enough. When I returned to my desk at Headquarters, I picked up my work where I had left off. No one asked about the SSCI interview, and the issue seemed to be closed.

After weeks of living in a pressure cooker, we were itching to get out of Washington. Joe was giving a speech at UCLA and he and I leapt at the kind invitation from Norman and Lyn Lear to spend that weekend at their home in Los Angeles. Norman had contacted Joe after he saw him on the PBS show *NOW with Bill Moyers*. They became fast friends and we looked forward to meeting Norman and his wife in person. The year before, Norman had purchased one of the few existing original copies of the Declaration of Independence at Sotheby's for $8.2 million. He sent it around the country so ordinary citizens could see the birth certificate of this great country.

When Lyn called a few days later to say that she was throwing a small dinner party for us. I was thrown into a panic. What to wear? What to do with my hair? The visit was a welcome, lighthearted diversion from the reality of our lives that fall. In the Lears' warm Provençal-style home with modern masterpieces hanging on every wall, it was delicious fun to chat with these huge Hollywood figures. Defying the stereotype of a star as somewhat dim or narcissistic, they were extraordinarily smart, well-informed, politically passionate, and witty. Joe and I seemed to be as much of a curiosity as they were for us. They asked probing, sophisticated, and detailed questions about the run-up to the war, the CIA, the leak, and the growing insurgency in Iraq. Their keen interest and understanding was reassuring, but I began to feel just a little bit like the zebra in the petting zoo. When Warren Beatty held my chair as I sat at the lavish dinner table, I thought that my life had taken a surreal turn, unimaginable only six months before.

Returning to Washington, life picked up again at its unrelenting pace. *Vanity Fair* magazine had done an extensive interview with Joe and one blustery November day, a small band of photographers, assistants, makeup artists and stylists—all dressed in the chic black New York uniform—showed up at our home to take pictures of Joe to accompany the story. I had been at the park with the children that morning and came into the house windblown, tired, and not feeling too well. When I entered the kitchen where they were making up Joe for his photos, the *Vanity Fair* team turned as if one and beseeched me to consider getting my photo taken as well. Caught up in the glamorous moment and feeling somewhat beaten down, I reluctantly agreed, but only if I could not be recognized. To be honest, it was a "what the hell" moment. I did not listen to my instincts and threw my extreme caution about public exposure to the wind. In no time, the beauty team had me made up, outfitted in a Hermès scarf and dark glasses thoroughly concealing my face and sitting in Joe's Jaguar, which they parked in front of the White House. We finished up quickly and Joe and I went home, not giving the photo session another thought.

When the January 2004 *Vanity Fair* hit the stands with the photo of me and Joe, the furor from the Right was deafening. Some suggested that I had "outed" myself by appearing in the photo. Others saw it as a publicity stunt or self-promotion. Those who were spinning the view that Joe's op-ed and the subsequent leak of my name were inconsequential called it flagrant and outrageous. Those attacks were expected. But I had not bargained for being called to the CPD Chief's office and given an angry dressing-down. Mark was absolutely furious that I had not told him of the *Vanity Fair* photo and he was right—I should have. My only explanation is that in the craziness of my life at that time, my judgment suffered. I have never been spoken to so harshly by a supervisor and I left his office nearly in tears. I was humiliated and worse, I had lost his respect. The next day, I returned to Mark's office and offered my sincere apology and offered to go find another job in another division if he no longer wanted me to work in CPD. He accepted the apology and told me to stay. But I had obviously broken his trust and he was always frosty with me after that.

Almost two years later, I found out that during that very same time period, he had started an affair with someone in his direct chain of command. When I heard the stories about their escapades circulating throughout the Division, I thought back to my dressing-down and mused that even Mark's judgment suffered sometimes as well. To this day, I'm ambivalent whenever the *Vanity Fair* photo is flashed on the TV screen when an aspect of the leak case is discussed.

In the midst of the swirl of photographs, work, children, and media frenzy, the small but respected publishing house of Carroll & Graf offered Joe a contract to write a book. He agreed, pleased to have an opportunity to tell his story about Niger and Iraq, as well as to write about his diplomatic career and war and peace in Africa and the Middle East. Our neighbor recommended his cousin by marriage, Audrey Wolf, as Joe's literary agent, and she immediately suggested that with all the publicity surrounding the leak, Joe could get a much larger advance than the ten thousand dollars already informally agreed upon with Carroll & Graf if he allowed several publishers to bid on the book. Joe declined because he had a gentleman's agreement with the editor, Philip Turner, that he felt obligated to keep.

As is his character, Joe immediately threw himself into the project with intensity and passion. When he wasn't traveling or giving a radio interview, he was up at 4:30 A.M. every morning hunched over the computer keyboard for hours before going to work. When we went to my parents' home in Pennsylvania for Thanksgiving he took along his laptop and continued writing, taking time out only for the turkey dinner. Not surprising, his discipline paid off and he had a manuscript ready for the editor in four months. We were living together in the same house, but in parallel universes. I was dealing with my work, the children's needs, and trying to come to terms with my new overt CIA status. Joe was writing his book, responding to steady media requests for interviews, and traveling across the country to speak to college students or a variety of civic groups. Sometimes it seemed the only way we communicated was via yellow Post-its or cell phone messages. Once Joe's book was essentially completed, his travel schedule became even more demanding and I often felt like a single working mother whose life had taken a wrong turn.

When I married Joe in 1998, I happily took his name. This was not so much from a postfeminist backlash and return to tradition, but rather because I practically reasoned that *Wilson* was a much easier name to spell and pronounce. My days of spelling "P-L-A-M as in Mary-E" over the phone would be over. I was often a little wistful, however. I had done some sporadic genealogical research over the year, because my brother and I had grown up without ever knowing any relatives on my father's side of the family. My father had no idea if he had any family still alive anywhere, but seemed supremely uninterested in finding any family if my brother or I ventured to ask him about it. But the only two Plames that I could find in the country were my father and my brother.

My great-grandfather, Samuel Plamevotski, emigrated to Chicago in 1892 from a small Jewish hamlet in the Ukraine. Family lore said he was a rabbi and he left with his oldest son to avoid being drafted into the czar's army as well as the frequent murderous pogroms. My occasional work in the dusty microfilm bays at the National Archives in Washington and Chicago's City Hall yielded two precious documents. The first, dated 1892 and so presumably done shortly after he arrived, was Samuel's intent to declare U.S. citizenship. A scrawled "X" marks his signature. The second, bestowing U.S. citizenship ten years later in 1902, shows a carefully written "Samuel Plame" on its signature line. His son, my grandfather, Samuel Plame, Jr., came to Chicago with the rest of the family in 1894. In 1917, he met and married my grandmother in a love match. Unfortunately for them, my grandmother was a gentile descended from a rugged pioneer family related to Andrew Jackson, and the Plame family promptly sat *shiva* for Samuel, horrified that the son of a rabbi would dare to marry a *shiksa*, and cut off all contact with him forever. Their only child, my father, Samuel Plame III, was born in 1920 and had no memories of any family on his father's side. My religious upbringing and education were undertaken exclusively by my mother, who was Protestant. It was this void in my family past that led to my interest in my father's genealogy.

One day in the fall of 2003, as the name *Plame* was being bantered around the airwaves and newspapers for what seemed like the millionth time, my brother, Robert Plame, received an odd phone call out of the blue. "Is your father Samuel Plame?" asked the gentleman who had introduced himself as Leon Coleman. "Um, yes" my brother answered, somewhat warily. "Well, I think we're second cousins!" Leon exclaimed. Leon, it turned out, lived only a few miles from my brother in Portland, Oregon. He had a wealth of family stories and was able to help us piece together our Plame family tree. Through Leon's happy intervention, that spring Joe and I celebrated Passover Seder dinner with newly found relatives. As we worked through the ancient Haggadah text describing the trials of the Jewish people and their indefatigable optimism, and I nibbled on the traditional matzo and maror, I thought that this was a very positive, albeit unlikely, consequence of having the name *Plame* in the public domain.

On December 31, 2003, Attorney General John Ashcroft had recused himself from the leak investigation. No public reason was given, although his deputy, James Comey, said, "The attorney general in an abundance of caution believed that his recusal was appropriate based on the totality of the circumstances and the facts and evidence developed at this stage of the investigation." It was a belated but welcome Christmas present. Ashcroft had clearly given some thought to his extensive financial and personal ties to Karl Rove, who even then was believed to have had a significant role in the leak, and made the right decision. Several years later, we heard secondhand from a friend of Ashcroft that he was "troubled" and had "lost sleep" over the administration's actions. In 2006, Joe attended the Moroccan National Day and was standing by himself for a moment in the crowd. A man spotted Joe from across the room and headed directly for him, thrusting out his hand. The dark-haired gentleman introduced himself as a "leading member of the Washington evangelical movement" and Joe steeled himself for an expected tirade. Instead, the man said with whispered sincerity as he held his hand, "You should know that there are many of us that support you." When Joe asked why, the man continued, "because we believe in truth and we know that this government has lied." Perhaps the same consideration had stirred Ashcroft. In any case, Ashcroft's departure led to another Justice Department move that would bring great anxiety to the White House. Comey turned to the U.S. attorney for Illinois, Patrick Fitzgerald, to conduct the investigation. Comey said of Fitzgerald: "For those of you who don't know him, he is a total pro. I chose Mr. Fitzgerald, my friend and former colleague, based on his sterling reputation for integrity and impartiality. He is an absolutely apolitical career prosecutor. He is a man with extensive experience in national security and intelligence matters, extensive experience conducting sensitive investigations and, in particular, experience in conducting investigations of alleged government misconduct." Comey was right, and Fitzgerald's integrity and dogged determination to get to the bottom of any leak would haunt the White House. Joe and I heard nothing but positive things about Fitzgerald from many sources and we were heartened to see the justice system work as it was designed to.

Fitzgerald, in his early forties, had already earned an impressive reputation as a government prosecutor and his record of indictments was a strikingly diverse list of the powerful. In 1993, he won a guilty plea from Mafia capo John Gambino. He won a conviction against Sheik Omar Abdel Rahman for the 1993 World Trade Center bombing and built the first criminal indictment against terrorist Osama bin Laden. In late 2003, he indicted former Illinois governor George Ryan on conspiracy and fraud charges. In 2005, Fitzgerald's office indicted a number of top aides to Democrat Richard Daley, the mayor of Chicago, on charges of mail fraud and brought criminal fraud charges against Canadian media mogul and British lord Conrad Black. So Fitzgerald was not easily intimidated by wealth, status, or threats. In a *Washington Post* profile in 2005, he was described as, "a solidly built former rugby player who enjoyed getting muddy and bloody well into his twenties, Fitzgerald is nothing but confident in his own skin. Just as he does not fear bin Laden, he seems to fret little that he is now tangling simultaneously with the Bush White House and the *New York Times*, two of the nation's most powerful and privileged institutions." He was universally described by friends and critics alike as a man of integrity and zeal for pursuit of truth. We would soon have our opportunity to meet Fitzgerald in person and take his measure.

One cold and rainy winter day in early 2004, I left Headquarters and drove to a beautiful office building downtown. After passing through the security gauntlet complete with badge and x-ray machine, I took the elevator to the prosecutor's office. After being buzzed into the suite, I was ushered into a poorly lit conference room with standard-issue government furniture. After a moment, Fitzgerald entered with a deputy and firmly shook my hand. Despite a serious demeanor, he was warm and engaging. I felt at ease immediately and at his request, launched into a description of my career, and what I was doing prior to Joe's trip to Niger and the subsequent events. Fitzgerald did not take notes, but he listened intently, his eyes rarely leaving mine as I told my story. My impression of him was of a highly intelligent, compassionate person who probably had a good sense of humor. I read later that he particularly enjoyed playing practical jokes on his colleagues. As we stood to shake hands at the conclusion of the meeting, I told him that the only thing Joe and I hoped for was "a robust and fair investigation and that justice was served." Fitzgerald said that he "would do all he could to see that this happened." I believed him completely.

CHAPTER 11

The Year from Hell

When Joe's book, *The Politics of Truth*, was published in April 2004, we hosted a festive party at our home. On a warm evening in the Washington spring, just as the azaleas were blooming in a riot of color, dozens of friends and supporters stopped by to sip champagne and offer congratulatory words and handshakes. Book parties tend to be a dime a dozen in Washington—everyone seems to write a book eventually—but for the author, of course, it's special and Joe was rightly proud of his work. He was particularly delighted to have the opportunity to write about his twenty-five-year career rather than just the leak; it was a rich slice of diplomatic history. His former Foreign Service colleagues uniformly appreciated his realistic portrait of the hard and unglamorous work that diplomats do in the trenches around the world. The initial reviews were mostly positive and the book quickly found a spot on the *New York Times* best-seller list, much to our surprise. I even began watching the book's Amazon ranking—taking secret pleasure as it climbed higher each day. Very few authors make any significant money on a book, and my financial plans for any royalties that might come our way were modest: I hoped for enough to rebuild the splintering and rotting deck on the back of our house. Joe was amused by the idea of being a genuine published author and kept joking that I should buy him a corduroy jacket with elbow patches. It was a happy time.

A few days later, a wealthy and well-known Democratic fund-raiser graciously offered to hold a book party in our honor at her soft pink Georgetown mansion. It was one of the first times that Joe and I had appeared out in public and, despite my pride in Joe, my further visibility made me uncomfortable and guarded. I bristled at the idea of myself as a public personality. As Joe chatted easily with the guests, told stories, and posed for photos, I stood off to the side by the piano, soaking in the heavenly aroma of lilies from all the flower arrangements as well-wishers came by to shake my hand. Many people told me that they thought Joe and I were heroes; he for speaking out and I for my public service in a difficult profession. Of course it was gratifying to hear their compliments, but it also made me want to shake with embarrassment. Neither Joe nor I considered ourselves heroic in any way—we did our jobs and tried to do the right thing as citizens in a democracy. We did understand, however, that we were symbols of push-back against an administration that appeared to be an unstoppable juggernaut that spring—Joe was in a lonely club of those that had spoken up publicly to question what appeared to be an increasingly arrogant and deceitful White House. Still, it was not a role I ever anticipated that either one of us would play, and it felt strange. I had not yet found my footing in this new world, and I felt very vulnerable, but tried to smile and say something cogent. That evening was to be one of the last pleasant memories we would have for a long time; the forces on the other side preparing their counterattack.

With 2004 being an election year, the good book reviews and

cheers for Joe were countered by harsh editorials and cutting commentary from those on the right. The good coverage that the book was receiving seemed to infuriate those who saw Joe and his criticisms of the yellowcake and the leak as a threat, or at least an insult, to the president's presumed victory in November. Tellingly, the critics didn't attack any of Joe's facts or the book itself; their strikes tended to be quite personal in nature. For example, journalist and former Republican National Committee staffer Cliff May wrote that "after a wet-kiss profile in *Vanity Fair*, [Joe] gave birth to a quickie book sporting his dapper self on the cover, and verbosely entitled [it] *The Politics of Truth: Inside the Lies That Led to War and Betrayed My Wife's CIA Identity: A Diplomat's Memoir.*" May then perversely claimed that Novak hadn't outed me—Joe had: ". . . So if Novak did not reveal that Valerie Plame was a secret agent, who did? The evidence strongly suggests it was none other than Joe Wilson himself."

Other reviews from right-leaning sources were equally mean-spirited. Having lived through the first spate of harsh attacks on Joe's credibility and character in the wake of the leak, I thought I had acquired some armor. I was wrong. I knew the comments were politically motivated, but they were still painful to read, and once again we felt under siege. In the midst of this tangle of emotions, Joe embarked on several long national tours to market his book, leaving me to cope as best I could and shield Samantha and Trevor from the whirlwind just outside the house.

With so much vitriol in the air and Joe away, threats to our security, which had begun months earlier, took an ominous turn and I became increasingly concerned about our safety. We received a steady stream of disturbing letters, crank phone calls, even death threats. One spring day, four-year-old Trevor picked up the ringing phone and proudly answered, just as I'd taught him: "Wilson residence. May I help you?" I could tell immediately from his puzzled expression that the caller was not a well-meaning friend. I lunged for the phone, heard the raw ramblings of a seriously deranged person, and hung up, shaking. Until this passed, my children would not be answering the phone or be out of a trusted adult's sight for a moment.

Only a few days later, the green secure phone rang at my desk at Headquarters. A colleague, ██████, with whom I had once worked on a sensitive project ████████████████, called me from her posting in the northeast part of the country. She was the new boss at her office and an experienced and competent operations officer. Not wasting any time on pleasantries, ██████ started right in on the purpose of her call: "Hi there. It's ██████. I want to give you a heads-up on something that's come across my desk. ███████████████████████████████████

██████████████ that got the immediate attention of the CIA's protective security branch, which swung into action. This branch is used to dealing with the constant barrage of threats, primarily from mentally unstable individuals, typically directed toward the DCI and other top CIA officials. Now, with the latest information coming in about ████████ looking particularly menacing, the branch's first priority was to convince the bureau not to relinquish surveillance in order to assess further how great a risk he might be. As I drove home that evening, I conjured up possible dreadful scenarios. I tried to stifle my rising panic about harm coming to Trevor or Samantha as a consequence of my exposed CIA affiliation. All of a sudden, it wasn't "just political." It was very real and it was placing my family in jeopardy. I felt I could handle whatever happened to Joe or me; my children were another matter. Rounding the corner to my street, I tried to see my home from the perspective of someone who was seeing it as a target. What were its vulnerabilities? Where were my escape routes? How predictable were our schedules and those of the children? I was used to running this kind of internal inventory and analysis while living overseas—it was normal and prudent. A great deal of our deployment training had been devoted to constructing and understanding good security practices. But I was not used to doing it in my quiet Washington neighborhood. I felt cheated. Then I got furious.

In the wake of the leak, in October 2003, the CIA had sent out an officer to review our security situation at home. They recommended doing things like cutting back tree branches that partially covered an outdoor lighting fixture and putting a deadbolt on the front door. I didn't feel perceptibly safer, but I was not yet ready to request 24/7 security. Now, months and many crank phone calls, disturbing letters, threats, and one ▓▓▓▓▓ later, I thought I had no choice.

Fury is not an effective emotion when dealing with a bureaucracy. I had learned long ago not to take bureaucratic obstacles personally; you had to relentlessly work the system. I drafted a polite, succinct memo to the head of CIA security. Given the recent threat information about ▓▓▓▓▓▓, and the stream of intelligence reporting pertaining to the increased threat of an Al Qaeda attack in the run-up to the presidential elections, I requested a 24/7 security presence at my residence until the November 2004 elections. I understood that this would require significant resources but I would never have forgiven myself if I hadn't asked and something had happened to my family. I hand-carried my memo to the office of the head of security on Headquarters' seventh floor. The secretary cheerily told me that they would get back to me "as soon as possible."

The next day I received an interim response from the head of security while his office "determined the specific threat situation." He said that the Agency had notified the Washington Metropolitan Police Department of my concerns and requested they increase patrols in my neighborhood. To my pleasant surprise, I soon began to see D.C.'s finest cruise by our home once in a while and I knew that they were doing their best. The memo concluded that their review would be completed in thirty days, at which time I "would be notified."

Nearly two months later, at the start of the hot Washington summer, the chipper secretary called me to say that a memo from the Director of Security was waiting for me in their offices. I hustled over, and after scanning the first few lines, walked back to my office in a fog. The CIA had decided to deny my request for any security coverage. The security director's rationale was that a month of "observe and report" coverage of my residence—that is, frequent, nonpredictable drive-bys—had indicated to them that there was no "specific or credible threat to the safety of you or your family." The memo gave me a pat on the back for my use of good security practices and, if anything changed, I should let them know. When I told my immediate supervisor, Jim, who had been extremely supportive and helpful over the last few months, of the latest development, his eyes opened wide and he looked at me in sheer disbelief. Jim is the master of understatement and he croaked, "I imagine you must be disappointed in their decision."

To say that the CIA response "disappointed" me doesn't begin to touch the betrayal I felt. After ███████████████ loyal service, I expected the Agency to come through on its standing promise to protect its "family," something that had always been a point of CIA pride. I thought of ████████████ other potential targets: Tenet, Ashcroft, Rove. All had 24/7 secret service protection at home and en route to work. They and their families didn't have to worry about surprise unwelcome visitors. Threats to ranking, high-profile U.S. officials are an unfortunate part of public life, more so during war time, but they were well protected. Although far from being a top U.S. official, because of unique circumstances I was just as vulnerable. Clearly, I was on my own. I went home, taught our nanny, Monique, the basics of surveillance detection, bought her a cell phone with a one-button 911 dial, instructed her not to let the children out of her sight, called Joe on the road, and told him what happened, and tried not to be consumed by bitterness.

Fourteen months after President Bush had landed on the aircraft carrier the USS *Abraham Lincoln* and spoke to the cheering troops in front of an enormous "Mission Accomplished" banner strung above the vessel's bridge, American soldiers were still bringing Iraqi scientists suspected of working on Saddam's WMD programs into detention for questioning. ████████████

██████████████████████████████████████

████████████████████████████████████ The imminent peril of WMD, the crucial selling point of this war of
choice, had yet to be found, and the occupation of Iraq was cost-
ing ever-increasing numbers of U.S. troops. Close to a thousand
American troops had been killed since the beginning of the war
and tens of thousands of Iraqis. The costs of the war, in blood,
treasure, and our international credibility, were beginning to
penetrate the public consciousness. The appalling Abu Ghraib
prison scandal had exploded in April, shocking every American
with its vivid photographs of Iraqi prisoners being subjected to
inhumane treatment. When CBS broke the story, followed
quickly by Seymour Hersh's investigative piece in the *New
Yorker*, Americans were outraged. It was heartbreaking. What
had we become as a nation? But in a July speech at Oak Ridge
National Laboratory, President Bush told the cheering crowd,
"Three years ago, the ruler of Iraq was a sworn enemy of America, who provided safe haven for terrorists, used weapons of mass
destruction, and turned his nation into a prison. Saddam Hussein was not just a dictator; he was a proven mass murderer who
refused to account for weapons of mass murder. Every responsible nation recognized this threat, and knew it could not go on
forever. . . . Although we have not found stockpiles of weapons
of mass destruction, we were right to go into Iraq. We removed a
declared enemy of America, who had the capability of producing
weapons of mass murder, and could have passed that capability to
terrorists bent on acquiring them. In the world after September
the 11th, that was a risk we could not afford to take." It was as if
there were two wars: the one that the administration touted with
pride, and the one that everyone else followed on their TVs and
that wasn't going as promised.

As I reviewed some of the latest depressing reports from the
field, I heard a tap on the office door and one of my colleagues

asked if he could come in. I was happy for the diversion, but as soon as he sat down, I could tell this wasn't going to be a social conversation over coffee. His round face was flushed and his eyes, behind glasses, looked close to tears. I had worked with him for the last two years, through many stressful days, and I had never seen him so emotional or distressed. He glanced anxiously at the closed door before speaking. "They twisted my testimony," he said in a low, tight voice. I had no idea what he was talking about. "*I* recommended Joe for the trip, don't you remember? I told the committee this, but they didn't include it in the report."

His words rang in my ears. A few days earlier, on July 7, Joe had come home in a state of full fury with a copy of the Senate Select Committee on Intelligence (SSCI) *Report on the U.S. Intelligence Community's Prewar Intelligence Assessments on Iraq*, which was released the next day. Joe dropped the two-inch stack of papers on the kitchen table and marched upstairs to change clothes, his every motion emanating hostility. I grabbed the report and read most of it without moving from the kitchen. It seemed to be a jumble, and then I got to the sentence, "The plan to send the former ambassador to Niger was suggested by the former ambassador's wife, a CIA employee." This was the first "conclusion" in the "Additional Views" section, written by Republican senators Pat Roberts, the committee chairman, Christopher Bond, and Orrin Hatch. Even more bizarre, "The Committee found that, for most analysts, the former ambassador's report lent more credibility, not less, to the reported Niger-Iraq uranium deal." I could not believe what I was reading. How could this be? What analysts were saying Joe's report *lent more credibility*? Why? What was going on here? I felt like Alice falling down the rabbit hole: what was once white was suddenly black.

I somehow managed to get dinner on the table. Midway

through the silent meal, Joe abruptly got up, dumped his unfinished plate in the sink, and left the room in a wordless rage. The kids immediately picked up on the unspoken tension and starting acting up. They were irritable and naughty, I was exhausted and bewildered. Later that evening, after putting the children to bed, Joe came into our bedroom, brandishing the report. "What is this about a memo you did?" He was referring to a comment in the report that said I drafted an e-mail in which I wrote, "my husband has good relations [in Niger] with both the PM [prime minister] and the former Minister of Mines (not to mention lots of French contacts), both of whom could possibly shed light on this sort of activity." That was the e-mail I'd written at my supervisor's request and it was routine procedure to inform division management of ███ our office's activities. It wasn't the sort of thing I would have come home and told him about—it was standard procedure. I had forgotten about it. Certainly the e-mail was not evidence that I had suggested sending Joe to Niger. But the SSCI had construed it as such and were using it to conclude that I had, in fact, been responsible for his trip. Despite my best efforts to explain the innocence of the e-mail, Joe was too upset to listen. He just glared at me and mumbled something about a rebuttal and left the room. I lay down on the bed, miserable over my husband's deep anger, the Republican senators' complete disregard for the truth, and my own naïveté. Joe told me years later that for him, reading this report and learning that I had written that e-mail were his lowest points in this entire ordeal. It made me feel sick all over again.

The next day, Joe drafted an eight-page rebuttal to all the senators on the intelligence committee. Joe pointed out many of the reports inaccuracies, such as its conclusion that his 2002 trip strengthened analysis that Iraq was seeking uranium from

Niger. In truth, other facts in the report suggest the exact opposite:

- In August, 2002, a CIA NESA [Near Eastern and South Asian Analysis] report on Iraq's Weapons of Mass Destruction capabilities did not include the alleged Iraq-Niger uranium information. (pg. 48)
- In September, 2002, during coordination of a speech with an NSC [National Security Council] staff member, the CIA analyst suggested the reference to Iraqi attempts to acquire uranium from Africa be removed. The CIA analyst said the NSC staff member said that would leave the British "flapping in the wind." (pg. 50)
- The uranium text was included in the body of the NIE but not in the key judgments. When someone suggested that the uranium information be included as another sign of reconstitution, the INR [State Department Bureau of Intelligence and Research] Iraq nuclear analyst spoke up and said that he did not agree with the uranium reporting and that INR would be including text indicating their disagreement in their footnote on nuclear reconstitution. The NIO said he did not recall anyone really supporting including the uranium issue as part of the judgment that Iraq was reconstituting its nuclear program, so he suggested that the uranium information did not need to be part of the key judgments. (pg. 53)
- On October 2, 2002, the Deputy DCI [Director of Central Intelligence] testified before the SSCI. Senator Jon Kyl asked the Deputy DCI whether he had read the British White Paper and whether he disagreed with anything in the report. The Deputy DCI testified that "the one thing where I think they stretched a little bit beyond where we would stretch is on the points about where Iraq seeking uranium from various African locations." (pg. 54)

- On October 4, 2002, the NIO for Strategic and Nuclear Programs testified that "there is some information on attempts . . . there's a question about those attempts because of the control of the material in those countries. . . . For us it's more the concern that they (Iraq) [have] uranium in country now. (pg. 54)
- On October 5, 2002, the ADDI [Associate Deputy Director for Intelligence] said an Iraq nuclear analyst—he could not remember who—raised concerns about the sourcing and some of the facts of the Niger reporting, specifically that the control of the mines in Niger would have made it very difficult to get yellowcake to Iraq. (pg. 55)
- Based on the analyst's comments, the ADDI faxed a memo to the Deputy National Security Advisor that said, "remove the sentence because the amount is in dispute and it is debatable whether it can be acquired from this source. We told Congress that the Brits have exaggerated this issue. Finally, the Iraqis already have 550 metric tons of uranium oxide in their inventory." (pg. 56)
- On October 6, 2002, the DCI called the Deputy National Security Advisor directly to outline the CIA's concerns. The DCI testified to the SSCI on July 16, 2003, that he told the Deputy National Security Advisor that the "President should not be a fact witness on this issue," because his analysts had told him the "reporting was weak." (pg. 56)
- On October 6, 2002, the CIA sent a second fax to the White House which said, "more on why we recommend removing the sentence about procuring uranium oxide from Africa: Three points 1) the evidence is weak. One of the two mines cited by the source as the location of the uranium oxide is flooded. The other mine cited by the source is under the control of the French authorities. 2) the procurement is not particularly significant to Iraq's nuclear ambitions because the Iraqis already have a large stock of uranium oxide in their inventory. And

3) we have shared points one and two with Congress, telling them that the Africa story is overblown and telling them this in one of the two issues where we differed with the British." (pg. 56)

- On March 8, 2003, the intelligence report on my trip was dis-seminated within the U.S. Government according [to] the Sen-ate report (pg. 43). Further, the Senate report states that "in early March, the Vice President asked his morning briefer for an update on the Niger uranium issue." That update from the CIA "also noted that the CIA would be debriefing a source who may have information related to the alleged sale on March 5." The report then states the "DO officials also said they alerted WINPAC analysts when the report was being disseminated because they knew the high priority of the issue." The report notes that the CIA briefer did not brief the Vice President on the report. (pg. 46)

Not surprising, the committee never acknowledged receipt of Joe's letter. The "Additional Views" section of the SSCI report was a political smear if ever there was one and liberally put forth distortions and outright lies. Yet it continues to be cited today by Joe's critics as proof of his lack of credibility. Months later, Joe asked a senior Democratic senator on the committee how they could have issued such a warped report. His response was simple and direct: there was simply too much "incoming" and "far more serious substantial disputes" on the table. Major battles had erupted between Democrats and Republicans over every single issue and the Democrats couldn't fight them all. They had to let it go without comment. In other words, with more pressing politi-cal fights to take on, they made a calculated decision to sacrifice Wilson. This was politics as usual—but a bitter lesson for me and Joe. Ironically, the worst blow came from Senator Evan Bayh, a Democrat from Indiana with national leadership ambitions, who in a July 22, 2004, interview with Salon.com said that "we were agnostic on Wilson." It's hard to forget things like that.*

The report got other important points wrong, too. For example, the SSCI didn't learn about the case of Iraqi foreign minister Naji Sabri, recruited as a CIA source and potentially a gold mine, until after the release of the report. According to Tyler Drumheller in an interview on *60 Minutes*, Sabri was recruited by the CIA in the summer of 2002. The White House was thrilled to have a source from Saddam's inner circle, but when Sabri told the CIA that Iraq had no fissile material for a nuclear bomb and no viable chemical or biological weapons programs, the White House no longer wanted to hear from him. Drumheller was interviewed twice by the SSCI committee after it found out about Sabri from the March 2005 Robb-Silberman Report, issued by the Commission on the Intelligence Capabilities of the U.S. regarding WMD. CBS News noted that Secretary of State Condoleezza Rice said that the Iraqi foreign minister "was just one source, and therefore his information wasn't reliable." John Prados wrote on TomPaine.com in September 2006 that "when Michigan Senator Carl Levin tabled an amendment that would have put in citations to National Intelligence Estimates (NIEs) on Iraqi weapons from before 2002, which apparently illustrate CIA uncertainties more clearly, the Republican majority not only slapped down the initiative but tacked on a minority report asserting that the very effort to add this perspective 'reveals a fundamental misunderstanding of the

---

* Although the complete report was supposed to have appeared before the 2004 presidential election, Senator Roberts was able to defer the second part—and potentially more damning one—on the political use of the available intelligence. What was produced that July was a poorly written, convoluted, overt political whitewashing that deflected any blame for the claims about Iraq WMD prior to the war away from the White House and on to any available target, usually the CIA.

role of the NIE.' " In the end, the Republicans issued the flawed report because as the majority, they could force their version through and their purpose was to shift the blame for the faulty intelligence from the administration to the CIA and to derail the investigation into the leak of my name.

What was missing from the SSCI report was just as telling as the distortions it contained. The "Additional Views" section signed by Roberts, Hatch, and Bond had concluded, "The plan to send the former ambassador to Niger was suggested by the former ambassador's wife, a CIA employee." However, the senators omitted that as reported in the July 21, 2003, *Newsday* column by Timothy Phelps and Knut Royce, "a senior intelligence officer confirmed that Plame was a Directorate of Operations undercover officer who worked 'alongside' the operations officers who asked her husband to travel to Niger. But he said she did not recommend her husband to undertake the Niger assignment. 'They (the officers who did ask Wilson to check the uranium story) were aware of who she was married to, which is not surprising,' he said. 'There are people elsewhere in government who are trying to make her look like she was the one who was cooking this up, for some reason,' he said. 'I can't figure out what it could be.' 'We paid his [Wilson's] airfare. But to go to Niger is not exactly a benefit. Most people you'd have to pay big bucks to go there,' the senior intelligence official said." The SSCI spent close to seventeen pages on the Niger uranium question building its smear against Joe, but it did not bother to include the text of his original *New York Times* op-ed.

The fallout from the SSCI report was immediate and relentless. On July 10, my close circle of college friends and I had agreed to meet at Hershey Park, Pennsylvania, for what was supposed to be a carefree summer weekend with our children. As I waited for everyone in the hotel lobby that Saturday morning I kept one eye on my four-year-old twins running circles around the couch, and idly picked up a copy of the *Washington Post*. Thumbing through the pages, I was stopped cold. Susan Schmidt had written an article headlined "Plame's Input Is Cited on Niger Mission—Report Disputes Wilson's Claims on Trip, Wife's Role." As I scanned the article, my heart sank. "Former ambassador Joseph C. Wilson IV, dispatched by the CIA in February 2002 to investigate reports that Iraq sought to reconstitute its nuclear weapons program with uranium from Africa, was specifically recommended for the mission by his wife, a CIA employee, contrary to what he has said publicly." I was so furious I could barely speak when my friends asked me what was wrong. The full attack was on and I felt helpless to do anything to defend my husband and myself.

Naturally, the *Wall Street Journal* editorial page wasted no time in using the SSCI report as more ammunition for the smear campaign. I was at my CIA desk when I read the July 20 editorial titled "Mr. Wilson's Defense: Why the Plame Special Prosecutor Should Close Up Shop." One sentence put everything into sharp focus: "In short, the entire leak probe now looks like a familiar Beltway case of criminalizing political differences. Special Prosecutor Patrick Fitzgerald should fold up his tent." That was it! I had missed the larger aim and strategy of the smear campaign until that moment. The SSCI report and the resulting damage to Joe's reputation and motives were to be used to derail the leak investigation, which was sniffing dangerously close to the White House. Now I understood the ferocity of the attacks on Joe. In the coming months, many reliable sources told us that before the report was issued, there was considerable collusion between the vice president's office and Senator Pat Roberts on how to craft the report and its content. So much for checks and balances and the separation of powers.

So when my colleague, the Reports Officer, came to my office a day after the SSCI report came out, he confirmed what I had felt to be true—that I had not suggested Joe at all—but was afraid to voice without knowing for sure. He also reminded me of how the phone call to Penny had started this chain of events. A wave of apprehension swept over me. I wanted to urge my colleague to come forward again with the truth, but I couldn't tell him what to do—to do so could be witness tampering. He would have to figure it out for himself. Unfortunately, I could hear the fear and uncertainty in his voice and knew there was no telling what he would decide. I thanked him for letting me know and watched as he stood up and left.

A few days later he came back and closed the door again. From his breast pocket, he removed a crumbled piece of paper, unfolded it, and pushed it across the desk. It was a memo he had drafted that stated his SSCI testimony had been taken out of context and that *he*, not I, had suggested Joe for the trip. The memo closed with a few complimentary sentences about Joe's and my patriotism and commitment to our country. I was filled with gratitude. Then he said he'd shown the memo to his supervisor and asked that he be allowed to testify again to the SSCI to correct the record, but was told unequivocally that that was not possible. He then mentioned that he talked to his wife about it the night before and she had said "they would do to us what they did to the Wilsons." She would not allow him to do anything more on the matter. I could only utter a weak "thank you," lower my head, and turn back to my reading.

With the clear wisdom of hindsight, I should have immediately approached the senior management of CPD and asked for their support to correct the report's omission of the junior CPD officer's testimony. I should have aggressively pushed for an investigation into how the report distorted the issue of how and why Joe was selected for the mission to Niger. I should have asked to make a photocopy of my colleague's memo and put it into a safety deposit box for insurance. I should have asked my former supervisor to clarify his role in Joe's selection (he was then in language training, preparing to go out to a Middle East post again). But I did none of those things. I was much too passive, feeling boxed in, afraid of repercussions. If I spoke out I would lose my job. If I didn't, it might doom my marriage. It was a miserable time for me and Joe—both of us existing in separate but connected rooms in hell.

The SSCI report set the stage beautifully when the Republican attack machine shifted into high gear for the Democratic National Convention in Boston, held July 26–29. Joe was invited to speak at various events and every morning he had to respond to the reporters' queries about him and the SSCI report. He learned from reporters that every day, the RNC sent a "blast fax" to all media outlets with talking points savaging him. It was clear that the attacks were a dress rehearsal of what was to come and Joe warned his friends in the Kerry campaign to beware. Within weeks the "Swift Boat" campaign used many of the same techniques and friendly media outlets that had been employed against Joe. Their tactics would have made Joseph McCarthy proud: fearmongering, defamation of character, shameless disregard for the truth, and distortions of reality. It was classic Karl Rove: go after your enemy's strong point. In Joe's case it was that he told the truth; in Kerry's case, it was his exemplary military service.

As the attacks rained down on us, Joe took the worst of the barrages, by far. The hard Right went after his international consulting business. When Joe retired from the State Department in 1998 after twenty-three years, he opened his own "boutique" firm. His clients included corporations, high-net-worth individuals, and nonprofits seeking strategic advice on trade and investment in high-risk environments in Africa and the Middle East. His diplomatic career on the African continent, during which he dealt with dictators and negotiated conflicts, had given him first-name relationships with many of its leaders. He had built a sterling reputation as being knowledgeable and honest in his dealings. In the waning years of the Clinton administration, he wanted to use that goodwill to bring corporate America to Africa, which seemed on the verge of a genuine economic resurgence fueled in part by American efforts to stimulate trade and access to American markets.

In the new Orwellian world that we inhabited, however, Joe's experience, his good standing throughout the African community, and his commendations from George H. W. Bush had little currency. Over the course of 2004, Joe's domestic and international clients left one by one, uncomfortable with his notoriety. His enemies learned who some of his clients were and publicized their names in their right-wing blogs, bringing them unwanted attention. New business dwindled to nothing. A nonpartisan Washington think tank that dealt with Middle Eastern policy did not renew Joe's unpaid position as an "adjunct scholar"—implying that a connection with Joe wouldn't be good for fundraising. At one point, a close business partner of Joe's was contacted by a powerful Republican operative and told in no uncertain terms that his continued association with Joe might cost him a valuable international contract. Fortunately, he was not intimidated by these Mafia-style tactics and responded with strong profanity. A longtime friend who ran an international consulting firm listed Joe on her Web site as a senior adviser. During a meeting with a potential client who happened to be a Republican with ties to the administration, she was questioned closely and skeptically about Joe and his involvement in her business. Joe's speaking engagements, upon which we had begun to rely more heavily for family income, all but dried up. Republican benefactors threatened to withdraw their support for universities if Joe were permitted to speak on campus. The few places that asked for Joe wanted him to speak for free, usually giving him a coffee mug or a plaque as a thank-you. The concerted attacks ultimately began to affect the sales of Joe's book.

My mother, struggling to understand what we were going through but always trying to be supportive, once expressed her hope that Joe would get a "real" job. I reacted defensively, but I knew what she meant—a normal job with a reliable paycheck. What she didn't understand was that it took all our energy just to keep going and push back. By the end of the summer, the damage had been done and Joe's business, which relied so heavily on personal recommendations and discretion, was on life support. Our income now mostly depended on my less-than-full-time government job. The bills, of course, kept flowing in.

Given our family's fragile financial health and the worsening political climate, it probably wasn't the best time for me to consider taking some time off work, but that's exactly what I began to do. I didn't know how much longer I could continue the act of "keeping it together." The succession of blows—the Agency's decision not to provide us with any security, followed by the horrifying SSCI report and its Additional Views section, then my colleague's inability or unwillingness to retestify before the SSCI, and the continuing media onslaught—were overwhelming. It was further exacerbated by my deepening disenchantment with the war in Iraq. As the insurgency flared and the road between the airport and the Green Zone in downtown Baghdad became known as the "highway of death" or "RPG alley" people traveling the deadly seven mile stretch were killed nearly daily by IEDs and ambushes. I struggled to justify sending young and inadequately trained CIA officers to deal with the volatile insurgency so they could continue the elusive "hunt for WMDs." CIA officers might have some military training, but they are not soldiers. Attacks became so frequent on the airport road that the U.S. Embassy closed it to embassy personnel in December. Our policies at every level seemed ineffective and everyone in my chain of command appeared paralyzed, unable to come to grips with the reality on the ground in Iraq. I could barely breathe. There was no relief at home or work. There never seemed to be time to think about next steps—everything was reactive.

I felt tremendous guilt as I thought of my young children who barely saw their father and had to cope with an incredibly stressed and impatient mother. I yelled at them like a fishwife and collapsed in tears when they wouldn't get into the bath when I asked. I didn't want to further burden Joe by telling him that I was near my breaking point, but I tried to make my case that I needed time to regroup. I remember putting it in terms of wanting to take time off to help support him in this fight. What I really needed was just some peace and quiet to get my footing again. So, despite my deep misgivings and swirl of emotions, in August I requested and was permitted a six-month leave from the Agency on what is called "Leave Without Pay" (LWOP).

I had high hopes that a break would offer some relief in our crazy lives, but as the wry saying goes, "Wherever you go, there you are." Without work, I simply had more time to think about how our lives had spiraled out of control and how I wasn't contributing to our family income. In mid-August, Joe's literary agent, Audrey, gave a cocktail party for us at her quaint family vacation home on Martha's Vineyard. I eagerly anticipated a few days with Joe away from Washington. The invitations mentioned a brief talk by Joe to be followed by a question-and-answer session. Over sandwiches at the town dock the day before the party, Audrey informed us that many of her longtime friends had called to cancel. The franker ones cited Joe's appearance as the reason. Others simply declined without comment. As I finished my lunch, it suddenly struck me that we had officially become pariahs.

The next night, in her garden overrun with violet hydrangeas and pink rose bushes, I spotted Art Buchwald. Buchwald had been gravely ill, but he was funny, gracious, and supportive. Later when Joe spoke from Audrey's porch to the small group, he noted that his parents, inspired by Ernest Hemingway's and Art Buchwald's writing and adventures in 1950s Paris, had taken him and his younger brother out of school and moved to Paris and to follow the bullfights in Spain. Joe remarked that it was the experience of those rather bohemian wanderings that led him to a diplomatic career. So Joe concluded, "I owe my current predicament to Art Buchwald." The crowd laughed appreciatively. Afterward, Art came up to Joe and said his only regret was "that Ernie isn't with us tonight to hear this."

Before we went home, Joe had a few book signings and speaking events in small resort towns in Connecticut along Long Island Sound. At one local library, the townspeople packed the small open space in front of the shelves; those not lucky enough to get a folding chair stood in the back. Without notes Joe launched into a powerful speech about his concerns over the war in Iraq, our reasons for entering it, and how we were prosecuting it, as well as the bigger issues looming over the leak case. He spoke about the social contract between the government and its people, enshrined in our Constitution, and appealed to the citizens of this little Connecticut town to hold our government to account for their words and deeds. We have a responsibility as citizens to be informed and engaged in our civic life—whether running for the school board, organizing a neighborhood watch committee, or stuffing envelopes for a political candidate. On the Niger uranium claim, he asked for a show of hands by any present who knew who put the infamous "sixteen words" into the president's address. No one raised a hand. Then he asked who did *not* know the name of his wife? Again nobody raised a hand. They all knew who I was. "What's wrong with this picture?" he asked rhetorically. "Nobody knows who put a lie in the president's mouth, yet everybody knows the name of a covert

CIA officer simply because she is married to a man who had the temerity to challenge the administration."

As he spoke, I glanced around the room and saw keen attention focused on Joe and more than a couple of folks nodding their heads. As he concluded his twenty-minute talk, I felt a swell of pride; Joe was speaking out because we thought it was the right thing to do. That belief would have to sustain us through more rough times just ahead.

CHAPTER 12

Stay and Fight

As the wretched summer of 2004 turned into fall and our twins entered pre-K, the solid and affectionate marriage that I always thought was the best thing to ever happen to me seemed balanced on a knife's edge. At times, to my horror, it was not clear to me what the outcome would be. Ironically, my temporary leave from work only served to exacerbate the growing tension between me and Joe because we were both around the house more, mostly getting in each other's way and under foot. In the early days of the leak, Joe had gallantly defended my honor, integrity, and (once it was acknowledged by the Agency) my covert status, and spoke often of our strong mutual attraction and happy marriage. He saw the attacks aimed at him that summer as an opportunity for me to defend him and he thought that I had failed miserably.

He deeply resented that I had not adequately come to his defense. I shared his rage and frustration at our limited ability to fight back against the unfair and ludicrous allegations directed toward us, but I felt helpless. As an Agency employee, I was not permitted to speak to the press and he knew that well. Never mind that I thought I would be fired from the Agency if I debunked the charges publicly; the only thing that registered with Joe was that he needed me and I wasn't there, and little noises to "ignore it" or "it doesn't matter" or "oh, it's just the usual right-wing BS" only made it worse. It was a strange situation, we were in it together, but we were experiencing it differently. And no one but us could really understand what we were going through.

With both of us walking around feeling deeply wronged, small disagreements quickly mushroomed into full-scale fights and constant bickering overwhelmed our communications. Normal interaction became increasingly difficult and fraught with peril. You never knew if an offhand comment or routine request would set the other one off. Never successful at "compartmentalizing" my problems, I moped around feeling miserable all the time, as I know Joe did, too. And even though I intellectually understood that he was displacing his anger at the situation onto me, it didn't make it any easier to endure. The frequent fights, seething accusations, hurtful words, and entrenched bitterness pushed us both to the brink. Joe is a formidable opponent in any circumstance, and I felt I was always on the losing side, unable to make my case coherently because so much emotion was involved and so much at stake personally. When communication nearly halted entirely, it became obvious that our marriage was in deep trouble. We retreated further into our shells and each began to contemplate life without the other.

The tension finally came to a head on a clear, blustery October afternoon. We were sitting on our deck, trying to stop the slow slide of our marriage into nothingness. We called the other's bluff about separating, trying to ascertain how much the other one wanted out of the painful relationship. We inflicted pain as only those who are most intimate can. After moving in wary circles around each other and reaching what was, for me, the depths of despair, we finally reassured the other that we would not throw in the towel just yet. Neither one of us was ready to call it quits. We had invested too much in the marriage and still had more fighting to do—with each other and against our enemies. Just as the conversation was winding down and I began to think we were easing over the worst of the fight, Joe turned to me and asked, "Why are you choosing the Agency and your career over your marriage?" The words fell like a physical blow, but however painful, the outburst finally brought the underlying problem out into the open. Joe felt deeply betrayed by my passive behavior and questioned my very loyalty to him and our marriage. I simply had no idea he had seen the conflict in these terms. It had not occurred to me that he perceived my actions (or inactions) as siding with the CIA at the cost of my marriage. I tried to convince him that my loyalty was never in doubt, but I did not want him to revisit his accusations in the years to come every time we had an altercation. Still, talking frankly seemed to lance the boil and for the first time in weeks, we spoke directly and without cloaking ourselves in self-pity and misinterpretation. I vowed that "they" could try to take whatever they could from us, but we wouldn't give them the satisfaction of letting them have our marriage as well. From that moment on, although there were still plenty of hard feelings and disagreements ahead, we both knew that we were in this together, wherever it might lead us.

As both of us tried to patch our marriage back together that fall, the full reality hit me that I could no longer perform the job ████████████ for which I had been highly trained—the job I loved and was so proud of: Covert Operations Officer. The exposure of my name and true employer in July 2003 and the ensuing media attention had closed that path for good. ██████ ██ ████████████ Only a very small and trusted circle of individuals know the officer's true affiliation and responsibilities. A future overseas assignment was out of the question for me—the inevitable publicity about my posting would jeopardize any operation or asset. Furthermore, being a widely known CIA operative overseas could potentially place my family in harm's way. I had no desire to be another star in the CIA Headquarters' lobby. I considered looking into other available careers under the Agency's vast umbrella, but nothing particularly appealed to me. I always thought that operations were the Agency's core mission and the most appealing aspect of working there—everything else came in a dull second. It was obvious to me that anyone working for the government better truly love what she was doing, because the modest pay and personal sacrifices wouldn't keep a good employee with any ambition around for long.

So I found myself exploring new jobs beyond the Agency for the first time ▮▮▮▮▮▮▮▮. I had always dreamed of being one of the ▮▮▮ women in operations to retire from the Agency's senior intelligence service (SIS) ranks, but that fall, I made the rounds of Washington think tanks on informational interviews, naïvely thinking that someone with nearly ▮▮▮▮▮▮ of operational experience and a security clearance in good standing might be of some interest. I knew that my experience was a little unusual but I thought of my strengths: a honed ability to think on my feet, responsibility for agents' lives, a capacity to produce even under extremely stressful conditions, managerial experience, and a pretty good understanding of how the intelligence community worked. Many of the experienced people I talked to were sympathetic to my situation but unable or unwilling to make any firm offers. I heard a lot of, "Well, keep in touch and let us know what your plans are." I felt like a kid right out of college, hoping someone would take a chance and hire me. I also briefly toyed with the idea of a job on Capitol Hill, perhaps as a staffer on one of the intelligence committees. I could continue in public service and get credits as a federal employee toward retirement. However, as I took the meetings, two things became crystal clear: one, that I was a political hot potato, whom no one was in any hurry to hire until the entire drama had unfolded, and second, that that was probably just as well. ████████████████████████ ██████████████ the thought of sitting at a desk all day and writing about the world was, well, dull. I also doubted I'd be very good at it. I am not an academic and my skill set just didn't seem to mesh well with what was out there and what I was seeing.

To expand my horizons a bit, I paid a call on a wealthy and handsome man-about-town businessman turned philanthropist. We had met at a social event earlier in the year and he kindly said that I was welcome to contact him for help or advice. He had plenty of life and business experiences and it was certainly worth getting his ideas on what I might consider next. He worked out of a large office suite near the White House on Pennsylvania Avenue, and, as I waited for him in the reception area, my eyes fell on the modern art and intricate Persian rugs that decorated the maze of rooms. The secretary materialized to show me to his office and he seemed genuinely pleased to see me. We discussed everything from various future career options ████████████ ███████████████████████████████████. Finally, he leaned back in his chair and smiled broadly. "Fuck 'em. Go back with your head high and make 'em sweat." He was absolutely right. I knew I could tough out almost any situation and I would be a fool to quit ██████████████████. Why should I leave ████████████████ just because it had become a little uncomfortable? His confidence in me and piquant advice were just what I needed to hear.

As the November presidential election loomed closer, Joe was home much more. His speaking engagements had tapered off to virtually zero—the occasional community college or high school talk. Our coffee mug collection slowly expanded. In the last weeks leading up to the election, the Right's attacks on Kerry intensified to a daily roar. Their attacks that summer against Joe had been a chance to test-market their tactics. The "Swift Boat" attacks, which the Kerry campaign at first ignored, started right after the Democratic convention, and ultimately had devastating effects. The Right went directly to the heart of what Kerry held dearest—his Vietnam service and his history of speaking truth to power about the unpopular war. Even those who supported Kerry were left wondering what had really happened that day on Bay Hap River when he and others had come under enemy fire. It was a stunning demonstration of what a well-financed and well-organized political opposition group could do and there is no doubt that the $22 million that the "Swift Boat Veterans for Truth" poured into their campaign hurt Kerry's standing in the polls right up to Election Day.

Two weeks before the election, the "Vote for Change" concert arrived in town. The rock and roll extravaganza featured such stars as Bruce Springsteen, R.E.M., Pearl Jam, the Dixie Chicks, John Mellencamp, Jackson Browne, James Taylor, and the Dave Matthews Band. An eleven-state tour was finishing up with a final evening in Washington. It was a dream concert, but our days of sleeping outside to be the first in line to buy tickets were long over and Joe and I assumed we would have to take a pass. Luckily, the day before the concert, a friend said she found that great seats were available near the stage—did we want to go? I found a babysitter in record time and went online to purchase our tickets. We rationalized that the steep $186 per ticket, which we really could not afford, was to a good cause; we felt a little like teenagers escaping adult supervision.

From the first note of Mellencamp's set the capacity crowd at the MCI Center was on its feet screaming and singing along with the music. At one point, a huge security guard in a tight T-shirt with "SECURITY" stenciled on the back appeared near our seats and motioned for us to follow him. He slipped passes over our heads and we walked fast to keep up with him through the rabbit warren of rooms and hallways backstage. As we hustled along the crowded corridors, I caught glimpses of hardened roadies, slinky blonde girlfriends, technicians carrying yards of wiring, worried-looking star wranglers on cell phones, and even toddlers, all doing what they do best. He finally parked us in front of a room with a hand-lettered "Pearl Jam" sign taped to the door. Joe had met Pearl Jam's lead singer, Eddie Vedder, in Seattle a few months previously and had struck up a genuine if improbable friendship. Eddie greeted us warmly. I felt incredibly old and unhip; I couldn't name one of their songs to save my life. As we turned to go and return to our seats, I walked straight into a large male torso. I stepped back somewhat embarrassed and looked up about three feet to see the smiling face of Tim Robbins. He's one of those stars about whom you can never say, "He's much shorter in real life." We exchanged brief greetings and tried to keep the guard in sight to get back to our seats.

Just as we were to step from behind the darkened stage to return to our seats, we were suddenly detained by more security guards. In a moment, we were surrounded by what I quickly realized were members of Springsteen's E Street Band, waiting to go on next. I was thrilled. The only day I had ever cut school was to buy *The River* album in October 1980. Joe, from a different musical generation than I was, was less impressed having "the Boss" just steps away. We shuffled to get out of the way while Bruce led his band on a preperformance pep rally. When Joe and I finally returned home at the unheard of time of 2:30 in the morning and let the babysitter go, we observed that at least our unwanted notoriety had some upsides. I was faintly amused when nearly a year later, *Time* magazine breathlessly reported that we spent $372 for our evening at an "anti-Bush fundraising concert," as though that alone made us suspect.

Finally, Election Day dawned. We proudly stood in line at our neighborhood polling place with the children before taking them to school. I said a quick silent prayer as I cast my vote; so much seemed to ride on the outcome of the bitterly fought election campaign. Never before had I felt so distant and disenfranchised from my country's leader. I deeply believed that Bush and his administration were pushing the country in the wrong direction in every aspect of their domestic and international policies. Still, I had no illusions about a sure Kerry win. Late that afternoon, Joe called me from a crowded Georgetown restaurant where he was enjoying a cigar with friends. He told me that the first exit polls, which had come out at around 4 P.M. seemed to indicate a decisive Kerry victory. I inhaled sharply—it was the first time I allowed myself to hope that Bush would be a one-term president. Joe also mentioned that he had run into *New York Times* journalist Judith Miller in the crowd. Miller had refused to reveal her sources on the leak to Special Prosecutor Patrick Fitzgerald, and he had held her in contempt of court. Her appeal was then slowly working its way through the courts. I distrusted her reporting in articles she had written in the run-up to the war. She became close to many Iraqi sources who gave detailed and sometimes spectacular interviews about Saddam Hussein's WMD programs. Yet since the invasion of Iraq in March 2003, not one of the allegations splashed on the *New York Times*'s front page had been proved accurate. In an article for her paper in July 2003, she blamed the failure of U.S. forces to uncover weapons of mass destruction on "chaos," "disorganization," "interagency feuds," "flawed intelligence," "looting," and "shortages of everything from gasoline to soap." Everyone was to blame except her and her heavy reliance on leads from Iraqi National Congress head Chalabi. Yet it was her reporting, more than anyone else's, that showcased the administration's WMD theories. Now she had introduced herself to Joe. As they shook hands, he mentioned that he was worried about the outcome of the election, to which she replied, "Don't worry, it's over. It's a done deal [Kerry's victory]. If I thought it was close at all, I'd be in the newsroom, working. In fact, I spent the afternoon shopping for prison garb." Judith Miller's conclusions about a Kerry victory were to be proved wrong.

That night we went to a party in one of Washington's toniest neighborhoods to watch the returns. We went in high spirits, as the late-afternoon exit polls continued to give Kerry a substantial lead. I hurried into my host's living room where a number of TVs were tuned to different news channels. My first glance at the TV showed a map of the country being slowly swallowed in red, and my heart sank. I'm no political expert, but I knew it was over. I wanted to leave immediately—there was no point in staying—but Joe had already been drawn into the thick crowd. As I desperately looked around for him, I was pulled into a conversation with Sally Quinn and her son, but I was in no mood to be especially social or polite with anyone. Other Washington boldface-name types were there, but I just wanted to leave. An hour or two later, I finally wrangled Joe to the door, and there was near silence in the car on the way home. Once there, I went straight to bed, while Joe stayed up much of the night watching the drama of the 2000 election repeat itself in Ohio.

The next day was cold and gray, perfectly matching our moods. Although I never assumed Kerry's win, I had trouble processing Bush's. I understood that the country was reluctant to desert their commander in chief in a time of war, but the mistakes and arrogance and intolerance in the administration in so many areas were deplorable. I had trouble comprehending why my fellow citizens would want four more years of the same course. There was morose humor in the headline of British newspaper the *Daily Mirror*. Above a picture of George W. Bush ran the question, "How can 59,054,087 people be so DUMB?" My dear friend Janet was staying with us and we visited Ford's Theatre and the house across the street where Lincoln died. The melancholy spirit of those places fit our moods and I thought of that noble president who led our country through the bleak years of the Civil War. In the car on the way home, I heard on the radio the expected news that Kerry had conceded the election. The country's future, and our own, seemed bleak.

I turned over in bed, restless, kicked the sheets around, and realized Joe wasn't next to me. The illuminated clock on the bedside table read 2:30 A.M. Joe liked to get up early and exercise, but this was ridiculous. I got out of bed, put on my robe, and went downstairs. I checked the dark TV room. No Joe. I went to see if he was on the computer in our home office. No Joe. I was getting worried. It was the middle of the night in the dead of winter and my husband was nowhere to be found. When I returned to the dark kitchen, an eerie blue light out on the deck caught my eye. I walked over and tugged open the door. An icy blast came into the room as my heart sank. There was Joe, wearing a puffy parka with the hood up, smoking a cigar. The blue light of his laptop computer illuminated his tired face.

I asked the obvious question, "What *are* you doing?" "Looking for real estate in New Zealand," he answered—way too cheerfully for the hour. "Look at this beautiful oceanfront property in Napier, pretty cheap, too. What do you think?" His question cut to the quick of our piecemeal conversations over the last few months that had accelerated with Bush's reelection. Fitzgerald's investigation into the leak appeared to have ground to a halt. My career was at a dead end and Joe's didn't look so promising, either. We had children to raise and couldn't continue the way we were going. What were we going to do?

Our sense of outrage and alarm grew as we realized the country had to endure four more years of bad decisions. The administration was systematically destroying all the international institutions that had served our country and the world so well since the end of World War II. The credibility of the U.S. was at an all-time low. The neocon ideology, so pervasive in the corridors of power since 9/11, had yet to demonstrate that our war of choice in Iraq to "remake" the map of the Middle East would have the desired outcome. Our society was becoming more of "haves" and "have nots" with each passing year. The vaunted middle class, the backbone of this country, was under increasing pressures. Basic civil liberties were under attack. America no longer felt like our country—something neither of us had ever experienced before.

When Bush was pronounced the winner of the 2000 election courtesy of the Supreme Court's decision to stop the ballot recount in Florida, Joe and I were upset. However, our concern was focused much more on the unprecedented and clearly partisan decision by the highest court in the land than on the election's winner per se—even though it was someone we did not endorse. We reasoned that the country was at peace, the economy was chugging along just fine, and we liked Bush père, who had appointed Joe ambassador and with whom Joe enjoyed an occasional but sincere correspondence. As devastating as it was to see the revered justices throw the election, we naïvely figured *how bad could it get anyway*? The ongoing bloodshed in Iraq demonstrated that just when you thought it was bad, the news could get worse.

I had been following the profound changes at the CIA while I was on temporary leave. Tenet had left as DCI in June 2004 on a decidedly bittersweet note. According to MSNBC, "The White House strongly denied that Tenet had been forced out, saying his decision came as a surprise to Bush. Tenet told CIA personnel afterward that his resignation 'had only one basis in fact: the well-being of my wonderful family, nothing more and nothing less.' " We all knew there was more to it than those bland public statements, but CIA employees were caught by surprise when DDO Jim Pavitt resigned just one day after Tenet. He also cited the popular reason of "wanting to spend more time with my family." Both men were crucial to the Agency's mission, especially in wartime, and their departures heightened everyone's anxiety. In a move that had been rumored since Tenet's departure, the president had named Porter Goss as DCI in September. Goss, a CIA Operations Officer through most of the 1960s, then a congressman from Florida who became head of the House Permanent Select Committee on Intelligence, arrived at Headquarters with the clear intention to houseclean, and from the beginning he was seen more as a crusader and occupier than former colleague. He brought with him several loyal Hill staffers, known for their abrasive management style, and immediately set to work attempting to bring the CIA—with special emphasis on the often wild and willful operations directorate—to heel, per White House orders. White House officials had suspected that CIA officials had leaked information prior to the election about the intelligence surrounding the war in Iraq that put the Agency in a better light. Thus, Goss's orders from the administration were probably along the lines of "get control of it."

Although there was an overwhelming sentiment within Headquarters that long-needed reforms about how intelligence was shared, packaged, and used were critical to rebuilding the tarnished prestige of the Agency, Goss's heavy-handedness was bitterly resented. He was criticized for not interacting with senior Agency managers; for spending little time with the heads of foreign intelligence services (all of whom the CIA relied on for cooperation in counterterrorism and counterproliferation matters); for not being sufficiently engaged in day-to-day activities; and for being unable to master some of the details of operations. In a March 2005 interview, Goss said "he was a little amazed" at his workload. Employees' worst fears about the creeping politicization of the CIA were realized when shortly after the November presidential election, Goss e-mailed a memo to all CIA workers that said in part, "We support the Administration, and its policies, in our work as agency employees. . . . We do not identify with, support or champion opposition to the Administration or its policies. We provide the intelligence as we see it—and let the facts alone speak to the policy-maker." Although a CIA spokesman explained the memo as a statement of the Agency's nonpartisan nature, it appeared to be just the opposite. It had a kind of creepy Orwellian Ministry of Truth ring to it—further dismaying CIA staffers who believed the Agency was rapidly losing credibility and power as partisan politics began to degrade its work product.

Strangely, this disturbing e-mail came out only hours after the tough and respected DDO, Steve Kappes, resigned in a fury after Steve's Deputy, a highly valued officer named Mike Sulick, criticized Goss's powerful Chief of Staff, Pat Murray. According to Tyler Drumheller, in his book *On the Brink*, the relationship between Goss's office and the office of the DDO was disintegrating over a variety of issues and came to a head when Murray sent Sulick a "truly obnoxious email" that "accused Sulick and

1

Looking my best at four and a half. My mother made many of my clothes, including this dress. *Courtesy of the Author.*

2

With my father and brother at Shaw Air Force Base, South Carolina. At two and a half I was eager to fly. My father belonged to the base aeroclub. *Courtesy of the Author.*

3

With my parents on my first trip to Europe, 1973. It was sweltering hot in Venice, Italy. *Courtesy of the Author.*

4

Posing in Cody, Wyoming, on my family's second driving vacation across the country in 1974. *Courtesy of the Author.*

5

My good-looking parents on their sixteenth wedding anniversary, 1976. *Courtesy of the Author.*

6

Tailgating before the football game at Penn State with some of my best friends, 1981. That's me in the back row, center. *Courtesy of the Author.*

7

Windswept in front of the ancient Parthenon, Athens, Greece, in 1990. *Courtesy of the Author.*

With my loving and protective big brother, Bob Plame, 1998. *Courtesy of the Author.*

Bliss, wedding day, 1998. *Courtesy of the Author.*

Still managing to smile as I
leave the house to have the
twins, January 11, 2000.
Courtesy of the Author.

11

Joe proudly holding his second set of twins, January 2000. *Courtesy of the Author.*

12

Roly-poly Trevor and Samantha at eight months. *Courtesy of the Author.*

Blessed with two sets of twins! Our 2000 family Christmas card photo, taken on the steps of our Washington house with the eight-month-old twins and twenty-year-olds, Sabrina and Joe Wilson V.
Courtesy of the Author.

Attending the Washington equivalent of "the prom"—the White House Correspondents Dinner, April 2006.
AP Photo/Haraz N. Ghanbari.

At the National Press Club to announce the filing of our civil suit in July 2006. I was very nervous about speaking publicly for the first time. *© UPI Photo/Roger L. Wollenberg/Landov.*

An unusually light moment during my testimony before the House Committee on Oversight and Government Reform, March 2007. *AP Photo/Dennis Cook.*

Kappes, two of the most experienced, respected men in the building, of being fools and lacking integrity." Murray then ordered Kappes to fire Sulick, but he refused. Over the weekend, Kappes and Sulick came to a decision that's almost never made in Washington. They both resigned on principle. This shock was magnified over the coming weeks and months as dozens of senior Agency officers left, no longer able to abide working for an organization that had strayed so far from its mission. According to the *Washington Post*, by January 2005, over twenty senior CIA officials had retired or resigned since Goss became DCI. At least one thousand years of hard-earned operational experience walked out the door when our country's national security needs were greatest. It was devastating.

After I went on leave back in August, I constantly heard from my colleagues that morale was dangerously low, and there was a spirit of outright revolt toward Porter Goss and his "Gosslings." Everyone was calculating the benefits of staying or jumping from the fast-sinking ship. I had my own doubts about Goss and his agenda. Just after Novak's column appeared in 2003, Goss, Chairman of the House Permanent Select Committee on Intelligence, gave an interview to his hometown paper in Florida. He was asked if the committee would investigate the leak. His demeaning response: "Somebody sends me a blue dress and some DNA, I'll have an investigation." That comment alone, offhand as it might have been, spoke volumes about Goss's optic on the politicization of intelligence, and revealed his disdain for CIA employees.

As I looked over Joe's shoulder at the real estate listings on the screen, the idea of moving to New Zealand wasn't so far-fetched. In fact, there was a bit of excitement and relief thinking about removing ourselves from what had become a very painful situation in all respects. I had once visited New Zealand ███████ ███████████████ and had been taken with the country's stunning physical beauty, charming and ethnically diverse people, and—most of all—its distance from Washington. I don't believe you can go any farther than New Zealand without starting to return home again. Joe scrolled down the screen. "What about that one?" I said, pointing at a charming cottage overlooking the dark blue sea.

One cold January morning, about ten days before Bush's second inaugural in 2005, I awoke with a start and nudged Joe in the ribs to wake him, too. "We have to get out of this town," I said. "I simply cannot stay here and live through the inaugural hoopla feeling like we do about this administration. Can we take the kids and go skiing somewhere instead?" Perhaps because he wasn't awake yet, he agreed instantly. By the end of the day, we had all our plans in place. In an unprecedented stroke of luck, we got four airline tickets using frequent-flyer miles and Joe had called his good college buddy, George, who lived in Salt Lake City, Utah. George and Donna kindly invited us all to stay at their home near the university, and we could drive every day to the famous Alta ski resort, an easy forty-five minutes away up a steep and narrow canyon. We bought ski clothes and gear, tried to stoke the kids' enthusiasm about a sport they had never seen before, and got out of town just as jubilant Republicans streamed into it to celebrate "W's" second term.

Joe had not skied in thirty-two years. The last time he was on skis, he was twenty-three years old and broke his leg at Tahoe. The intervening years traipsing around Africa had not offered much in the way of snow sports, but he was game to pick it up again. That is, until I looked behind me on our first run down an easy intermediate slope at sunny Alta and saw a huge ball of white powder rolling down the mountain spewing profanities the entire way. Oh, this will be a fun vacation, I thought as the very angry ball of snow came to a rest at my feet. However, by the end of the week, helped by our ski instructor and two new pairs of parabolic-shaped skis that practically make the turns for you, both of us were back in form and willing to try anything on the mountain. It wasn't always pretty, but we had a blast. As for five-year-old Samantha and Trevor, they took to the sport immediately and by the end of the week, were shooting down intermediate slopes with yelps of joyful abandon. They showed no fear, and it was obvious that they would outski both of us in a few years.

As our skiing improved, our spirits began to heal, too. Taking in the majestic, heartbreaking beauty of Utah's Wasatch mountains, we felt our troubles slip to the back of our minds. No one knew who we were or cared, except to ask if we were having a good time skiing. When asked where we were from, we simply said, we were visiting from Washington, and most of the locals smiled and said, "Oh, lots of rain up there." We usually didn't correct them.

Through the gifts of time and space, we came to several fundamental decisions. First, keeping our marriage healthy was paramount. We vowed to press on as a team, as partners, understanding that if we were apart, neither one of us stood a chance of succeeding on any level. Second, we would not move away from Washington or out of the country just yet; it was *our* United States, too, and we were going to fight for it. Moving away would have been interpreted by our enemies as a sign of weakness or defeat, and that was the last thing we would do. Although we knew there were still many difficulties ahead, we felt we had been tested and found strong enough. I would not wish the pain we had experienced over the last year on my worst enemy, but we found there is truth to the saying "what doesn't kill you makes you stronger." Joe's critics wanted to destroy him, and they nearly succeeded. The Republicans would have loved nothing better than for Joe and the leak investigation simply to go away—both had a funny way of reminding the public about the abuse of governmental power. But our considered, joint decision was to fight back. We certainly weren't going to make it easy for them.

I never thought I would see my name and "gay male prostitute" in the same story, but it happened shortly after we returned home from Utah in February 2005—a further indication of how twisted the whole *l'affaire Plame* had become. Jeff Gannon, an accredited White House reporter for two conservative Web sites, Talon News and GOPUSA, attended a January press conference, and asked the president, "How are you going to work with people who seem to have divorced themselves from reality?" Liberal bloggers immediately began to investigate Gannon's credentials. What they turned up in no time embarrassed everyone. Naked pictures of Gannon, whose real name is James Dale Guckert, appeared on many gay escort Internet sites where he advertised his services for two hundred dollars an hour. Once his moonlighting became public, Gannon resigned and turned in his White House press pass. He was indignant he would be fired for "past mistakes" and asked if it was "right to hold someone's sexuality against them." The bloggers had a field day trying to figure out how Gannon had gotten through the White House security background check. Oddly enough, Gannon had interviewed Joe before the election. In the interview, Gannon refers to an "internal government memo prepared by U.S. intelligence personnel" that said I had suggested Joe for the trip to Niger. As a result, the FBI paid him a visit in their leak investigation, but Gannon said he never had nor saw the memo and was not asked to appear before the grand jury. It was a bizarre, but thankfully short episode.

Later that spring, before I returned to work at the CIA, Joe and I were invited to a swank dinner in New York. In keeping with our resolution not to go away like our critics would have liked, we accepted and looked forward to a chic evening of some celebrity watching. During cocktails on the vast terrace of the New York State Supreme Court building, I felt a little tap on my shoulder and whirled around to see Marlo Thomas smiling and introducing herself. *That Girl* was an icon from my childhood days. I watched the popular sitcom after school and learned from the character of Ann Marie, who was a single, independent modern woman. And she had a never-ending mod wardrobe that was a wonder. Marlo was delightful and we chatted at some length. When we parted, she said, "You seem much more open as a person that I would have expected." I was taken aback, but realized that *That Girl* got it right. I was reverting to the person I had been before my CIA career had compelled me to be wary and closed to any and all approaches.

In May 2005, I returned to the Counterproliferation Division at CIA, where I had worked before my leave, and I intended on doing the best job I could. Although much of my driving ambitions had been tamped down by having children and further curtailed because of the events of the last two years, I was flattered and surprised to be given a good operations job with responsibility. It was all about keeping WMD, especially the nuclear kind, out of the hands of rogue states. My job was essentially to oversee the work done by our officers, making sure that cables went out to the field promptly and accurately, ensuring that our innovative operations stayed within the legal boundaries, coordinating with others in our Division and throughout the Agency, and providing solid operational advice and experience when needed. Although our branch was relatively small, it was doing some of the most creative ████████ work of the entire Division. This was the part of the work that I loved—developing and then figuring out if some of the most outlandish operational proposals would actually work. What could be more fun or satisfying than thwarting people with evil intent? For me, one of the best aspects of the job was the opportunity to work with Junior Officers—many who had yet to serve in the field—who still held tightly to the idealism and enthusiasm that brought them to the CIA in the first place. They were all highly intelligent, multilingual, ambitious, and best of all, perhaps, curious about the world around them. I felt like I had a stable of thoroughbreds and my job was to give them all the right conditions to run their best race.

I was thrilled to pass along some of my hard-earned experience and operational smarts to my junior charges. There are so many things in CIA operations that you can only learn by doing—things they don't teach you at the Farm, or even openly discuss. As I prepared these Officers for their maiden postings, I tried to advise them of the possible pitfalls and obstacles, I thought to myself that I was just hitting my stride ▓▓▓▓▓▓▓▓▓▓ ▓▓▓▓. Maybe I'm just a slow learner, but it is a complicated and ever-changing field. I enjoyed the company of several Senior Officers in our branch who had retired from the Agency, but were back working on contract—"green badgers," we called them. Over the last few years, the Agency had welcomed a huge influx of green badgers to cope with the burgeoning workload. Just as I tried to impart some experience to the Junior Officers, I continued to learn from my elders about the spy business. Their stories, gossip, suggestions, and insights proved invaluable to my learning and expertise. So much of what a Case Officer learns is on the job. They talked candidly of their own blunders and about the things that could go alarmingly wrong when an agent was put on the "box" (slang for the polygraph machine), close calls with foreign police officers, technical spy gadgets that didn't work as promised, and unlikely recruitments.

I found the work challenging and fulfilling, and my immediate colleagues were of the highest caliber but, as spring turned to summer, my heart wasn't in the job as it should have been. I sometimes felt disconnected and at other times, very uncharacteristically self-pitying. One day, I sat in CPD's large conference room with the rest of the Division as my peers received promotions. With a stab of regret, I knew that if things had been different, I would have been up there, too. But I was beginning to ponder how much I still cared. The CIA I had joined and served loyally was experiencing profound change and terrible morale. The congressional 9/11 Commission had created the "Director of National Intelligence" position and in February, the president installed ambassador John Negroponte, who was given authority to oversee the heretofore powerful DCI. From that moment on, the name "Central Intelligence Agency" became a misnomer. Promises were made to the CIA's workforce that the new DNI structure would not just be an "extra bureaucratic layer" over the CIA, but that's exactly what it would become. It seemed to me that the White House was intent on emasculating the CIA by blaming it for the failures in Iraq and anything else they thought they could throw at the Agency and have stick. The newspapers were full of stories about "secret CIA prisons" in Europe used for the administration's war on terror. The *New York Times* carried a front-page story detailing how careless CIA officers had led to the discovery of supposedly secret flights to and from Cairo, Baghdad, and Kabul ferrying detainees in the "war against terror." The paper wrote about shell companies and front companies used by the Agency for their "renditions" and gave many details on how it all worked, ▮▮▮▮▮▮▮▮▮▮▮▮▮▮▮
▮▮▮ It was just damn embarrassing to the CIA ▮▮▮▮▮▮▮
▮▮▮▮▮▮▮▮▮▮▮▮▮▮▮▮▮▮▮▮▮▮ Around the same time, the *Washington Post* broke the story of several CIA officers abducting a radical Islamic cleric from the streets of Milan. The

ensuing details that emerged about the abduction showed extremely lazy tradecraft and an arrogance that led to the operation's ultimate compromise. In early June 2007, the trial opened in Italy—less the twenty-six American defendants. According to the *Guardian*, among those indicted were the Station Chief in Rome and the boss in Milan. Opening the paper each day to yet another new and unflattering revelation about the CIA had everyone holding their heads in their hands. I began to seriously consider the notion that my CIA career was over for good and that it was time, and best for me and my family, to move on.

As Washington's summer began to heat up, so did the showdown between special prosecutor Patrick Fitzgerald and the two reporters who had refused to comply with the grand jury subpoenas and reveal their sources for his investigation: the *New York Times* reporter Judith Miller and *Time* magazine writer Matt Cooper. In October 2004, the district court in Washington had consolidated their appeals. We had seen *Time* managing editor Jim Kelly at a dinner in April, and he told us, rather morosely while swirling the whiskey in his glass, that *Time*'s legal defense of Matt Cooper had cost them more than two million dollars, and the fight wasn't over. Finally, on June 27, 2005, the Supreme Court refused to hear their appeal. The lower court's ruling compelling the reporters to testify before the grand jury stood and Miller and Cooper faced the very real and dismaying prospect of jail time.

One evening not long after the Supreme Court decision, Joe and I were walking with good friends to a Lebanese restaurant in Georgetown for a rare dinner out, when we passed Matt Cooper and his wife, Mandy Grunwald, on the sidewalk. While our friend Jackie and I continued walking on toward the restaurant, Cooper stopped Joe and our other friend. After opening pleasantries, Cooper paused for a moment, obviously struggling to say something. Finally he asked, "Could you do something for me?" He wanted Joe to write the judge on the leak case and request leniency for Matt in the hope that it would help keep him out of jail. Joe was taken aback. "Well, I'll talk to my lawyer," he said. Later in the restaurant, as we ate hummus, baba ghanoush, wrapped grape leaves, and other Mediterranean delicacies, the four of us marveled over this strange request. Had Matt momentarily lost his mind? A request from Joe for leniency on Matt's behalf would carry little or no weight with the presiding judge. More pointedly, it was obviously in our interest to have the reporters testify. We, along with the entire country, wanted to hear what they would say under oath. We wanted to know what sources in the administration had leaked my name to the media, thereby undermining our national security.

In the debate over whether reporters should be compelled to reveal their sources, it seemed to me that some of the leading advocates of reporters' First Amendment rights had lost sight of a basic fact in this case: people in the administration had *used* reporters to advance their own political agenda. That alone is not unusual, or even criminal. But the reporters' refusal to testify would not help to uncover *government wrongdoing*, but assist officials who wanted to *cover up their illegal behavior*. It was the Pentagon Papers or Watergate turned on its head. A lot of well-meaning but self-righteous talking heads expressed their devotion to First Amendment rights but could not see that this particular case was not about the freedom of the press, or about reporters' roles as watchdogs on behalf of the governed, the citizens of this country. These reporters were allowing themselves to be exploited by the administration and were obstructing the investigation. It didn't make much ethical sense to me.

CHAPTER 13

Indictment

On July 6, 2005, Judith Miller was sentenced to four months in jail for civil contempt. It was two years to the day after Joe's *New York Times* op-ed piece on Iraq and Niger had appeared. When Miller suggested that home detention and being denied cell phone and e-mail access would be adequate punishment, Fitzgerald held firm to jail time and noted dryly, "Certainly one who can handle the desert in wartime is far better equipped than the average person jailed in a federal facility." He added that Miller "could avoid even a minute of separation from her husband if she would do no more than just follow the law like every other citizen in America is required to do." And he added for good measure, "Forced vacation at a comfortable home is not a compelling form of coercion." Fitzgerald was clearly prepared to push the system hard to get Miller and Cooper in front of his grand jurors.

Ten days later, the *Washington Post* reported that the special prosecutor was contemplating additional criminal contempt charges for Miller if she continued to defy the judge's order to testify, potentially extending her jail time. Miller maintained that she needed to protect the identity of her source; Judge Hogan held that the source had, in fact, released Miller from her obligation. Miller's attorney, well-known First Amendment lawyer Floyd Abrams, said, "Judy's view is that any purported waiver she got from anyone was not on the face of it sufficiently broad, clear, and uncoerced." The *Post* mentioned that among those who had received waivers was Vice President Cheney's Chief of staff, Scooter Libby, who had answered questions from the special prosecutor. Another was Matt Cooper, who was spared jail time in an eleventh-hour reprieve, when he said that his source had released him from his promise of confidentiality. "That source gave me a personal, unambiguous, uncoerced waiver to speak to the grand jury," Cooper told reporters. He would not disclose the source. *Time* then released a statement saying that "by personally and directly releasing Matt from his obligation to confidentiality, his source has made the decision for Matt to testify a simple one, as other journalists have already testified in this case after being released by their sources." On June 30, *Time* turned over to the court all of Cooper's pertinent e-mails and notes. Although legally joined at the hip for months through the appeals process, Cooper and Miller were now poised to go in very different directions.

On July 10, *Newsweek* reporter Michael Isikoff wrote that Karl Rove was Matt Cooper's source. The article printed an e-mail written by Matt Cooper to his editor at *Time* in July 2003; "Spoke to Rove on double super secret background for about two mins before he went on vacation . . ." He concluded, "please don't source this to rove or even WH [White House]" and in Isikoff's words, "suggested another reporter check with the CIA." According to Cooper, Rove was very disparaging toward Joe, unsurprisingly. In a *Washington Post* story, Cooper cleared up the mystery of the phrase "double super secret background"—he said it "was a play on a reference to the film *Animal House*, in which John Belushi's wild Delta House fraternity is on Double Secret Probation."

The next day at the White House press briefing, press secretary Scott McClellan endured what had to be one of his hardest days on the job as reporters competed to ask the next question. The following transcript gives an inkling:

Q: Does the president stand by his pledge to fire anyone involved in the leak of a name of a CIA operative?

McClellan: Terry, I appreciate your question. I think your question is being asked relating to some reports that are in reference to an ongoing criminal investigation. The criminal investigation that you reference is something that continues at this point. And as I've previously stated, while that investigation is ongoing, the White House is not going to comment on it. The president directed the White House to cooperate fully with the investigation, and as part of cooperating fully with the investigation, we made a decision that we weren't going to comment on it while it is ongoing.

Q: Excuse me, but I wasn't actually talking about any investigation. But in June of 2004, the president said that he would fire anybody who was involved in this leak. And I just want to know, is that still his position?

McClellan: Yes, but this question is coming up in the context of this ongoing investigation, and that's why I said that our policy continues to be that we're not going to get into commenting on an ongoing criminal investigation from this podium . . .

Q: Do you stand by your statement from the fall of 2003 when you were asked specifically about Karl and Elliott Abrams [National Security Council] and Scooter Libby, and you said, "I've gone to each of those gentlemen, and they have told me they are not involved in this"—do you stand by that statement?

McClellan: And if you will recall, I said that as part of helping the investigators move forward on the investigation we're not going to get into commenting on it. That was something I stated back near that time, as well.

Q: Scott, I mean, just—I mean, this is ridiculous. The notion that you're going to stand before us after having commented with that level of detail and tell people watching this that somehow you decided not to talk. You've got a public record out there. Do you stand by your remarks from that podium, or not?

McClellan: And again, David, I'm well aware, like you, of what was previously said, and I will be glad to talk about it at the appropriate time. The appropriate time is when the investigation—

Q: Why are you choosing when it's appropriate and when it's inappropriate?

McClellan: If you'll let me finish—

Q: No, you're not finishing—you're not saying anything. You stood at that podium and said that Karl Rove was not involved. And now we find out that he spoke out about Joseph Wilson's wife. So don't you owe the American public a fuller explanation? Was he involved, or was he not? Because, contrary to what you told the American people, he did, indeed, talk about his [Wilson's] wife, didn't he?

McClellan: David, there will be a time to talk about this, but now is not the time to talk about it.

Q: Do you think people will accept that, what you're saying today?

McCLELLAN: Again, I've responded to the question. . . .

Q: Do you recall when you were asked—

Q: Wait, wait—so you're now saying that after you cleared Rove and the others from that podium, then the prosecutors asked you not to speak anymore, and since then, you haven't?

McCLELLAN: Again, you're continuing to ask questions relating to an ongoing criminal investigation, and I'm just not going to respond any further.

Q: When did they ask you to stop commenting on it, Scott? Can you peg down a date?

McCLELLAN: Back at that time period.

Q: Well, then the president commented on it nine months later. So was he not following the White House plan?

McCLELLAN: John, I appreciate your questions. You can keep asking them, but you have my response. Go ahead, Dave.

Q: We are going to keep asking them. When did the president learn that Karl Rove had had a conversation with the president— with a news reporter about the involvement of Joseph Wilson's wife and the decision to send—

McCLELLAN: I've responded to the questions.

Q: When did the president learn that Karl Rove had—

McCLELLAN: I've responded to the questions, Dick. Go ahead.

Q: After the investigation is completed, will you then be consistent with your word and the president's word that anybody who was involved would be let go?

McClellan: Again, after the investigation is complete, I will be glad to talk about it at that point.

Q: And a follow-up. Can you walk us through why, given the fact that Rove's lawyer has spoken publicly about this, it is inconsistent with the investigation, that it compromises the investigation to talk about the involvement of Karl Rove, the Deputy Chief of staff?

McClellan: Well, those overseeing the investigation expressed a preference to us that we not get into commenting on the investigation while it's ongoing. And that was what they requested of the White House. And so I think in order to be helpful to that investigation, we are following their direction.

Q: Scott, there's a difference between commenting on an investigation and taking an action—

McClellan: Go ahead, Goyal.

Q: Can I finish, please?

McClellan: You can come—I'll come back to you in a minute. Go ahead, Goyal.

In an act of desperation, McClellan acknowledged Raghubir Goyal of the *India Globe*, who could reliably be counted on to ask foreign policy questions about India and Pakistan. Watching a few minutes of the commotion on TV that night, I almost felt sorry for McClellan, who was perspiring and had that deer-in-the-headlights look to him.

To our great relief, positive articles began appearing that helped to explain what had really happened and why it mattered. Stories headlined "So What's the Story on Bob Novak?," "Ambassador Joe Wilson—Still Fighting the Bush Administration's Culture of Unaccountability," "New Explosive Rove Revelation to Come? Time to Frog-March?," "What Karl Rove told Time magazine's reporter," "Ex-Diplomat's Surprise Volley on Iraq Drove White House into Political Warfare Mode," "Operation Cover-up," "CIA Leak Case Recalls Texas Incident in '92 Race," "A CIA Cover Blown, a White House Exposed" told the tale in unvarnished terms. One of my favorites, which I excitedly e-mailed to friends as evidence of the beginning of a sense of vindication, was from the *Los Angeles Times* on July 18: "Top Aides Reportedly Set Sights on Wilson: Rove and Cheney Chief of staff were intent on discrediting CIA agent's husband, prosecutors have been told." That said it all. As Karl Rove and Scooter Libby and their actions of May and June 2003 came under close scrutiny, our personal lives once again felt like a circus. The phone rang off the hook at all hours. Unexpected visitors showed up at our door. Sleep was elusive—but this time I wasn't so reluctant to take any sleep aids. Joe and I began getting sidelong looks and double takes when we went out in public together. However—unlike the summer of 2004—Joe and I now had a certain satisfaction that the truth was beginning to seep out, even as our anxiety mounted about what would happen next in the case.

The polls continued to show steady decline in confidence in the administration; in June 2005, the president's approval rating was an anemic 43 percent despite continued White House extortions that "amazing progress is being made" in Iraq. In early July, just hours after bombs ripped through the London underground, Egypt's envoy to Iraq, who had been kidnapped just a few days before, was executed by an insurgent group claiming ties to Al Qaeda. Later in the month, Defense Secretary Rumsfeld made an unannounced visit to Baghdad and spoke privately to transitional Prime Minister Ibrahim Jaafari. Rumsfeld's message to him was that the United States wanted to begin pulling troops out of Iraq within a year, and the country's leadership needed to get tougher and establish enough stability for the U.S. to be able to do so. The administration's inept and befuddled response to Hurricane Katrina in late August exacerbated the public's feelings of anger and resentment toward the White House. The president's approval ratings continued to plummet. Gradually, strangers on the street started greeting Joe with "Keep it up!" and "We're with you!" When he drove around town in his well-known (thanks to the *Vanity Fair* photos) dark green convertible, people beeped and gave him the thumbs-up. The tide was changing and the future seemed more promising than it had for some time.

One day that July while I was at my desk at the Agency, I glanced out my office door at the TV—mounted from the ceiling and tuned to Fox News as it often is in Headquarters. My picture was on the screen. The newspaper holder outside my door showed many of the nation's leading dailies with the leak story on page one. I had more or less come to terms with the notion that my days of privacy were over, but something else was bothering me deeply, and I had trouble putting my finger on it. I stewed for a while, and then finally realized what it was. No one, in the bustling office ███████████████████████, had said one word to me about the news of the last weeks. It was like the big elephant in the room that no one had mentioned. I began to feel a little paranoid and panicked. Was I being isolated? Was management freezing me out? Would they slowly pull away my access to sensitive information? What was going on? Was there a hidden surveillance camera above my desk? How could no one in the office mention what was going on out there?

Before leaving work that day, I stepped into the Deputy Branch Chief's office and closed the door behind me. I got right to the point and asked him if he—and all the others—had been instructed *not* to speak to me about the case. ███ There was an awkward pause. He tried to quickly assure me that no, no, there had been no such instructions from on high. It was simply a matter of people not knowing what to say and wanting to "respect my privacy." "Thanks," I responded, "but I'm not an ogre!" I told ▆▆▆ that I didn't mind at all if people talked to me about the case—it would make me feel more normal and not like such a freak. In fairness, he must have passed along the message to the group, because after that, my colleagues stopped by, shyly at first, then more frequently, and talked about the latest developments that began to pile up ferociously. I still felt like the odd one out, but at least my paranoia eased.

While "Little Miss Run Amok," as Judith Miller said she called herself at the *New York Times* because "I could do whatever I wanted" was doing her time in an Alexandria, Virginia, detention center, she hadn't been completely forgotten, even though the London subway bombings had happened the day after she went to jail and knocked her story off the front pages. She had no Internet access and had to share a cell with another woman, but Miller had plenty of elite visitors. According to the *Washington Post*, "the who's who of friends, supporters and Washington and New York luminaries" included John Bolton, then U.S. ambassador to the United Nations; former senator Robert Dole; billionaire publisher Mort Zuckerman; and Gonzalo Marroquin, president of the Inter American Press Association and director of the Guatemalan daily *Prensa Libre*. Miller got mail, too—including from the vice president's Chief of staff, Scooter Libby. Libby closed his note to Judy with these cryptic lines, "You went into jail in the summer. It is fall now. You will have stories to cover—Iraqi elections and suicide bombers, biological threats and the Iranian nuclear program. Out West, where you vacation, the aspens will already be turning. They turn in clusters, because their roots connect them. Come back to work—and life. Until then, you will remain in my thoughts and prayers." No one knew what he was talking about.

On September 29, 2005, Judith Miller was released from jail after agreeing to testify before the grand jury about conversations with her confidential source, who was publicly revealed to be Scooter Libby. How Miller finally got out of jail is a curious tale. On the day of her release, Joseph Tate, one of Libby's attorneys, said he had told Floyd Abrams that Libby's waiver was voluntary and that there was no objection to Miller testifying about the pair's conversations. "We told her lawyers it was not coerced," Tate said, contradicting Abram's and Miller's expression of doubt in July about the validity of her source's waiver. Tate said he had been contacted a few weeks earlier by Miller's successor counsel Robert Bennett, and was "surprised" to learn that Miller had not accepted the offer of a year ago as authorization to speak with prosecutors. After Bennett and Tate checked with the special prosecutor to ask whether their respective clients could speak without being accused of obstructing justice, Miller and Libby spoke by telephone. Sometime around September 19, the lawyers wrote to Fitzgerald to say that Miller now accepted Libby's representation that the waiver was voluntary. According to an article that Miller wrote for the *New York Times* on October 16, she had been confused over what that first waiver meant. "At the behest of President Bush and Mr. Fitzgerald, Mr. Libby had signed a blanket form waiver, which his lawyer signaled to my counsel was not really voluntary, even though Mr. Libby's lawyer also said it had enabled other reporters to cooperate with the grand jury. But I believed that nothing short of a personal letter and a telephone call would allow me to assess whether Mr. Libby truly wished to free me from the pledge of confidentiality I had given him. The letter and the telephone call came last month." Somehow that account doesn't square with Tate's later comment: "We are surprised to learn we had anything to do with her incarceration." The day after she was freed, Judith Miller testified before the grand jury for four hours.

Alongside Miller's article the *New York Times* ran a lengthy piece by three of her colleagues at the paper. David Lindorf wrapped up the essence of the article well in his Counterpunch.com piece published October 18: "Without outright calling their co-worker a liar and a shill for the Bush administration's war marketing campaign, they left almost no doubt in the reader's mind not only that this was in fact what she was, but that the Times' senior management and many of her colleagues at the paper thought exactly the same thing." In Miller's personal piece, this Pulitzer Prize–winning journalist could not remember why the name "Valerie Flame" (I said to friends later that it was my exotic-dancer stage name) showed up in her notebook. And she couldn't remember who told her the name "Valerie Wilson." Lindorf continued, "Equally funny was Miller's continued effort to explain why she just couldn't accept Libby's attorney's assertion to her that she was free to reveal his identity and the content of his conversations with her to the prosecutor. She couldn't do that, she insisted, unless she spoke in person with Libby and was sure he wasn't being 'coerced.' As though Libby's leaks, which were part of an administration campaign to smear Wilson, hadn't been approved by higher-ups. As though, in other words, her source was some kind of whistleblower in need of protection from his bosses."

The grand jury's term was scheduled to expire on Friday, October 28, and any possible indictment would have to be that week or never. For the third time that morning, I resolved to concentrate on my work— ▮▮▮▮▮▮▮▮▮▮▮▮ ▮▮▮—but it seemed that no matter how many times I started, I was distracted by the miniature CNN broadcast in the corner of my computer screen with the sound muted. Whenever they flashed a picture of Fitzgerald, Scooter Libby, Karl Rove, or me, I turned the volume up. Every few hours or so Joe would call to pass along some tantalizing bit of gossip or read me something of interest from a blog. Although I told myself repeatedly that the only decision and opinions that counted were Fitzgerald's, I couldn't help but be drawn into the world of rumor, speculation, and innuendo. Who would be indicted? Had the targets received letters? Had anyone turned snitch? What was the mood in the White House? I desperately wished I had more insight, but properly, neither the FBI nor the prosecutor's team had shared one word of their nearly two-year-old investigation with us. Virtually every hour brought a new development and no matter how many Advil I downed, my throbbing headache would not ease.

I anxiously fiddled around my desk pushing papers into one pile and then another. I took my complete inability to concentrate as a sign that I should go home, when ███████████ ████████████ appeared at my doorway. "Well, are they finally going to get Rove?" she asked with a gleam in her eye. "You know I don't know anything more than what everyone else gets on CNN," I responded. I put away the sensitive papers on my desk, logged off my computer, gathered up my bag and coat, and stopped by the office of my Branch Chief to let her know I was leaving early. ████████, a smart and ambitious woman with bright blond hair whom I had come to admire, smiled wryly. She had been supportive since my arrival at her branch nearly six months ago and liked my work ethic and management style. However, even she could see I was losing the battle that week. "Go home and good luck," she said.

Joe had been on the West Coast for a speaking engagement earlier that week and I was extremely anxious for him to get home before any indictment announcement. During those days,

I'd peer out my children's bedroom window to see if any satellite trucks were lined up on the quiet street. I had made contingency plans to move with the children to the welcoming home of nearby friends if the media invasion became too much, but I was hoping to avoid a forced relocation. Fortunately, Joe made it back in town the next day and we fell into bed that night exhausted but unable to sleep, like so many nights before.

The morning of Friday, October 28, we went through the motions of getting the five-year-olds off to school, and once the kids were out of the house it was suddenly quiet and we had nothing to do but wait. It was excruciating. Shortly before noon, the phone rang. We jumped, looked at each other, then Joe picked up. Someone from the special prosecutor's office was on the line to let us know that indictments would be filed within the hour and that Fitzgerald would hold a press conference at 2 P.M. Joe thanked them for the heads-up and hurried upstairs to dress for an interview. I was so busy channel surfing for any new news that hadn't been played a hundred times before that I barely noticed as Joe left the house.

Just before 2, our lawyer came by to watch the press conference with me. When Fitzgerald took the podium with his trusted and experienced lieutenant, FBI agent Jack Eckenrode, at his side and began to speak, I held my breath. As the conference went on, his slight initial nervousness wore off, and his natural ability to speak extemporaneously and passionately about his investigation came through. Fitzgerald announced that a federal grand jury had indicted Vice President Cheney's Chief of Staff, Scooter Libby, on five counts relating to the probe of the leak of my identity: one count of obstruction of justice, two counts of perjury, and two counts of making false statements. "What we see here today, when a vice president's Chief of Staff is charged with perjury and obstruction of justice, it does show the world that this is a country that takes its law seriously, that all citizens are bound by the law," Fitzgerald said. Libby resigned that same day. By the time he finished, I was exhilarated. Our attorney left for the federal courthouse. Later on TV I watched him read a short statement on behalf of Joe and me:

> The five-count indictment issued by the grand jury today is an important step in the criminal justice process that began more than two years ago. I commend Special Counsel Patrick Fitzgerald for his professionalism, for his diligence, and for his courage.
>
> There will be many opportunities in the future to comment on the events that led to today's indictment. And, it appears that there will be further developments before the grand jury. Whatever the final outcome of the investigation and the prosecution, I continue to believe that revealing my wife Valerie's secret CIA identity was very wrong and harmful to our nation, and I feel that my family was attacked for my speaking the truth about the events that led our country to war. I look forward to exercising my rights as a citizen to speak about these matters in the future.
>
> Today, however, is not the time to analyze or to debate. And it is certainly not a day to celebrate. Today is a sad day for America. When an indictment is delivered at the front door of the White House, the Office of the President is defiled. No citizen can take pleasure from that.
>
> As this case proceeds, Valerie and I are confident that justice will be done. In the meantime, I have a request. While I may engage in public discourse, my wife and my family are private people. They did not choose to be brought into the public square, and they do not wish to be under the glare of camera. They are entitled to their privacy. This case is not about me or my family, no matter how others might try to make it so.

This case is about serious criminal charges that go to the heart of our democracy.

We, like all citizens, await the judgment of the jury in a court of law.

Thank you.

I switched off the TV and the house was eerily silent. No phones rang, no camera crews pulled up outside. I wandered upstairs to our bedroom and turned the TV on again to watch the brief follow-up remarks by President Bush on the South Lawn before he left for a Camp David weekend. The president delivered what I thought were tepid and uninspired words about Libby:

> Today I accepted the resignation of Scooter Libby. Scooter has worked tirelessly on behalf of the American people and sacrificed much in the service to this country. He served the vice president and me through extraordinary times in our nation's history. Special Counsel Fitzgerald's investigation and ongoing legal proceedings are serious, and now the proceedings—the process moves into a new phase. In our system, each individual is presumed innocent and entitled to due process and a fair trial. While we're all saddened by today's news, we remain wholly focused on the many issues and opportunities facing this country. . . .

The president then got into his waiting helicopter. I looked out our window, with its expansive view of the Washington Monument and I could make out Marine One rising from the White House lawn, its rotor blades pushing through the air. I watched as it glided toward our house, which happened to be in its northward path, and then flew, at what seemed like a very low altitude, directly over it. All I could think about was what a sad time this was for our country.

In the days and weeks that followed, I felt as if I were underwater, hearing only muffled sounds as people talked. Although it was deeply gratifying to hear good wishes and congratulations from friends and strangers alike, and to watch demand for Joe on the lecture circuit spike upward, our personal lives remained unsettled. One week after the press conference, I left the house for work early one morning to find Trevor playing on the lawn before going off to school. I gave him a quick kiss on the forehead and tossed a ball a few times with him. As I picked up my purse and started walking toward the car, out of the corner of my eye I noticed a photographer across the street, camera raised. In a surge of maternal protectiveness, I envisioned tackling the photographer, pinning him to the ground in a wrestling move, and pulling the film out of his camera in a rage. Instead, I scooped Trevor up in my arms and hustled back into the house, shaking with anger.

I thought that with the indictment behind us, I could exhale a bit, but I was wrong again. As Dorothy Parker once quipped, "What fresh hell is this?" On November 5, retired Army General Paul Vallely made the startling accusation that Joe had casually revealed my CIA employment over a year before the Novak column appeared while Vallely was waiting with Joe in the greenroom of Fox News. He said that in addition to his conversations with Wilson, the ambassador was proud to introduce Plame at cocktail parties and other social events around Washington as his CIA wife. "That was pretty common knowledge," he said. "She's been out there on the Washington scene many years." "This whole thing has become the biggest non-story I know," he concluded, "and all created by Joe Wilson." I was shocked. That a general of the Army, an institution that set high moral standards for its officer corps, would say such obvious lies was outrageous. As Joe pointed out, publicly in response to Vallely, he had not told anyone about my true employer—not any Democratic senator, close friends, not even his brother. Why would he have told someone he didn't even know? It defied logic. After changing his story several times, and receiving a strongly worded letter from our attorney, Vallely faded from public view. People like him—and we had seen our share of them since this affair started—are contemptible.

Later that same month, another bombshell. Exalted Watergate reporter and prolific writer Bob Woodwood testified under oath on November 14 that another senior administration official—not Libby—had told him about me and my position at the CIA nearly a month before Novak's July 2003 column. According to a statement that Woodward made to the *Washington Post*, the paper where he nominally serves as assistant managing editor, he did not believe the information about me to be "sensitive or classified." In light of this new information, the dynamics shifted again and Libby's lawyers hastened to claim that it undermined the case against their client. Apparently, Woodward did not disclose his involvement in the case to the *Post*'s executive editor because he feared being subpoenaed by the special prosecutor. He later apologized to his editor. "I explained in detail that I was trying to protect my sources. That's job No. 1 in a case like this," Woodward told the paper. "I hunkered down. I'm in the habit of keeping secrets. I didn't want to do anything out there that was going to get me subpoenaed." When news of Woodward's unconscionably late testimony broke, I was deeply disappointed that he had chosen to react as a journalist first and a responsible citizen only when his source "outed" him to the special prosecutor. As David Corn noted in his blog for *The Nation*, "What compounded his problem was that Woodward had gone on television and radio shows to dismiss the leak investigation and criticize Fitzgerald, without revealing that he had had a personal stake in the matter because a source of his had been a target." It was not Woodward's best moment.

Now I had to seriously consider my career and what to do next. For ▓▓▓▓▓▓▓▓▓▓▓▓ I had loved what I was doing, but I could no longer continue to do the undercover work for which I had been trained. My career had been done in by stupidity and political payback, and that made me angry. If I resigned, I would lose my modest, but dependable, government paycheck. Given Joe's dearth of consulting business, it was an important consideration. What could I do next? Did I actually have any marketable skills? In spite of all that had happened and my own deep disappointments over how the Agency had responded throughout the leak episode, leaving the Agency "family" was difficult. However, I could not shake the image in my mind of sitting in my government office at fifty, with figurative cobwebs hanging from the desk and chair. I finally decided that I had not come this far to be scared by the unknown. I would wait until ▓▓▓▓▓▓▓▓▓▓▓ ▓▓▓▓ January 2006, and resign—sadly, but on my terms. When I did resign, my boss ▓▓▓▓ literally begged me to reconsider my decision, and despite my respect for her and my belief in the mission, I was not tempted for a moment. Leaving was the right choice for me and my family. I was ready to close this chapter in my life.

On my last day, my office threw me a farewell party and invited many of the colleagues and friends I had worked with over the years. Besides putting out a lovely luncheon in one of the conference rooms, friends brought flowers, cakes, and best of all, cards inscribed with sincere sentiments. I was touched and buoyed by their gestures. The young officers whom I had supervised were particularly outraged at what had happened and at the increasing politicization of intelligence that my case exemplified. Like me, they had entered the Agency filled with energy, hope, and patriotism, only to emerge a few years later with a realization of their own vulnerabilities, the danger of politicians meddling in intelligence matters, and a clearer sense of the moral ambiguity that characterizes even the most honorable institutions. After our lunch I rose to address my assembled colleagues. I hoped that I could maintain my composure and wanted to express my deep belief in the importance of keeping the nation's intelligence free from political interference. Our counterproliferation mission (and that of counterterrorism) was too important to our national security. The nodding heads and smiles around the room told me I had many supporters.

I used the days after my resignation to take stock of where I was and what I wanted next. I was thrilled and relieved to realize that my marriage had not only survived a prolong period of unbelievable stress, but was thriving. We thought and moved as a team more often. Our enemies had taken many things from us, but they had failed to ruin us and our commitment to our country and each other. We also recognized that for the first time we could decide where to live based on what kind of life we wanted and our goals beyond government service. We instituted a rule that either one of us could discuss potential locations without an automatic veto from the other. It was a useful exercise that helped to clarify our ambitions and desires for the next phase of our adventures together. And it began to make us feel as if we were reasserting some measure of control over our lives. Our conversations helped us reconfirm our core values, deepening our commitment to each other and to our family. It felt like a new beginning.

CHAPTER 14

Life after the Agency

I looked forward to beginning the next chapter in my life, but first Joe and I thought it would be a good idea to take some time away from Washington to unwind. Far away. Several friends had told us about an unpretentious, beautiful, peaceful retreat in Baja, Mexico, called Rancho la Puerta, and we decided to look into going. As soon as my parents confirmed that they could watch the children while we were away, the vacation was booked. Joe offered moderate resistance, imagining that he would have to do yoga all day and wouldn't be able to get messages on his Black-Berry. However, he saw that I was determined to go—with him or not—and he agreed to join me after finishing a speaking engage-ment in California. His concern that his BlackBerry would go blank was well placed, but within hours, the natural beauty of the setting, the low-key environment, the privacy, and the sheer quiet won him over. There were no telephones anywhere, and to read a magazine or newspaper or watch TV, a guest had to make a real effort to find them in one small casita on the grounds.

During our daily sunrise hikes in the rock-strewn mountains behind the resort, I began to mull over the idea of writing a book as a way to process all that had happened to us over the last three years. A few nights, by the light of the fireplace in our room, I started to jot down notes. Many memories, some of which I would have preferred stayed buried in the past, were stirred. I played with different ideas about how to tell our story and thought long and hard about my motivations for doing so. Although I had never spoken publicly on the leak and I had no plans to do so, I believed that writing a book would help me understand what we had lived through and reflect upon the much larger forces swirling around us. I knew for certain that I wanted to convey my pride in my work at the Agency and encourage young people to consider a career in public service. I wanted to make the point to college students that although not nearly as lucrative as working on Wall Street, a career in the Agency could certainly be more exciting and have more impact on our world. I saw it as a way to make a difference while having fun. In the insecure world we live in today, our country needs as many talented and dedicated officers as possible. Our story could also illuminate the much larger issue of the importance of holding our government to account for its words and deeds, as well as underscore the responsibilities and rights that we enjoy as citizens of this great country.

During our week at the resort, very few people recognized us, which was just fine with Joe and me. We attended exercise classes, took walks, and simply relaxed, setting the craziness of Washington aside for a bit. That is, until one day as I was putting on my shoes after a yoga class, a woman quietly tapped me on the shoulder and whispered, "Did you know your picture is in *Time* magazine?" Hmmm. I walked over to the casita and tried to reach as casually and nonchalantly as I could for the latest issue of *Time* on a low coffee table. It was the one proclaiming their *Time* Person of the Year, which, in a departure from their usual practice, had been awarded to two people in 2005: Bill Gates and

Bono of U2 "for making mercy smarter and hope strategic and then daring the rest of us to follow." As I paged through the magazine, wildly hoping that the woman had somehow made a mistake, I stopped short. There was a two-page black-and-white photo of Joe on our living room couch looking unbelievably tired and worn. It must have been taken in late 2003, as the initial media frenzy over the leak was at its height. I vowed I would not let Joe see the magazine and my heart ached when I saw how the pressures we were under had manifested themselves so clearly on his face. I felt terrible for him, or at least I did until my eyes traveled to the background of the photograph and I saw that I was in the frame, too. Then I felt even sorrier—and embarrassed— for myself. There I was, in my pajamas, barefoot, my hand in my hair, looking rumpled and worried and undone. I tried to remember the photo shoot and had a vague memory of Trevor scampering into the living room and having to shoo him out of the way. The photographer had caught me in his frame as I crossed the room. To say it was a candid shot would be an understatement. Later some people tried to console me, arguing that it was an honest and powerful portrait of two individuals in a marriage under incredible strain. Maybe so, but they weren't in *their* pajamas in *Time* magazine.

By the time we left the resort, I was more comfortable in my decision to write a book, even though the only writing I had done to date had been relatively dry and factual intelligence reports. I knew that a book would invite more publicity and incite the radical right to further criticism of us. However, I figured that our enemies would have loved nothing better than to see us go away, never to be heard from again. They could continue to make us the object of their irrational rants, but I wasn't going to give them that satisfaction.

•   •   •

The first weeks of post-Agency life matched my naïve expectations that our lives would return to some degree of normalcy. I delved into the minutiae that had been ignored for months: doctors' appointments, trips to the dentist, thank-you notes, house repairs, activities with the children. The absence of any reporting on the leak case in the first months of 2006 lulled me into a false sense that the worst of the storm was behind us.

Suddenly, on April 11, the *New York Times* published a front-page article, "With One Filing, Prosecutor Puts Bush in Spotlight," which described the investigator's scrutiny of the White House. The article reported on a filing Fitzgerald had made just a few days earlier that stated in direct, clear language, "There was 'a strong desire by many, including multiple people in the White House' to undermine Joe Wilson." According to the *Times*, "Mr. Fitzgerald's filing talks not of an effort to level with Americans but of 'a plan to discredit, punish or seek revenge against Mr. Wilson. It is hard to conceive of what evidence there could be that would disprove the existence of White House efforts to punish Wilson.' " Reading those words brought us a rush of relief; Fitzgerald's dogged efforts seemed to put to rest any doubts of what we had believed happened all along. What satisfaction to read: "Every prosecutor strives not just to prove a case, but also to tell a compelling story. It is now clear that Mr. Fitzgerald's account of what was happening in the White House in the summer of 2003 is very different from the Bush administration's narrative, which suggested that Mr. Wilson was seen as a minor figure whose criticisms could be answered by disclosing the underlying intelligence upon which Mr. Bush relied. It turned out that much of the information about Mr. Hussein's search for uranium was questionable at best, and that it became the subject of dispute almost as soon as it was included in the 2002 National Intelligence Estimate on Iraq."

Strange things were happening in the fishbowl of Washington's political and intelligence community. In mid-April, long-time senior CIA officer Mary McCarthy was fired for allegedly disclosing classified information to reporters. At the time of her dismissal, after an apparently difficult polygraph exam, Mary was working in the CIA Inspector General's office. Supposedly, a CIA inquiry had identified Ms. McCarthy as having supplied information for a November 2, 2005, article in the *Washington Post* by Dana Priest, a national security reporter, that revealed that the Agency was sending terror suspects to clandestine detention centers in several countries, including sites in Eastern Europe. McCarthy's dismissal was unprecedented in the CIA and served as yet another example of the Bush administration aggresively punishing leaks that they believed were harmful to national security. During the same time frame, the *New York Times* reported that the National Security Agency wiretapped citizens without warrants, and the administration was also investigating who had leaked information about the warrant-less program to the press. Joe and I shook our heads at the irony of the administration taking an aggressive stance against leaks when it had been clearly established that someone who had been involved in the leak of my name to the press (which arguably also harmed our national security), Karl Rove, still had his security clearance and went to work every day at the White House.

By coincidence, Joe and Mary McCarthy had worked to-gether on the National Security Council during the Clinton administration. Mary was always professional, respected, and very good at her job. A few days later Mary's attorney said that she had not leaked any classified information and was not the source for Priest's article on secret prisons. According to her lawyer, she had been fired for having undisclosed contacts with journalists, in violation of her secrecy agreement. By firing Mary,

who was only ten days away from retirement, the CIA management under Porter Goss was sending a clear signal that no one
was to step out of line and if they did, the results would be harsh.

On April 26, 2006, Karl Rove made his fifth appearance
before the grand jury. Those who had long seen Rove as a malevolent force in the White House and national politics were beside
themselves with glee. Would Fitzgerald finally get his elusive target? That day, Joe and I were in New York. We had been invited
to a lunch at a chic Manhattan restaurant, Michael's, favored by
the power brokers in publishing, public relations, and entertainment. As we paused at the corner of Fifty-fifth Street and Fifth
Avenue to get our bearings, several passersby approached us and
offered their support and kind words. Suddenly, there was a tap
on my shoulder and there stood the writer Dominick Dunne,
beaming and introducing himself. Dunne, perfectly dressed in a
dark suit, chivalrously kissed my hand and told us how much he
admired what Joe had done. We chatted a moment, and it turned
out that he, too, was having lunch at Michael's. As we waded into
the crowded and noisy dining room, almost every table was filled
with a recognizable face. Many of the patrons came over to our
table to shake our hands and offer words of cheer and congratulations. After enduring and absorbing so much vile criticism, it
was a lighthearted and welcomed change.

That evening we attended an event hosted by *Vanity Fair* editor Graydon Carter in conjunction with the Tribeca Film Festi-
val. The dinner was the kind of glittering affair that *Vanity Fair*
does to perfection. Celebrities were scattered about, photographers' flashbulbs went off, cigarette smoke wafted above our
heads, and waiters appeared bearing silver trays of champagne
flutes. At the end of the evening, I went to retrieve my wrap and
was gently pulled aside by a New York society woman with perfect hair and makeup. I had no idea who she was. She whispered
to me quickly, in a rather conspiratorial way, that she had voted

for Bush in 2004, but now she was "just so sorry. It was a terrible mistake." As she adjusted her fur stole she glared at me and squeezed my hand tightly. "I wish you and your husband good luck." With that, she walked off.

It was nearly midnight. We were leaving very early the next morning to return to our normal life with our children. As we stepped into the car taking us back to our hotel, we both let out a big sigh. I pulled off my high heels and settled into the plush backseat. As the car raced through the empty streets, I marveled, as I do every time, at the wonder that is New York at night. Stopped at a light at Rockefeller Center, my eye caught the red news ticker that stretches around an NBC Studios building. "Rove Makes Fifth Grand Jury Appearance in the Valerie Plame Affair" was running along the strip.

On May 5, while sitting in tiny chairs during a parent-teacher conference at the children's elementary school, Joe's BlackBerry started going off incessantly. I glared at him to shut it off and he glanced at it and tucked it away into his coat pocket. As soon as we were finished and out the door, he pulled it out and told me that CIA Director Porter Goss had been effectively fired. Although Goss said he was "stepping aside" during an Oval Office meeting with President Bush, it seemed pretty clear that he had been pushed to do so. According to the *Washington Post* front-page article the next day, "senior administration officials said Bush had lost confidence in Goss, almost from the beginning and decided months ago to replace him." As columnist David Ignatius wrote on May 7, "Goss was dumped by a president who doesn't like to fire anyone. That was a sign of how badly off track things had gotten at the CIA."

Once John Negroponte became the de facto intelligence czar as Director of National Intelligence (DNI), a job created by

Congress over a year before, Goss's effectiveness, prestige, and daily access to the president had been considerably diminished. This, in turn, further degraded and undermined the organization he led. During a time of driving massive change, which Goss and other senior intelligence managers were attempting to do at the Agency, effective and clear communication with all levels of the organization is critical. Goss failed completely at this task and the cost was high. During his tenure, according to the *Washington Post*, "In the clandestine service alone, Goss lost one director, two deputy directors, and at least a dozen department heads, Station Chiefs and division directors, many with the key language skills and experience he has said the Agency needs. The Agency is on its third counterterrorism Chief since Goss arrived." Criticism of Goss's eighteen-month tenure poured in from all sides; he had been a poor fit from the beginning. In an underperforming bureaucracy such as the CIA, a strong leader, respected by the rank and file, is essential to managing needed change and modernization. On a personal note, I was not sorry to see him go.

Goss's abrupt departure served to highlight what those of us concerned about the intelligence community already knew: the reorganization recommended by the 9/11 Commission that was supposed to bring greater coordination was thus far an abysmal failure. I remember standing in Counterproliferation Division's large conference room in early 2005 when the creation of the DNI was announced to the Division workforce. Our Chief swore that the DNI would not be just another layer of useless bureaucracy—everyone acknowledged that we already had plenty of that. The veterans of intelligence reorganizations past made cynical comments under their breath. According to the DNI diagram, there are sixteen separate intelligence units under its aegis. As of April 2006, Negroponte's budget was close to $1 billion and none of us knew what his staff of nearly 1,500, who were temporarily housed at Bolling Air Force Base in Washington, D.C., was doing with their time. According to the DNI's own Web site, its mission is "a unified enterprise of innovative intelligence professionals whose common purpose in defending American lives and interests, and advancing American values, draws strength from our democratic institutions, diversity, and intellectual and technological prowess."

The lore of the CIA was that it was created after Pearl Harbor to prevent such a disaster from happening again. According to a study ordered by President Bush in 2001 and edited by the head of the CIA Historical Staff, Michael Warner, "The explosions at Pearl Harbor still echoed in Washington when President Harry Truman and Congressional leaders passed the National Security Act of 1947. A joint Congressional investigation just a year earlier had concluded that the Pearl Harbor disaster illustrated America's need for a unified command structure and a better intelligence system. Indeed, the President and many of his aides rightly believed that the surprise attack could have been blunted if the various commanders and departments had coordinated their actions and shared their intelligence." Isn't that what Congress was attempting to do again with the DNI, prevent another 9/11 attack? Perhaps in their haste to respond to the recommendation of the 9/11 Commission report, Congress failed to see that although the CIA might have serious problems that needed to be addressed, attempting to smother them with another layer of bureaucracy was not the solution.

The early summer sun was just above the horizon on June 13 when I came down the stairs on my way to the kitchen to make some coffee. My thoughts were on the end-of-school-year activities for the children and our upcoming trip to Florida to visit my parents. I passed Joe in the family room, on the phone. It was way too early to be having a business conversation, and I wondered what had happened. Was someone sick? I looked up when Joe came into the kitchen and knew instantly that something was terribly wrong: "Rove's not going to be indicted," Joe said in an unusually flat tone. The day before, Fitzgerald had told Robert Luskin, Karl Rove's attorney, that his client would not be charged with any crimes relating to the leak of my name. And just like that, months of speculation over Rove's fate, watched with equal zeal by both Democratic and Republican partisans, ended. Only days before, the blogosphere had been rife with rumors that the grand jury had handed down an unnamed sealed indictment and that it was being held over Rove's head to ensure his full cooperation with prosecutors. It was hard to process that someone who had appeared before a grand jury five times, and had admitted that he had spoken to Robert Novak and Matt Cooper in the week before my name was published, would face no consequences for his actions.

I was puzzled and angry but more concerned about Joe. He had convinced himself that Rove would be indicted and now that wasn't going to happen. Joe is a congenital optimist, which is one of the reasons I married him. He's the guy who buys one lottery ticket just knowing that the $200 million prize will be his. He is a great believer in what is possible, and has a winning way of persuading others that it will happen. It's not naïveté or idealism, but rather his positive approach to life that I find so appealing. So to see him reeling from the news of the nonindictment, in direct refutation of his belief that justice is usually served, was tough. And I felt powerless to say or do anything to comfort him. While our faith in Fitzgerald's skills and integrity remained unshaken, we couldn't help but wonder, along with everyone else, what the special prosecutor had received or heard from Rove to prompt his decision.

It is true that bad news comes in threes. Shortly after learning about Rove, we received a stark form letter from the IRS informing us that our 2004 taxes would be audited. That's a letter no one wants; neither one of us had ever been audited and we had no idea what to expect. I immediately contacted our accountant who had prepared our taxes for years. According to Rich, there was nothing in our tax return that would have triggered an audit: no unusual claims that would have caused a red flag, no strange activity, no excessive income (that's for sure). I am not conspiratorially minded, but after talking to Rich I really had dark thoughts about Nixonian "enemy lists." Didn't Nixon use the power of his office to unleash IRS audits on those he deemed to be his enemies? A 1971 memo from White House Counsel John Dean to a Republican businessman explains the purpose of the "list": "This memorandum addresses the matter of how we can maximize the fact of our incumbency in dealing with persons known to be active in their opposition to our Administration. Stated a bit more bluntly—how we can use the available federal machinery to screw our political enemies." After several weeks, many hours of pulling paper and files, and two thousand dollars in accountant fees we were completely cleared by the IRS. Our taxes were in perfect order. My concerns that we were the targets of yet another political attack were strengthened several months later when we learned that a journalist friend of ours had been also singled out for an audit. He had just published a book highly critical of the Bush administration and it felt like payback. But, then again, maybe the audits were just a strange coincidence.

It was around that same time in early summer that the owner of the lawn service company we had used for some time was walking around the house, surveying the garden. By chance, he noticed something very strange. I was writing at my desk, on our lower level when John knocked on the glass door and gestured at me to come out on the deck. I stepped outside and looked up to where he was pointing. Several of the enormous bolts that held the upper deck to the side of the house were inexplicably missing. It was not as if they had fallen out: there were none on the ground. Our upper deck is probably fifty feet above the ground and a collapse with people on it or below it would be fatal. It didn't make sense—we had rebuilt the deck the year before and used a reputable local firm that had done other projects for us. I called Joel, the owner of the firm, and asked him to come out. The next day he took a close look at the support beams and bolts and was as alarmed as John had been; he told us to stay off the decks until they were fixed. Joel was at a loss to explain the missing bolts; he trusted his workers and couldn't imagine that they had forgotten to put in several large, important bolts. It was all unnerving. As the saying goes, "Just because you're paranoid doesn't mean that they aren't out to get you."

Joe and I had talked for months about filing a civil suit against Cheney, Libby, Rove, and others who had been targets of the leak investigation. Even back in late 2003, following my "outing," Joe raised the prospect of filing a lawsuit several times but every time he broached the subject, I got angry, defensive, and overly emotional. I didn't want to talk about it: the leak was still too raw for me and I wasn't ready yet to think rationally through what such an action would mean. For a long time, the idea of a civil suit was another point of unspoken friction between us. But after we lived life for a while as the public Joe Wilson and Valerie Plame Wilson, I began to tally up the costs of the campaign to smear Joe and to out me carelessly: the near destruction of Joe's reputation and his consulting business, the end of my career, the wholesale invasion of our privacy, threats to our physical security, the chronic level of stress that adversely affected our health in myriad ways, and two small children wondering why their parents were fighting again. A lawsuit couldn't completely remedy the situation, but to me, it began to look more appealing.

It wasn't until the spring of 2006 that I was finally ready to sit down and talk through the possibility of filing a civil suit. After some long conversations about what we were getting ourselves into, Joe and I narrowed our motivations down to three that we thought validated the anticipated legal pain. First, it was a means of getting to the truth of how the erroneous sixteen words about the uranium from Niger had made their way into the president's State of the Union address. Second, it would hold government officials accountable for actions that might be illegal or unconstitutional. Third, it would serve as a deterrent to future public servants who might think they are above the law. As a matter of self-preservation, we knew that the jackals of the Right would continue to attack us as long as they could get away with it. The only way to deal with schoolyard bullies is to confront them. We had seen how Watergate apologists had attempted to blur the historical record for a generation, and given what we had lived through for three years, we had no doubt that similar efforts would be made to whitewash the scandal, or worse, to make us the perpetrators of the whole thing. These fears were soon realized in September 2006, when the *Washington Post* editorial page actually said that Joe was responsible for the leak.

At the time—long before the November midterm election that put the Democrats back into the majority in both houses of Congress—we were also convinced that the president would likely grant a pardon to Libby long before his case went to trial. Our civil suit seemed to be the only means by which we could expose the administration's wrongdoing. In any case, whatever decision we made had to be made soon. The three-year statute of limitations on what we were going to claim would expire on July 14, 2006: the violation of our First Amendment right to freedom of speech, the violation of Fifth Amendment right to equal protection of the laws, violation of our right to privacy and property, conspiracy to deprive persons of their civil rights, action for neglect to prevent civil rights violation, public disclosure of private facts, and civil conspiracy.

Disappointment over the nonindictment of Rove receded, overtaken by a frenzy of activity. Our legal team was busy putting the final touches on the claim, continuing their research and polishing the language to ensure that the case was as compelling, direct, and well grounded in legal precedent as it could be. After all, we were naming powerful Vice President Cheney, presidential advisers Karl Rove and Scooter Libby, and "John Does" numbered 1–10 to provide for as-yet-unknown defendants. Adding the John Does turned out to be a prudent move, for in the months ahead, journalists and the ongoing criminal investigation indeed provided more potential defendants to our case. Everything had to be airtight because we were going after very big game and any mistake, legal or otherwise, could doom the entire effort. However, after having been the quarry for the last three years, it felt good to finally be the pursuer.

The coordination of what felt like a thousand moving pieces finally came together on July 14, a typically steamy Washington summer day. The suit had been properly filed with the court the evening before, and we had arranged a press conference at the National Press Club in downtown D.C. to announce what we were doing and why. Joe made a few remarks before an intimidating scrum of reporters and photographers. I followed, speaking publicly (with a dry mouth and shaking knees) for the first time since my name had appeared in Robert Novak's column.

I am proud to have served my country by working at the Central Intelligence Agency. I and my former CIA colleagues trusted our government to protect us as we did our jobs. That a few reckless individuals within the current Administration betrayed that trust has been a grave disappointment to every patriotic American; Joe and I have filed this action with a heavy heart but with renewed purpose. I feel strongly that those who acted so recklessly, and who acted in such a harmful way, need to answer for their shameful conduct and to explain their actions in a court of law.

Lawsuits, as everyone knows, cost a great deal of money. We are far from independently wealthy, and indeed, the last three years had been a financial disaster for our family. To help defray the cost of litigation, we set up a trust fund for donations. Concurrently, we developed a Web site, Wilsonsupport.org, as a means for people who believed in our cause to donate, and get updates on the case. Joe and I had no illusions that we would earn one penny from our lawsuit—that was never our intent. We decided that should the civil suit result in any award money, once the legal costs were paid, monies equal to what had been contributed to the fund would go back to the Wilson Trust, which would in turn distribute them to other charitable organizations working to protect First Amendment rights and defend whistle-blowers from retaliation.

In our view, victory in the civil suit would not even be defined in a verdict and monetary judgment. Instead, we thought we'd be successful if we were able to surmount the significant legal hurdles that our case presented—claims of absolute immunity by the vice president being the largest—and have our defendants provide sworn depositions on what had happened and why. We also knew it would take years for a civil suit to wind through the courts and so delay our deep desire to move past the leak and its aftermath. But we proceeded, convinced that it was the right thing to do.

Shortly after the suit was filed, Joe and I joined forces with a nonpartisan, nonprofit watchdog group called Citizens for Responsibility and Ethics in Washington (CREW). Led by the brilliant, intrepid, and respected lawyer Melanie Sloan, this small group is "dedicated to targeting government officials who sacrifice the common good to special interests and help[ing] Americans use litigation to shine a light on those who betray the public trust." Much to our delight, CREW accepted our case on a pro bono basis and got to work immediately. Joe and I knew we were in good hands.

At the end of August 2006, I received a phone call late one evening from David Corn. Back in July 2003, Corn had been the first journalist to raise the point that the leaking of my name could have criminal implications according to the Intelligence Identities Protection Act. His book, *Hubris: The Inside Story of Spin, Scandal, and the Selling of the Iraq War*, cowritten with fellow journalist Michael Isikoff, was due to come out any day. David called to give me a courtesy "heads-up" about a bombshell in the book—that deputy secretary of state Richard Armitage had been the first administration leaker of my name, when he gave it to Bob Woodward, who had interviewed Armitage in mid-June 2003 for his own upcoming book, *Plan of Attack*. "According to Woodward, his source [Armitage] referred to Valerie Wilson in a 'casual and offhand' manner. 'It was gossip,' Woodward later said."

Armitage went on to "gossip" more in an interview with Robert Novak on July 8, 2003, after Joe's op-ed appeared in the *New York Times* and before Novak's column was published. According to the account in *Hubris*, Novak asked, "Why in the world did they send Joe Wilson on this?" "To answer Novak, Armitage revealed a tantalizing morsel that was in a classified State INR memo: that Wilson's wife worked at the CIA on weapons of mass destruction and had suggested her husband for the mission to Niger. It was the same information Armitage had already shared with Woodward." As David conveyed the gist of this to me on the phone, my mind began to race, trying to figure out what this meant to our case and to understand the complicated sequence of events of June and July 2003. I thanked him for letting me know, and hung up. I knew immediately that the far Right would use this revelation to slander us further and distort the case. What I was not prepared for was the barrage of criticism and backlash toward us from the more mainstream media.

Within a few days of the publication of *Hubris* and its revelations about the initial source of the leak, the Right Wing was frothing at the mouth, claiming that in fact there was no "conspiracy" campaign to smear Joe Wilson, as he and the special prosecutor had alleged. The book provided ample opportunity to paint Armitage as a harmless gossip, someone who wasn't even part of the neocon cabal that took the nation to war; that everything about this case had been overblown. On September 1, I opened the *Washington Post* to read their editorial titled "End of an Affair":

> It follows that one of the most sensational charges leveled against the Bush White House—that it orchestrated the leak of Ms. Plame's identity to ruin her career and thus punish Mr. Wilson—is untrue. The partisan clamor that followed the raising of that allegation by Mr. Wilson in the summer of 2003 led to the appointment of a special prosecutor, a costly and prolonged investigation, and the indictment of Vice President Cheney's Chief of staff, I. Lewis "Scooter" Libby, on charges of perjury. All of that might have been avoided had Mr. Armitage's identity been known three years ago. . . . Nevertheless, it now appears that the person most responsible for the end of Ms. Plame's CIA career is Mr. Wilson. Mr. Wilson chose to go public with an explosive charge, claiming—falsely, as it turned out—that he had debunked reports of Iraqi uranium-shopping in Niger and that his report had circulated to senior adminis-

tration officials. He ought to have expected that both those officials and journalists such as Mr. Novak would ask why a retired ambassador would have been sent on such a mission and that the answer would point to his wife. He diverted responsibility from himself and his false charges by claiming that President Bush's closest aides had engaged in an illegal conspiracy. It's unfortunate that so many people took him seriously.

I was furious. I suddenly understood what it must have felt like to live in the Soviet Union and have only the state propaganda entity, *Pravda*, as the source of news about the world. One didn't always agree with an editorial, but there was an understanding that it should be grounded in reality-based facts. The *Post*'s claims that Joe was the one responsible for the end of my career and that his report about Niger had been debunked were flatly untrue. To suggest that Joe somehow eroded my cover by going to Niger and then writing about it showed vast ignorance about how our clandestine services function. The line "Mr. Wilson chose to go public with an explosive charge, claiming— falsely, as it turned out—that he had debunked reports of Iraqi uranium-shopping in Niger" is another demonstration of willful ignorance. In fact, the *Post*'s news department had written copiously over the last three years—and amazingly enough, in that very day's paper—about the unsubstantiated, empty claims made by the administration. For starters, the White House itself had acknowledged that the infamous "sixteen-words" in the State of the Union address in 2003 were a mistake. How could the paper's editorial board write such things? When I subsequently found out that the most likely author of the editorial was Fred Hiatt, a respected journalist who had served as a foreign correspondent for the *Post* for many years, this possibility deepened my disappointment. Although Hiatt presided over an editorial page that had endorsed the invasion of Iraq, he had a reputation for upholding the highest standards of journalism. Here was an editorial that had clearly strayed far from the known facts. Joe had threatened many times over the last few years to cancel our subscription to the *Post*, but I had always persuaded him to keep it, pushing aside principle for the more pragmatic reasons of having movie listings, local news, and the weekend activities guide. This time, however, I had enough and didn't even wait for Joe's expected rant. I called that morning and canceled the paper, noting that if the editorial writers couldn't be bothered to read the news sections in their own paper, then neither would I. It was a minuscule but important victory for my morale. I just wished I hadn't waited so long.

Unfortunately, the paper still arrived for a few more mornings and I didn't have the sense to toss it into the recycling bin. I read David Broder, who on September 7 in his column argued with righteous indignation that the media had treated Karl Rove shabbily by saying less than nice things about the man. Broder excoriated Sidney Blumenthal, Joe Conason, the special prosecutor, and Joe—among others—for being so quick to say Rove had something to do with the leak. For good measure, he finished up with "these and other publications owe Karl Rove an apology." Inevitably, the Wilson bashing turned to Fitzgerald bashing. The image of an out-of-control prosecutor was resurrected with the rationale that if Fitzgerald knew about Armitage's identity from the beginning of his investigation, and apparently he did, then why did he bother to continue? The *New York Times* article on September 2, noted that "the question of whether Mr. Fitzgerald properly exercised his prosecutorial discretion in continuing to pursue possible wrongdoing in the case has become the subject of rich debate on editorial pages and in legal and political circles." However, the fact of the matter is that FBI investigators knew about Armitage's role from October 2003. Fitzgerald was appointed special prosecutor in late December 2003, but the FBI didn't shut down the investigation because they had good reason to believe that Libby and Rove were lying to them. There was another reason for the FBI to continue its investigation beyond Novak and Armitage. A September 28, 2003, *Washington Post* story reported, "Yesterday, a senior administration official said that before Novak's column ran, two top White House officials called at least six Washington journalists and disclosed the identity and occupation of Wilson's wife. 'Clearly, it was meant purely and simply for revenge,' the senior official said of the alleged leak." As the astute blogger "emptywheel" (Marcy Wheeler) wrote, "In other words, Armitage's admission didn't answer the range of questions we know to be placed before the FBI, to say nothing of the evidence included in the CIA's referral." What even the most seasoned journalists couldn't seem to comprehend, much less report, was that the Armitage revelation did not preclude the real possibility that there was a parallel effort within the White House to slander Joe and therefore discredit his article and findings about Niger. Although Armitage's actions may have been absent of malevolent intent, they still showed that a ranking government official, who should have known better, was extremely sloppy and careless in his handling of classified information. In a CBS interview, Armitage said, "Oh, I feel terrible. Every day, I think I let down the president. I let down the Secretary of State. I let down my department, my family and I also let down Mr. and Mrs. Wilson." Although Armitage may have thought his apology would get him off the hook, too much damage had been done. With our consent, our lawyers at CREW added Richard Armitage to our case as another defendant. He was our first "John Doe."

• • •

There was another revelation in *Hubris*, but it did not receive nearly as much media attention as the sensational leak from Armitage. The original version of the memo on the Niger trip prepared at undersecretary of state Marc Grossman's request by State's Bureau of Intelligence and Research (INR) for Scooter Libby stated that the meeting at CIA Headquarters was "convened" by me with the idea of sending Joe to Niger. Although that version fit nicely into the administration's claim of nepotism, the problem was that it wasn't true. The Africa analyst for INR, Doug Rohn, had come late to the meeting at CIA Headquarters in February 2002 and he wasn't sure about my role (I had already left the meeting after Joe's brief introduction). By the time the INR memo was written in June 2003, Rohn had left INR to become the Consul General in Karachi, Pakistan. So another analyst, Neil Silver, was tapped to write the memo for Grossman using Rohn's old notes. According to *Hubris*, "In the memo for Grossman—which had been triggered by Libby's request—Silver stated as a fact that the meeting at the CIA had been 'convened' by Valerie Wilson, whom he described as a 'CIA WMD manager.' " What the memo had dropped—and there is no reason for Silver to have foreseen the later importance of this—was Rohn's original phrase "apparently convened." "Inadvertently," Corn and Isikoff state in *Hubris*, "Rohn's uninformed impression was now portrayed as a hard-and-fast truth. It would soon become, in the hands of White House spinners, a political charge."

Other than the erroneous assertion that I had convened the meeting at CIA Headquarters, the INR memo was very clear in what had happened to generate Joe's trip to Niger. The memo says, "From what we can find in our records, Joe Wilson played only a walk-on part in the Niger-Iraq uranium story. . . . [H]e previewed his plans and rationale for going to Niger, but said he would only go if the Department thought that his trip made sense." The INR memo also noted, "Two CIA WMD analysts seemed to be leading the charge on the issue. . . . INR made it a point, gently, to tell them that the Embassy has very good contacts and the Ambassador is a [President Mamadou] Tanja confidant."

As all of this was churning in the press in the early part of September, I finished up the first draft of this book. I had worked on the book every day over the summer. I would start when Joe took the children to camp in the morning, and finish before I picked them up in the early afternoon. Much to my surprise, I found that I liked writing, and that it helped me understand events that had gone by too fast to make much sense of them at the time.

When I joined the Agency, I had signed, as all employees do, a secrecy agreement, which said among other things that I would submit any future writings for public consumption to the CIA's Publications Review Board (PRB) to ensure that I would not reveal classified information that could potentially harm national security. This seemed sensible to me. By the time I handed in my manuscript, I had already been in contact with the PRB. That spring, I received two rather stern letters from the PRB, reminding me of my obligations in regard to the secrecy agreement and Agency regulations. These letters were sparked by media accounts in May 2006 that I had signed a publishing contract for a book. I assured them that I had every intention of cooperating fully with the PRB and would remain in full compliance with Agency regulations regarding classified material. I was seeking to tell my personal story of joining the CIA as ███████████ ████████████████████████████████, serving my country, and then dealing with the sudden harsh media attention following the leak of my name to the press. During the summer, over a series of telephone calls and e-mails, I reached an agreement with the PRB to submit to them three to four chapters at a time for review while I continued to work on later chapters. My publisher, Simon & Schuster, was pleased with this agreement because it meant that the book could be reviewed in a timely manner and therefore go to press as quickly as possible. However, in midsummer, the PRB reversed its decision and said I needed to hand in the entire manuscript at once. An e-mail from them informed me,

> As you might expect, certain references in later submissions might impact directly or indirectly on earlier passages and could affect our review. Additionally, as you are continuing to write your first draft, you may find it necessary to include changes to the text of previously-submitted sections. In order that we will not have to re-review portions of the text that have been modified, we will wait for your final submission before formally starting the review process.

I was nonplussed at this sudden change after they had agreed to a rolling submission, but wanted to remain in complete compliance with the Agency and their requests. I would simply write more and write faster to get them an entire manuscript by the end of summer. Thus began one of the most difficult passages I've been through in this life. Looking back, it felt like betrayal all over again by a government I had loyally served for ██████ ██████.

CHAPTER 15

Alice in Wonderland

I was not naïve: I knew that for a former Agency officer to shepherd a book through the system and get it approved for publication is a harrowing, frustrating, and at times capricious process. With the added notoriety and political elements of my case, I was prepared to have my patience challenged and for the review to take much longer than usual. The PRB plays a vital role in ensuring that classified information is not released to the public and it is understandable that the back and forth between what the CIA seeks to protect and what the author seeks to publish will be fractious at times. But because I believed deeply in protecting our national security interests and that the Agency would act in good faith, I was determined to be as cooperative as possible.

In the beginning of the book review journey, I had reason to be cautiously optimistic. In the last decade alone, the Agency has approved at least twenty books for publication by former staffers. Some were done by former Operations Officers and gave very revealing insights into the esoteric training done at the Farm, such as Lindsay Moran's *Blowing My Cover* in 2004. Frankly, I was surprised at how much latitude they had granted to Moran for her book. Other books written by former intelligence analysts, such as Michael Scheuer's *Imperial Hubris: Why the West Is Losing the War on Terror*, which was also published in 2004, presented a very critical view of the administration's policy toward the war on terror. However, I was not very far into the process for my own book when I realized that my optimism was misplaced.

When I handed in my manuscript to the PRB in early September 2006, I was told that the "give-and-take" process with the PRB about what could and could not be left in the book would begin by mid-October. This seemed normal and I knew that the PRB would probably object to certain words, phrases, or passages I had used if they deemed them "classified." That was their job and I expected to work amicably with them to find mutually agreeable solutions in each instance so that my publisher and I could schedule the book's publication in a timely manner. I was therefore mildly concerned when I received a phone call in mid-October from a PRB staff member. She was not calling to set a meeting as I expected, but to request that it be moved back to early November. The PRB was "not yet ready" for the review and, furthermore, they still needed to work out "some issues" with the "seventh floor"—CIA slang for senior management. She declined to identify further what the issues were—after all, it is the CIA, so no need to say more than is absolutely necessary—and I hung up.

Fortunately, I had something interesting to keep my mind off what was or was not happening with my book while I waited to hear back from the Agency. Joe had been asked by Norman Lear to serve as the keynote speaker at the twenty-fifth anniversary gala for People for the American Way. Started by Lear in 1981 in reaction to the religious Right's encroachment on our civil rights for their own narrow political agenda, the foundation has since grown to over one million members and volunteers "to fight for our values and beliefs: equal rights, freedom of speech, religious liberty, and equal justice under the law for every American." It is an important organization in our civic society that, according to their Web site, serves as "an energetic advocate for the values and institutions that sustain a diverse and democratic society." At the dinner in a hotel ballroom in Los Angeles, Joe gave what I think was one of his best speeches ever. In a break from his usual method of preparation, Joe worked on it until a few minutes before he was to appear on the stage. The effort paid off: he received a long and sustained standing ovation. He said in part:

> I stand before you this evening as a proud American. Proud to have served my country for twenty-three years as a diplomat. My service included such glamorous postings as Niamey, Niger, and Baghdad, Iraq, during the Desert Shield portion of the first Gulf War. Hardly boondoggle posts, whatever Dick Cheney might think.
>
> I served not because I believe Americans are inherently better people than anybody else on this globe. We are not. We are all human beings with our respective virtues as well as vices. No, I served because I believed then, as I believe now, that the value system that has underpinned the contract between the governed and those who govern us for some 217 years provides the best guarantee of the commitment of our forefathers to the right of people to life, liberty, and the pursuit of happiness. . . .
>
> Our personal fight, or at least the one to which our name is attached, is not, in fact a fight on behalf of Joe and Valerie Wilson. This is not about us and never has been. Indeed, whatever hardship we may have suffered in the past three years at the hands of our government is mere inconvenience compared to what this nation of ours, and in particular

those brave men and women who wear the uniforms of the armed services, and their families have suffered.

The article I wrote for the *New York Times* challenged sixteen words in the president's State of the Union address. The next day the White House spokesman acknowledged that those sixteen words did not quote "rise to the inclusion in the State of the Union" unquote. Why then, do we not know who put the lie in the president's mouth? Why do we know instead the name of a covert CIA officer who happens to be my wife?

George Orwell once wrote, "in times of universal deceit, telling the truth is a revolutionary act." This is a fight against universal deceit. . . .

This is still a nation where a citizen can get up every morning and shout at the top of his lungs that the President, Vice President, Secretary of Defense, and Secretary of State are lying sons of bitches, and survive to see the sun go down. I know. I do it most days. Don't take my word for it. Ask Valerie.

But we will only remain free if we remain vigilant. Benjamin Franklin said 250 years ago, "They that can give up essential liberty to obtain a little temporary safety deserve neither."

We cannot, we will not, we must not compromise the Constitution of our great country. It is not, Mr. President, as you call it, "just a goddamn piece of paper." . . .

Back in Washington, I finally received word that the PRB was ready to sit down with me. So, on a rainy day in early November, I drove to a nondescript building in the Washington suburbs for my first personal meeting with the board. I was excited and nervous, but determined to reach a good outcome for all. This is when I first learned what "issues" the PRB had taken up with the seventh floor. According to the PRB chairman, the Agency had taken the position that ██████████████████████████ ████████. In other words, ██████████████████████ ██ ████████████████████████ My mind flashed back to the week just before Special Prosecutor Fitzgerald indicted Scooter Libby, in October 2005. At that time, Fitzgerald had requested and received permission to say the following in his indictment: "At all relevant times from January 1, 2002, through July 2003, Valerie Wilson was employed by the CIA, and her employment status was classified. Prior to July 14, 2003, Valerie Wilson's affiliation with the CIA was not common knowledge outside the intelligence community." I assumed that ████████████████ was chosen because it included the run-up period when the vice president's office inquired about the report claiming Iraq was seeking uranium from Niger. At the time, it seemed to be an appropriate statement ████████████████████████████ ████████ because it was not germane to the case against Libby. Now, the PRB was telling me ████████████████████████ ██████████████ and would not move off this position, for unknown and unexplained reasons. Writing a memoir ████ ██ ██████████████ would clearly be problematic with this rule in place.

Naturally, as we sat around a fake wood conference table, I expressed my puzzlement and dismay at this turn of events to the PRB chairman and his staffers. They agreed completely, using terms like "ludicrous" and "absurd" to describe the decision made by unnamed senior managers. ██████████████████████ ██ ██ ██████████████. Type "Valerie Wilson" or "Valerie Plame" into

Google's search engine; the latter name will yield over two million Web pages. I wasn't seeking to reveal classified information that could harm our national security—I simply wanted to tell my personal story, which included ▮▮ years of public service to my country. The PRB folks shook their heads and looked troubled as well, but said their hands were tied by higher-ups and there was nothing more they could do. The chairman said he didn't understand the reasons for the decision, either. "What are they trying to protect?" he asked rhetorically.

Perhaps looking to compensate for the bombshell they just dropped, they set down in front of me the ▮▮▮▮▮ half of my manuscript, covering my story ▮▮▮▮▮▮▮▮▮▮▮, and said I could give it to my editor. I leafed quickly through the pages, seeing the expected black slashes over areas that had been redacted. The PRB staffers hastened to point out that the manuscript—the half I had, anyway—really wasn't heavily redacted at all. The redactions, as I expected, were primarily the use of certain words and phrases that they would consider classified. ▮▮▮▮▮▮ Sentences that might begin with "In my ▮▮▮▮▮▮ career, I had never seen such a thing," for example, were dutifully blacked out. I could not, however, take the ▮▮▮▮▮ half of the manuscript with me then—they wanted it to be accompanied by a formal letter from the PRB. And they would have to hold on to ▮▮▮▮▮ part of my manuscript, ▮▮▮▮▮▮▮▮▮▮▮▮▮▮▮ ▮▮▮▮▮▮▮▮▮▮▮▮▮▮▮▮▮▮▮▮▮▮▮▮▮▮ ▮▮▮▮▮▮▮▮▮▮▮▮▮▮▮. I tried to keep my composure when I asked what was next. How could we find a compromise to break this deadlock? The PRB staffers said that the decision ▮▮▮▮▮▮▮▮▮ was still being hotly debated on the seventh floor and candidly admitted that there were deep divisions in management about how to proceed. They finished our session by saying, somewhat sheepishly, that a "final decision" would be made "soon." I left deeply anxious over the fate of my book.

On Election Day, November 7, 2006, I was nervous. Our hearts had been broken in the aftermath of the 2004 presidential election and thus I put no stock in the pundits' predictions that the administration's mishandling of the war in Iraq, combined with a sense of widespread Republican corruption that was exacerbated by late-breaking news about Republican congressman Mark Foley's inappropriate behavior with male House pages, would turn Congress over to the Democrats for the first time in years. I figured that if all the exit polls got it so spectacularly wrong about Kerry, then they could be off by just as wide a margin for this election. At a dinner party that evening, we all anxiously watched the election turns on TV. Early indications looked good for a Democratic triumph in the House, but I still held my breath. It wasn't until we stopped by a party at another friend's house at about eleven that night that victory was assured, and we toasted the occasion with champagne. The Senate, which earlier had not seemed to be in play, had close races in several states. A few days later, when all the votes were counted, Democrats had won a decisive victory in the House, and a close but clean win in the Senate. Joe and I were buoyed by the message that Americans had sent to Washington: the status quo would not be tolerated anymore and voters wanted their elected officials to move in a new direction. Unfortunately, as was so often the case in our journey since 2003, delight was followed quickly by bad news. The day after the election, the Agency called my lawyers and informed them that the ████████████████████ ████████████████ would stand. Supposedly I had no right ████████████████████████████ ████████████████ . The prospects of getting my book

published ██
dimmed considerably.

My lawyers feverishly researched and analyzed the legal basis of what the Agency was claiming. It defied common sense, logic, and possibly, my constitutional rights. I did not want to set a precedent or reveal anything that was truly classified in nature. I did want to say, however, that I had served my country ████████ ████████ The tale began to take on a distinct *Alice in Wonderland* quality, but without any guarantee that it would end up well. My lawyers and I compiled an extensive list of articles and interviews done by the mainstream media since I was outed in 2003 that discussed ██████████████████ the Agency ████████████ , my assignments ████████████████ , education, and other personal information. All of that was considered to be in the "public domain." Of particular note was Joe's book, *The Politics of Truth*, published in early 2004 and itself sent through the Agency's PRB process and approved for publication. Joe writes about when we met in 1997 ██ ██ What *is* explicit, however, is the passage describing my reaction to reading my name in Novak's column for the first time in July 2003: "When I showed it to Valerie, she was stoic in her manner but I could see she was crestfallen. ██████████████████████████ ██ There it was. ██ ████████████████ Still, they would not budge. The CIA, through its uncompromising and rigid application of this "bright line" rule, was essentially seeking to classify information ████████ that was already in the public domain and dictate that I could not talk or write about any of those episodes. I kept thinking back to what the PRB chairman had said to me: "What are they trying to protect?" Anyone not living in a cave for the last few years knew I had a career at the CIA—so, what was going on?

Three weeks after the Agency told my lawyers that its decision ▓▓▓▓▓▓▓▓▓▓▓▓▓▓ would stand, I received a formal letter from the PRB. It began, "The Central Intelligence Agency has reviewed for classification certain information that is contained in your manuscript, and has determined that this information remains currently and properly classified. Thus, your manuscript is disapproved for publication as it is currently written." There was no reason given for the decision. It then went on to list on a line-by-line basis all the deletions in the second part of the text. One week later, my two publishing lawyers, David B. Smallman, a First Amendment specialist who had once been a litigator with the prominent law firm Simpson Thacher & Bartlett and was longstanding outside counsel to Investigative Reporters and Editors, Inc., and Lisa E. Davis, a Harvard-trained entertainment attorney with Frankfurt Kurnit Klein & Selz, traveled to Washington from New York to meet with the Agency lawyers and the head of the PRB to discuss the letter and possible next steps. The meeting, which was cordial, began with David stating that while I would continue to work closely with the PRB to guard national security and ensure that all properly classified information remained fully protected, no logical reason or legal basis existed that would justify broad censorship of unclassified information. The Agency's acting General Counsel (GC) made it clear that the CIA "did not want a confrontation" over the book. In fact, the General Counsel had taken the unusual step of reading my manuscript and declared it "not problematic." In the postmortem meeting with my lawyers at my home later that day, we were all relieved that there might be some way to work around the seemingly insurmountably obstacle of the Agency's determination ▓▓▓▓▓▓▓▓▓▓▓▓ . We had no desire to pursue litigation. Perhaps a compromise could be hammered out that would uphold the Agency's regulations and still allow me to publish the book.

I was called back to meet with the PRB on December 1. I walked into the meeting willing to find a workable compromise for the book. The head of the PRB opened with some pleasantries and then got to the point, giving me two possible options to getting the book published under the existing Agency decision. ███

███

███

███

██████████████████████████████████████ I could write that I ███████ worked for the CIA—and ████████████ was somehow given significant responsibilities for worldwide operations to look for WMD in Iraq. ████████████████████████ Dumbfounded, I looked at the Chairman. When I finally found my voice, it was tight and strained. "You mean to tell me that after all my husband and I have lived through over the last three years you want me to write ███████████████████████ ███████████ People will think I'm insane." I said this last sentence with particular emphasis and alarm, but without raising my voice. I found out later that the Chairman was "offended" that I didn't take to this solution as he had hoped I would. █████████████

███

███

███

█████████████████████ . My reaction to this option was much the same as the first, but I didn't say anything. I just nodded and said I would give it some thought. And I meant it—I was skeptical of making such an approach work, but I was willing to consider (almost) any compromise. As I left, feeling somewhat shellshocked, the PRB handed me the redacted version of ████████ half of my manuscript so that I could send it to my editor at the publishing house. As I drove home in busy Washington traffic, I tried to stifle the rising panic I felt. My family's financial security made it crucial that I fulfill my publishing contract. I felt I had no choice but to keep fighting to get the decision reversed.

As Joe and I discussed my bizarre situation, we speculated that the new CIA Director, General Michael Hayden, had not been fully briefed on the issue. Hayden had a good reputation for being smart and a "straight shooter" throughout his distinguished career, and so keeping the Agency rooted to an absurd and possibly unconstitutional position did not sound like the pragmatic man people described. As a consequence, we decided to seek out the assistance and advice of a highly respected, high-ranking Democratic senator. At a minimum we thought that the senator could relay a back-channel message to Hayden about the unfolding situation without embarrassing anyone. At the meeting in the senator's office, attended by two senior staffers, the senator asked tough questions that I answered to the best of my ability. When the meeting was over and we were walking back to our car, I told Joe that I didn't think the senator was inclined to help us. Joe assured me that I was wrong and pointed out that it was the senator's job to ask the tough questions (like "Isn't this just a commercial issue?") before committing anything. Sure enough, Joe was right. The next day I was told by the senator's staffers that the senator had spoken to General Hayden right after our meeting and wanted to find a compromise that would protect whatever the Agency deemed classified, while still allowing me to publish my book. The general told the senator that he would call me himself to explain further the Agency's position. I was surprised and grateful for the senator's intervention on my behalf and settled in to wait for the general's call. It was a highly unusual move, but few things surprised me anymore.

I waited. And waited. Finally, on the fifth day after I was given the message that General Hayden would call me directly, and getting a little antsy hanging around the house so I wouldn't miss this important call, the phone rang. It was not the general. It was a PRB staffer, requesting that I come into the PRB offices again the next day. "Of course, what time?" I replied. This time the meeting was not in the conference room but in the chairman's office. I sat across from his desk while the chairman read carefully from his notes. "As, uh, a result of the, uh, senator's call to the general the seventh floor wanted to be sure they were uh, very, very clear on their decision." The chairman then proceeded to repeat what had already been determined at the previous two meetings: that senior Agency management, for still unknown reasons, ███████████████████████████████████████ ███████████████████████████████████████ ██████████████████████████████████████. It was the bureaucratic equivalent of *Groundhog Day*—the movie in which Bill Murray lives the same day, over and over. He can only escape by becoming a better person. In my version of *Groundhog Day*, I was being told the same thing by the Agency, but with apparently no hope of escape. I felt like I was being treated like a slow learner who doesn't understand the words the first time. No, I got it, loud and clear—I just wasn't willing to give up. The only bit of hope I grasped was the PRB's promise to release █████████ half of the manuscript, in redacted form, so I could have something to work on with my editor in trying to reshape the story. I was skeptical that any sense of story could be salvaged, but I was willing to try and was glad that they were at least willing to provide me ███████████ half of my book.

Unfortunately, my faith and trust in the Agency's word took a fresh beating when I received a letter from the PRB reneging, again, on their promise to provide me with █████████ half of my manuscript. Actually, the letter was sent to my parents' home in Florida, where the PRB knew I was spending the Christmas holiday. We indeed had been there, but the day the letter arrived, Joe and I and the kids had flown to Utah to stay with friends and get in some skiing over New Year's. When I called my mother, she told me a letter had arrived from the CIA, and I instructed her to read it to me over the phone. The letter was written in full-on bureaucratese: "As we explained in our letter of 21 November 2006 and as we discussed during our recent meeting, pages 1 through 124 of your manuscript, as currently drafted, would reveal classified information primarily because of the context in which the information appears and the timeframes associated with the material." The agency was clearly hoping that I would just get tired of trying to move the mountain and go away. I was feeling betrayed by the very institution that I served loyally ▆▆▆ ▆▆ .

Thoughts of something more nefarious than bureaucratic obstinacy had begun to occupy me. In mid-December 2006, a respected writer had experienced the White House's unprecedented political meddling in the CIA's review process. Flynt Leverett, a career government official, had worked at the CIA, the State Department, and the National Security Council during the George W. Bush administration. He was now working at a Washington area think tank. He was the author of books, articles, working papers, and public policy op-eds that had all been dutifully submitted to the PRB for clearance, which had always been granted. Suddenly, in mid-December the White House forced the CIA to heavily censor a thousand-word op-ed planned for the *New York Times* on U.S. policy toward Iran. This was extraordinary. The Agency's PRB process is designed to identify and redact classified information so that it does not appear in public, and should work without political oversight or influence. A furious Leverett released a statement blasting the White House that was picked up by several blogs:

Until last week, the Publication Review Board had never sought to remove or change a single word in any of my drafts, including in all of my publications about the Bush administration's handling of Iran policy. However, last week, the White House inserted itself into the prepublication review process for an op-ed on the administration's bungling of the Iran portfolio that I had prepared for the *New York Times*, blocking publication of the piece on the grounds that it would reveal classified information.

This claim is false and, I have come to believe, fabricated by White House officials to silence an established critic of the administration's foreign policy incompetence at a moment when the White House is working hard to fend off political pressure to take a different approach to Iran and the Middle East more generally. . . . Officials with the CIA's Publication Review Board have told me that, in their judgment, the draft op-ed does not contain classified material, but that they must bow to the preferences of the White House.

The White House is demanding, before it will consider clearing the op-ed for publication, that I excise entire paragraphs dealing with matters that I have written about (and received clearance from the CIA to do so) in several other pieces, that have been publicly acknowledged by Secretary Rice, former Secretary of State Colin Powell, and former Deputy Secretary of State Richard Armitage, and that have been extensively covered in the media. For the White House to make this claim, with regard to my op-ed and at this particular moment, is nothing more than a crass effort to politicize a prepublication review process—a process that is supposed to be about the protection of classified information, and nothing else—to limit the dissemination of views critical of administration policy.

Their conduct [the PRB] in this matter is despicable and un-American in the profoundest sense of that term. I am also deeply disappointed that former colleagues at the Central Intelligence Agency have proven so supine in the face of tawdry political pressure. Intelligence officers are supposed to act better than that.

On December 22, the *New York Times* printed the redacted op-ed piece by Leverett and his wife, Hillary Mann Leverett, herself a former foreign service officer who had worked on Iranian issues, titled "What We Wanted to Tell You About Iran." The paper, however, also included the public citations for the redacted portions so the public could see for itself that the original op-ed had not contained any classified information. Was the White House also responsible for the stalling of *my* book?

About a month or so before I resigned from the Agency in January 2006, I talked to the human resources folks to try to figure out what, if any, annuity benefits might be due to me. ▮▮▮▮▮▮▮
▮▮▮
▮▮
▮▮▮▮. I found it hard to believe that I was the only one in Agency history to leave with ▮▮▮▮▮▮▮▮▮▮▮▮▮ of service, but for whatever reason, the staff doing the calculations had trouble finding the appropriate regulations ▮▮▮▮▮▮▮▮▮▮▮▮▮▮▮▮▮▮▮▮▮▮▮▮.
When my last day at the CIA arrived, the Agency promised to continue researching the question ▮▮▮▮▮▮▮▮▮▮▮▮▮▮▮▮
▮▮▮▮▮▮▮▮▮▮. Nearly six weeks later, I received an ▮▮▮▮▮▮
letter dated February 10, 2006, in the mail, via regular post, on CIA letterhead from the Chief of Retirement and Insurance Services. ▮▮▮▮▮▮▮▮▮▮▮▮▮▮▮▮▮▮▮▮▮▮▮▮▮▮▮▮▮▮▮▮▮▮▮▮
▮▮

████████████████████████████████████. I tucked the letter away and did not think any more about it, but it would later come to have great significance.

In early 2007, with the new Democratic-led Congress in place, Congressman Jay Inslee of Washington state dusted off a bill that his office had drafted over a year earlier. The bill, written simply, sought to provide me with an annuity ████████████ ██ ████████████████. Attached as supporting documentation was the ██████████ letter I had received from the Agency in early 2006 ██ ████████████████████████████On January 16, 2007, the letter was entered into the *Congressional Record*. Inslee demonstrated tremendous political courage by doing this, knowing how politically explosive my case was, and Joe and I will always be grateful to him. It took a few days before it dawned on the Agency what had happened. Three days later, the Agency fired off a letter to me, ostensibly sent by the Chief of Retirement and Insurance Services, demanding that I return the original letter. It said, "The letter [of February 10, 2006] was not properly marked to indicate its national security classification. The absence of a national security classification marking was an administrative error and information contained therein remains classified." The real problem for the Agency was that once something is officially acknowledged, ██ ████, the law says it cannot then be reclassified. The genie was out of the bottle. Without any explanation or fanfare the Agency finally returned an unclassified version of the manuscript in late February.

In exchanges between the Agency lawyers and mine over the next few weeks, it was very clear that the Agency wanted that annuity letter back, badly. The letters to me and my lawyers began to read like this:

Alice in Wonderland | 279

To be clear, Ms. Wilson has a legal obligation to return the 10 February 2006 letter and any copies that she may have in her possession. The 10 February 2006 letter contains currently and properly classified information. We disagree with your characterization of our 10 February 2006 letter as an official acknowledgement of classified information that would require a reclassification action to protect. Please be advised that reclassification is only required when classified information is formally declassified by an official with declassification authority.

More ominous, the Agency also began to accuse me of not being willing to meet with the PRB and discuss "different revision approaches" to the book. This was patently false—I was always willing to meet with the PRB at any time—and it was also clear that the only "approach" they wanted to pursue was one where ████████████████████████████████ so thoroughly it would make the book unfit to print or read. In fact, during one conversation between General Hayden and the senator who was working on our behalf, he relayed the lie to the senator—seeking to characterize me as an uncooperative and disgruntled former employee. When word of that exchange got back to me, my frustration and puzzlement at why this was happening flashed to deep anger. I was a loyal CIA employee. I was not seeking carte blanche to reveal state secrets. But now I was being painted as "unwilling" to work with the PRB. After thirteen months of being as patient, cooperative, and respectful as I could be with the process, I had gotten nowhere.

I began to feel like what the Soviets termed a "nonperson." You simply ceased to exist in the eyes of the state. The Agency— because of apparent political meddling from the White House— ██ ████████████ for reasons that had nothing to do with protecting national security. It was becoming obvious that any remedy to correct the absurd situation would have to be found in the legal system. While I dreaded the idea of yet more litigation, I felt I had little choice. I needed to publish the book to assist my family financially and, just as important, I wanted to be able to say that had I served my country, proudly, for ▮▮▮▮▮▮▮▮▮▮. As Joe and I discussed the implications of suing the Agency over the publication of my book, the Libby trial finally began.

CHAPTER 16

The Libby Trial and Farewell to Washington

I. Lewis "Scooter" Libby's trial began on January 23, 2007, forty-three long months after I was "outed" as a CIA operations officer and fifteen months after the vice president's Chief of staff was indicted on one charge of obstruction of justice, two counts of perjury, and two counts of making false statements to a grand jury in the investigation of the leak of my name. After several initial delays to accommodate Libby's lawyers' packed trial schedule, it was a relief when it finally got under way. The jury selection process had been fraught with pitfalls, and took two days longer than expected, highlighting how difficult it was to find a pool of "politically neutral" jurors in Washington. It seemed nearly every potential juror had a link to the defendants or the long witness list of reporters and administration officials. As the *Washington Post* reported, "There is the software database manager whose wife works as a prosecutor for the Justice Department, and who counts the local U.S. attorney and a top official in Justice's criminal division as neighbors and friends. A housecleaner who works at the Watergate and knows Condoleezza Rice, not by her title of secretary of state, but as the lady who lives up on the fifth floor. And a former *Washington Post* reporter whose editor was now–Assistant Managing Editor Bob Woodward. He went to barbecues at the house of NBC's Tim Russert, a neighbor, and just published a book on the CIA and spying."

It was evident that Washington, despite pretensions to the contrary, is actually a very small town. Another problem was finding jurors in heavily Democratic Washington who were not avidly opposed to or biased against the administration and its policy on the Iraq War. If the task hadn't been so serious, it would have made a good sitcom plot. One woman told the judge, "I think there's been a lot of dishonesty, particularly with the Iraq War." Another man said, "I don't really believe the administration." It went on like this, one potential jury pool member after another. After four days, marked with many scuffles between the prosecution and defense, U.S. District Judge Reggie B. Walton managed to certify fifteen citizens as jurors: twelve permanent and three alternates. Opening arguments began the next day.

The trial started with fireworks from both sides. In his opening statement, Special Prosecutor Patrick Fitzgerald laid out a very narrow but compelling argument that Libby had lied, often, in response to investigators' questions about with whom he had discussed me and my CIA employment. Fitzgerald seemed to place Vice President Dick Cheney at the center of the case by saying that Cheney himself had disclosed my identity to Libby and later intervened to have White House press secretary Scott McClellan issue a misleading public statement clearing Libby of any involvement in the leak of my name to reporters.

Defense lawyer Theodore Wells surprised everyone with his opening statement by declaring that his client had been made the sacrificial "scapegoat" in this affair by Karl Rove and other current and former White House officials. The tactic ran against the conventional wisdom that Libby would play the good soldier, say nothing of value, and receive a presidential pardon if convicted. Hoping to rebut Fitzgerald's assertion that Libby had lied to save his job, Wells said, "Mr. Libby was not concerned about losing his job in the Bush administration. He was concerned about being set up, he was concerned about being made the scapegoat." According to Wells, Rove—described as the president's "right-hand man"—was behind the plot because his survival was essential for the president's reelection. Libby was so worried that he was being thrown under the bus that, according to Wells, in October 2003 he went to Cheney and bitterly complained, "I think people in the White House are trying to set me up. People in the White House are trying to protect Karl Rove."

Before the trial began, Joe and I had decided not to attend for two reasons. First, it wasn't about us—it was about the abuse of power. Second, we had no desire to add to the media stampede. The general public had to wait in long lines to get passes to the limited seating in the small courtroom in downtown D.C. The media was assigned to an overflow room. Fortunately for those who couldn't get a seat but wanted to follow the proceedings closely, the Libby trial was the first federal case in which independent bloggers received the same official credentials as reporters from traditional news media. The Web site Firedoglake (FDL), for example, rotated a team of six contributors "blogging" live from the courtroom. The site took pains to note that it was not an official transcript, but it was as close to real time as one could get. The court did not allow any audio or video feed. Thus FDL "offered the fullest, fastest public report available. Many mainstream journalists use[d] it to check on the trial," reported the *New York Times*. Here was a site that not only captured nearly every utterance in almost real time, but provided witty and insightful commentary. Joe and I quickly realized that the Firedoglake bloggers were much more knowledgeable about the intricacies and minute details of the case than we were.

Every morning, Joe vowed that he would not become obsessed with the trial. Then he would find himself logging off at 5 P.M. after having read the entire day's trial proceedings. When I wasn't talking with my lawyers regarding the stalemate with the Agency over my book's publication, or working on fund-raising for our civil suit, I also checked FDL many times throughout the day. Despite FDL's unabashed enthusiasm for Fitzgerald and the close analysis of every perceived misstep by the defense, I never thought a conviction was a sure bet. Who knew what the jurors were absorbing from the many witnesses' testimony, and how it would affect their ultimate decision on Libby's fate?

Various reporters who took the stand exposed an ugly detail; the symbiotic relationship between the Washington press corps and the administration. Each feeds off the other to advance its particular agenda. The media relies heavily on access to unnamed "senior administration officials" to break, build, and corroborate stories, and the administration manipulates the media to promote its point of view. If reporters want to enjoy continued access to top White House decision makers, they have to toe the line. One prominent national journalist told Joe and me months earlier about an incident in which this journalist interviewed President Bush and managed to slip in some unscripted "troublesome" questions. Within hours, the journalist's boss received a phone call from the White House and was told in no uncertain terms that if the journalist ever wanted to be invited back to the White House to interview the president again, such impertinent questions would not be tolerated.

One of the most egregious examples of this was documented

on Bill Moyers's devastating PBS special, *Buying the War*. The White House leaked information to the *New York Times* that Saddam Hussein had been trying to acquire aluminum tubes to restart Iraq's nuclear centrifuge program, which the paper then reported using "anonymous administration officials." Vice President Cheney appeared on NBC's *Meet the Press* the same morning the story appeared on the front page of the *Times* and referred to the article as yet further proof of Iraq's WMD capabilities.

Like Moyers, I thought the testimony in the trial by some of the so-called premier journalists in the country showed how eagerly they accept spoonfed information from official sources. They appeared to make little effort to corroborate information or seek out other sources at the working levels who might have given them a different story. The trial did not show American journalism at its finest hour.

The Libby trial shocked me in showing just how recklessly senior government officials who should have known better, who should have been much more diligent in protecting me and every CIA officer, tossed around my name with those who had no need to know. All of these officials were fully aware that I worked at the CIA, and while they might have been unclear as to where exactly I worked there, the fact that it was the CIA should have raised a big red flag. All of the officials involved in the leak of my name signed oaths when they joined the government to protect national security secrets. They knew that the CIA goes to great lengths, and at significant taxpayer's expense, to devise creative "covers" for its employees.

On January 29, former White House spokesman Ari Fleischer testified that he learned my name and CIA employment from Libby during a lunch in early July 2003, the day after Joe's article appeared. A week later, while on a trip to Africa with the president, Fleischer repeated the information to NBC's David

Gregory and *Time* magazine's John Dickerson. "If you want to know who sent Ambassador Wilson to Niger, it was his wife, she works there" at the CIA, he said to them. Fleischer added at trial, "[Never] in my wildest dreams would I have thought that information was classified." I guess to him it was just some tasty gossip to be dished. I thought it was irresponsible and despicable. He says he was "absolutely horrified" when he learned that what he had done might be criminal. If he was so surprised that his actions might have adverse national security implications, then he's not smart enough to work in the White House. That goes for all the officials who thought that using my name as catnip was just playing the Washington game as usual.

Joe and I were relieved that many of the documents introduced into evidence at the trial refuted the attempted spin by the White House and its right-wing echo chamber about the genesis of the trip. The most telling of those may have been the June 2003 State Department INR memo written for Undersecretary Marc Grossman at Libby's request. As Larry Johnson wrote in the online *Huffington Post*,

> We know, thanks to the INR memo, that Joe did not want to go to Niger and supported the position of INR analysts who thought the US Ambassador in Niger was quite capable of investigating the matter. Ultimately the CIA prevailed and Joe was sent. Valerie was not in the room when the decision was made nor was she in an administrative position with the clout to send her husband on such a mission.
>
> The INR memo introduced in the Libby trial confirms Joe's account as well about what he told the CIA debriefing team.... [T]he CIA report produced from Mr. Wilson's trip ... made it very clear ... that Iraq had not purchased or negotiated the purchase of uranium.

The Libby Trial and Farewell to Washington | 287

Yet another clipping showed Vice President Cheney's hand-written note over the top of Joe's article "What I Did Not Find in Africa." Cheney wanted to know, "Have they done this sort of thing before? Send an Amb. to answer a question? Do we ordinarily send people out pro bono to work for us? Or did his wife send him on a junket?" Given Cheney's vaunted decades of government service, it was frankly unbelievable that he would ask such questions. He would have known that the CIA frequently sends U.S. citizens abroad, on a pro bono basis, to answer specific intelligence queries. It is even quite possible that the CIA debriefed employees of Halliburton, the multinational company that Cheney headed prior to becoming vice president, when *they* returned from business trips in restricted countries of interest to the United States. Cheney's marginal notes should be more accurately interpreted as marching orders to staff on how to spin Joe's story so that Cheney could stay as far from it as possible while simultaneously undermining Joe's credibility. In the Libby trial, the veil was being lifted on the immense power of the White House to frame a story the way they wanted to have it told—truth and fairness be damned.

So it went with each day of the trial. Joe and I were alternately elated then dismayed by the news coming out of the courtroom. The prosecution rested in mid-February after more than two weeks of damning testimony by the government's long parade of witnesses, all of whom blew big holes in Libby's "faulty memory" defense. Everyone was wondering how the defense team would cast Libby as the scapegoat in the affair and attempt to place the blame on the White House.

Shortly after his indictment in October 2005, Libby engaged a top-notch team of three lead lawyers with excellent reputations: Theodore Wells, William Jeffress, and John Cline. Cline, an expert on classified documents, was presumably hired to help the defense figure out how to "graymail" the government, that is, force the government to choose between prosecuting an employee for serious crimes or preserving national security secrets. The defense demands that every classified document ever touched by the accused employee be made public. The lawyers' fees were to be paid from Libby's legal defense fund, which had been set up a week after his indictment and was chaired by Melvin Sembler, a wealthy Florida real estate developer and former GOP finance Chief. Sembler, ironically enough, was President George W. Bush's ambassador to Italy when the embassy in Rome first received the forged yellowcake documents, whose contents precipitated Joe's trip to Niger and Libby's legal odyssey.

The defense fund board featured big names, including senator and actor Fred Thompson, now running for the presidency; former education secretary William Bennett (perhaps more notorious these days for his million-dollar gambling losses in Las Vegas); and Princeton professor Bernard Lewis, an enormous intellectual influence behind the decision to invade Iraq because the war would "modernize the Middle East." A name I did not expect to see was that of the Honorable R. James Woolsey, director of the CIA from 1993 to 1995. What was he doing on Libby's "advisory committee"? His tenure at the CIA was marked by a virtually nonexistent relationship with President Bill Clinton. The joke at the time was that the guy who crashed his small plane into the White House in 1994 was actually Woolsey, trying to get an appointment with Clinton. Woolsey was a member of the neoconservative Project for the New American Century, and signed its 1998 letter to Clinton arguing that regime change in Iraq was the only way to stabilize the Middle East and ultimately protect Israel. He was one of the first to publicly accuse Iraq of complicity in the September 11, 2001, attacks and was a strong proponent of the Iraq War.

Regardless of his political views, I could not see how Woolsey could give his name to the defense fund of a man accused of leaking the name of an officer in the CIA—the very place Woolsey had run a decade earlier. Just before the trial, CBS News quoted him as saying, "I would be sympathetic to anyone who was indicted for nonviolation of a statute." Woolsey was referring to the 1982 Intelligence Identities Protection Act, which makes it a federal crime to reveal the identity of a covert intelligence agent. "He was not indicted for any underlying crime," Woolsey said. Perhaps Woolsey acted out of personal loyalty or friendship to Libby, or just wanted to firm up his credentials with the neocon crowd. In any case, before the trial began, the fund had raised over three million dollars from wealthy Republican donors.

On February 13, the defense called John Hannah, a former aide to Libby who now serves as Cheney's national security adviser. Hannah was on the stand for nearly two hours, and explained to the jury that Libby had many responsibilities and dealt with issues like the Iraq War, North Korea and Iran's nuclear capabilities, and the WMD threats posed by Islamic militants. He also tried to substantiate the defense's arguments about Libby's faulty memory: "On certain things, Scooter just had an awful memory." When the defense finished, they had clearly scored some points, but within five minutes, Fitzgerald had reversed their momentary advantage. The *New York Times* described the cross-examination:

> Noting that Mr. Hannah had testified that he could usually have a few minutes alone with Mr. Libby only in the evening after the crush of business, Mr. Fitzgerald suggested that Mr. Libby would have devoted time only to matters of great concern to him in the week of July 6, 2003.
>
> "If he gave something an hour or two that week, it would

be something Mr. Libby thought was important, right?" asked Mr. Fitzgerald.

"Well, with regard to me, yes," Mr. Hannah replied.

Left unsaid in the exchange was undisputed testimony [from Libby himself] *that Mr. Libby spent nearly two hours on Tuesday, July 8, with Ms. Miller, then a* Times *reporter. Ms. Miller has testified that Mr. Libby told her in detail about Ms. Wilson at the meeting.* (emphasis added)

It was a Perry Mason moment.

That same day, Libby's lawyer Wells announced that neither his client nor the vice president would take the stand. This decision effectively wrapped up the defense's case after barely two days of testimony. Libby's legal team had obviously concluded that exposing either their client or the vice president to what was sure to be a withering cross-examination from Fitzgerald and his team company was not worth the risk. It was an unexpected decision, and Fitzgerald complained vigorously that the defense had engaged in a "bait and switch" tactic. Many of us had looked forward to what Cheney would say about his role in the affair, and what Fitzgerald might pull out of him.

The weekend before closing arguments, Victoria Toensing, a lawyer who served in the Reagan Justice Department, authored an absurd op-ed in the *Washington Post* titled "Trial in Error." As one of the drafters of the Intelligence Identities Protection Act, she popped up all over TV land as a self-proclaimed expert on the leak case. (Tellingly, when the op-ed ran, the *Post* failed to disclose a longtime personal relationship between Toensing, her husband and law partner Joe diGenova, and Robert Novak.)

In her op-ed, which included fabricated mug shots of Fitzgerald and Joe, Toensing "charged" Fitzgerald for "ignoring the fact that there was no basis for a criminal investigation from the day he was appointed," "charged" the CIA for "making a boilerplate criminal referral to cover its derriere," and "charged" Joe with "misleading the public about how he was sent to Niger, about the thrust of his March 2003 oral report of that trip, and about his wife's CIA status, perhaps for the purpose of getting a book and movie." For good measure, she finished by claiming, "Plame was not covert. She worked at CIA Headquarters and had not been stationed abroad within five years of the date of Novak's column."

Toensing apparently hadn't been following the trial very closely, or else she would have known that each of her "charges" had been refuted in ample documentary and witness testimony. As for her declaration that I wasn't covert, she was dead wrong. And furthermore, how would she have been so sure of my status anyway? She was not a CIA employee. If anything, her rantings pointed out the shortcomings of the bill she helped author—that is, the difficulty of prosecuting someone who had violated the law and passed along the covert identity of an operations officer to someone who did not have a security clearance. The fact that I was at Headquarters ███████████ prior to being "outed" doesn't mean that I (or any other Headquarters-based Operations Officer) didn't travel overseas from Headquarters on operational business. We use such things as alias passports, disguises, and other tradecraft secrets to do this. It's called clandestine operations. Just as a general is still a general whether he or she is in the field or serving at the Pentagon, an Operations Officer by definition has responsibilities that don't vanish depending on location.

On February 20, Fitzgerald and fellow prosecutor Peter Zeidenberg made a detailed closing argument that Libby had willfully lied to the grand jury as well as the FBI during the investigation of the leak. Fitzgerald's statements also made clear that Libby wasn't the only one on trial: "there is a cloud over the vice president . . . a cloud over the White House over what happened. We didn't put that cloud there. That cloud's there because the defendant obstructed justice. That cloud is something you just can't pretend isn't there." He suggested that the vice president was, at a minimum, complicit with Libby in the leak of my name.

In sharp contrast to Fitzgerald's businesslike demeanor, Libby's lawyer Theodore Wells gave an over-the-top, emotional closing argument, stalking the courtroom and changing the pitch and cadence of his voice like a seasoned Baptist preacher. Blogger Jane Hamsher wrote that Wells "sounded like he was a used car salesman trying to fob off a junker he had no faith in." Wells concluded with a personal plea: "This is a man with a wife and two children. He is a good person. He's been under my protection for the last month. I give him to you. Give him back to me." And then, to everyone's astonishment, Wells teared up, sobbed, and sat down.

When Fitzgerald began his rebuttal, he leapt up, and, completely out of character, took the floor yelling "Madness, madness!" According to FDL, he was "lacerating and precise, speaking so quickly that the court reporter couldn't catch up. His command of the material was a bit daunting, able to recall voluminous evidentiary document numbers simply by looking at some chart in his own brain." And then, just like that, the trial was handed over to the jury to decide Libby's guilt or innocence.

Despite the hard evidence and the weak defense, I did not have absolute faith that the jury would render a guilty verdict. I kept thinking back to the O. J. Simpson murder trial in 1995; although overwhelming circumstantial and physical evidence pointed to Simpson murdering his former wife, Nicole Brown Simpson, the jury, split along racial lines, acquitted the former football star. I had no idea how Joe and I would handle the devastating outcome if Libby were acquitted on all counts. Especially important to us was that he be convicted on the obstruction of justice charge because it went to the very core of why no one was indicted on the "original crime" as described under the Intelligence Identities Protection Act. It's a truism that when one is waiting for something, each day seems as long as a year.

A few days into the verdict watch, on February 26, we got the news that there had nearly been a mistrial. Apparently, despite numerous instructions and admonitions from the judge, a juror had seen or read something about the trial over the previous weekend. The judge decided not to throw away three days of deliberations and allowed them to continue with just eleven jurors. It felt like a bullet had been dodged. The waiting went on. The only thing I knew for sure was that Joe and I had to be sleeping better than Libby and Cheney.

Finally, on Tuesday, March 6, after ten days of deliberations, the jury announced it had reached a verdict. It would be read at noon. It was a bitterly cold but sunny day. Joe had scheduled a lunch meeting, so I settled down in front of the TV. To say I was a bundle of nerves—it felt like I needed two hands to stir the milk in my coffee—would be an understatement. A cable network correspondent relayed the verdicts rapidly from outside the courthouse as I literally held my breath: first count of obstruction of justice, "guilty"; second count of perjury, "guilty"; third count of making false statements, "not guilty"; fourth count of perjury, "guilty"; fifth count of making false statements, "guilty." I started to cry with relief and immediately called Joe on his cell phone. I assumed he was at a restaurant watching the verdict on a TV, but when he answered and tersely asked, "Well, what is it?" I knew he didn't know yet. I told him, trying to keep my voice even. All he said was, "Thank God. The charge of obstruction of justice was the most important." He hung up. I knew he would be crazy for the rest of the day satisfying media requests for interviews. I was grateful to be alone for a few minutes so I could collect myself before the phone started to ring off the hook. I read later that Libby was stoic as the verdicts were read, while his wife openly cried. My feelings of deep sadness over the entire affair were tempered by relief that our justice system still worked as intended.

Libby and his team came out of the courthouse into the winter sunshine. The grim looks on their faces told everything. Wells told reporters that he was disappointed in the verdict but that they would file a motion for a new trial, and if that was denied, would file an appeal. One of the jurors, Denis Collins, a former *Washington Post* reporter, offered his perspective. He said that he and his fellow jurors found that passing judgment on Libby was "unpleasant" but that in the final analysis, Libby's story was just too hard to believe: "We're not saying we didn't think Mr. Libby was guilty of the things we found him guilty of, but it seemed like . . . he was the fall guy." So it seemed that Libby's defense tactic of casting him as a "scapegoat" had worked, but not in the way they had intended.

Fox News stayed true to form in the wake of four out of five guilty verdicts with a news crawler saying "Scooter Libby found not guilty of lying to FBI investigators." However, I could now manage a small smile at the absurdity of Fox "news." H. D. S. Greenway of the *Boston Globe* offered a more reality-based appraisal of the trial.

What the perjury trial of I. Lewis "Scooter" Libby really revealed was the astonishing lengths to which Vice President Dick Cheney and others in the Bush administration went to discredit Ambassador Joseph Wilson for his 2003 claim that the administration had been dead wrong about Saddam Hussein trying to buy material from Niger to make nuclear weapons. The intensity of this pursuit leapt out from the testimony.

The decision to "out" a covert CIA officer, Wilson's wife, which is a federal crime, showed a kind of desperation. The concept that she had sent her husband to Niger on some kind of boondoggle, instead of to investigate the Saddam sale, is bizarre in the extreme. With all due respect, Niger is neither Wilson's, nor anybody else's, ideal boondoggle destination.

Second, the intensity of the Wilson smear campaign, long meetings with favored reporters in hotels and on the phone, even the using of classified information, seems obsessive . . .

. . . In the most dysfunctional administration of our time, the vice president's office felt free to use classified information to bolster a false impression of Saddam's nuclear capabilities—going to absurd lengths to keep the truth from the American people and perhaps even the White House. According to testimony, Cheney got Bush to declassify secret material, but the president was not told how Cheney was going to use it.

As for Wilson, his crime was to shout that the emperor had no clothes. And that had to be discredited and Wilson punished by hurting his wife. . . .

A chapter had ended for us and we were eager to move on. During the last few weeks of the trial, I had been getting ready to move our household to Santa Fe, New Mexico. Joe and I had discussed the possibility of moving since at least 2004 (our New Zealand conversations), but our need and desire to depart Washington for good had intensified over the last few months. The city felt toxic to us, and whether the Libby trial ended as win, lose, or draw, we knew we had to get out. I seriously thought that if we remained in D.C., a place of chronic stress, one or both of us would have a heart attack. I also worried about the continuing effect of our unsettled and tension-filled life on our young children. We all needed some breathing space, a place to simply *be*, a place where there were other things to talk about besides politics. During trips to California, we had always managed to fit in a little fantasy house hunting, with special focus on Santa Barbara, where Joe had gone to college in the late 60s and early 70s and where he still had dozens of friends. Santa Barbara is indeed lotus land; verdant mountains running right down to sandy beaches and the rolling surf of the Pacific. It is one of the few places on the California coast that is oriented east/west, and its unique geography creates an especially mild Mediterranean climate that makes this little city about an hour and a half north of Los Angeles nearly perfect. But the beauty, charm, and climate of Santa Barbara were no secret, and it is consequently one of the most expensive real estate markets in the United States (median house price in 2005 was $2.5 million). For a couple of former government workers, ███████████████████████████████ and no trust funds to dip into, this price tag was out of the question.

In another life that now seemed like ancient history, I had traveled often to Los Alamos, New Mexico, always staying "down the hill" in Santa Fe. Although my whirlwind business trips did not allow much in the way of sightseeing, I took notice of the breathtaking scenery, mild and dry climate (such a welcome change from humid Washington), and a thriving artistic and cultural community. I was also impressed by the community's outdoor activities and environmental consciousness. I didn't have plans to move there at that time, though. Joe and I were fully expecting that I would be posted overseas ████ with the CIA.

In September 2006, Joe and I went to Santa Fe together for the first time to help raise money for the Military Religious

Freedom Foundation. (Led by Mikey Weinstein, an Air Force Academy graduate and passionate believer in the Constitution, his nonprofit foundation fights against religious proselytizing in U.S. military academies.) While there, we arranged for a real estate agent to show us a few homes. Joe had always dreamed of settling in beautiful Santa Barbara, California. However, as we viewed a few Santa Fe properties that offered the right amount of privacy amid gorgeous mountain vistas, brilliant blue skies, and the absolute quiet, I could see the wheels turning in Joe's head. By the time we headed back to Washington, I was sold on Santa Fe, and I could tell that Joe was open to the idea as well. Within a few weeks, as Joe was busy on the Democratic campaign trail, I was back in Santa Fe and found a house that I knew Joe would love as much as I did.

Once the papers were signed, all we had to do was sell our home in Washington. Although I am not Catholic, I had no qualms about buying a small statue of Saint Joseph that I buried head down, in the garden, in front of the house because legend has it that it will help the house sell quicker. Finally, at some point during the trial, we got a fair offer on the house and we accepted on the spot. There was another blur of activity as we arranged closing and move out dates. We selected March 13 as the day to hand over the keys.

Once the Libby verdict had come in, I looked forward to concentrating my energies on the move. But then the staff of Congressman Henry Waxman of California, the new Democratic chairman of the House Oversight and Government Reform Committee, called to ask if I would testify before the committee the following week. Though I was already bursting with obligations, I was thrilled at the opportunity to set the record straight, under oath, and said yes immediately. As I filled and taped boxes, cleaned and scrubbed the house for the new owners, and went through the numbing real estate ritual of "closing," my mind was always distant, working and turning over my prepared statement to Congress. I tried to think of every possible question the committee could throw at me, and set up a mock session the night before my appearance, with two trusted and experienced friends. I had to be sharp to avoid giving any information that the CIA would deem sensitive or classified. It was a minefield. I also had learned that General Michael Hayden, the CIA Director, had met with the bipartisan committee staffers and explicitly approved the use of the term "covert" in describing my cover status. This was a critical point and I rushed to make some small but important edits to my prepared statement. Although I still wasn't able to say openly how long I had served my country, I could at least counter those who had suggested over the last few years that I was no more than a "glorified secretary."

For moral support, I drove to the early morning hearing at the Capitol with my dear friend Ellen, at whose home I was staying. While waiting in an antechamber to the hearing room, I was surrounded by lawyers, congressional staffers, and friends, each of whom had earnest advice to give. Even though I had lived with the glare of publicity for several years, the attention was unsettling. I tried to keep my thoughts focused on this unique opportunity to reply to serious questions under oath and, hopefully, set the record straight once and for all on issues such as who sent Joe to Niger, and the reality of my covert status.

Finally, a staffer signaled that the hearing was to begin. When I stepped into the large room, I was momentarily blinded by the photographers' flashbulbs. I knew there would be media present, but I had no idea there would be so many. I was expected to work my way through the middle of them to get to the long witness table in front of the large dais where the congresspersons sit. I tried to keep my composure and held on to the table for support. Luckily for my nerves, Congressman Waxman opened the hearing with a five-minute preamble during which I could try to calm my pounding heart. When it came time to be sworn in, I was ready.

Good morning Mr. Chairman and members of the committee.

My name is Valerie Plame Wilson and I am honored to have been invited to testify under oath before the Committee on Oversight and Government Reform on the critical issue of safeguarding classified information. I am grateful for this opportunity to set the record straight.

I served the United States of America loyally and to the best of my ability as a covert operations officer for the Central Intelligence Agency. I worked on behalf of the national security of our country, on behalf of the people of the United States, until my name and true affiliation were exposed in the national media on July 14th, 2003—after a leak by administration officials. Today, I can tell this committee even more. In the run-up to the war with Iraq, I worked in the Counterproliferation Division of the CIA, still as a covert officer whose affiliation with the CIA was classified. I raced to discover solid intelligence for senior policy makers on Iraq's presumed weapons of mass destruction programs. While I helped to manage and run secret worldwide operations against this WMD target from CIA Headquarters in Washington, I also traveled to foreign countries on secret missions to find vital intelligence. I loved my career because I love my country. I was proud of the serious responsibilities entrusted to me as a CIA covert operations officer—and I was dedicated to this work. It was not common knowledge that "everyone on the Georgetown cocktail circuit" knew where I worked. Only a handful of people knew the truth.

But, all of my efforts on behalf of the national security of the United States, all of my training, and all of the value of my years of service were abruptly ended when my name and identity were exposed irresponsibly.

In the course of the trial of Vice President Cheney's former Chief of staff, "Scooter" Libby, I was shocked and dismayed by the evidence that emerged. My name and identity were carelessly and recklessly abused by senior government officials in both the White House and the State Department. All of them understood that I worked for the CIA, and having signed oaths to protect national security secrets, they should have been diligent in protecting me and every CIA officer. The CIA goes to great lengths to protect all of its employees, providing at significant taxpayers' expense painstakingly devised and creative "covers" for its most sensitive staffers. The harm that is done when a CIA cover is blown is grave but I cannot provide details beyond this in a public hearing. But the concept is obvious. Not only have breaches of national security endangered CIA officers, it has jeopardized and even destroyed entire networks of foreign agents who, in turn risked their own lives and those of their families—to provide the United States with needed intelligence. Lives are literally at stake. Every single one of my former CIA colleagues, from my fellow covert officers, to analysts, to technical operations officers, to even the secretaries, understands the vulnerability of our officers and recognizes that the travesty of what happened to me, could happen to them. We in the CIA always know that we might be exposed and threatened by foreign enemies. It was a terrible irony that administration officials were the ones who destroyed my cover. Furthermore, testimony in the criminal trial of Vice President Cheney's former Chief of staff, who has now been convicted of obstruction of justice and perjury, indicates that my exposure arose from purely political motives.

Within the CIA, it is essential that all intelligence be evaluated on the basis of its merits and actual credibility. National security depends upon it. The tradecraft of intelligence is not a product of speculation. I feel passionately as an intelligence professional about the creeping, insidious politicizing of our intelligence process. All intelligence professionals are dedicated to the ideal that they would rather be fired on the spot than distort the facts to fit a political view—any political view—or any ideology. As our intelligence agencies go through reorganizations and experience the painful aspects of change, and as our country faces profound challenges, injecting partisanship or ideology into the equation makes effective and accurate intelligence that much more difficult to develop. Politics and ideology must be stripped completely from our intelligence services, or the consequences will be even more severe than they have been and our country placed in even greater danger. It is imperative for any president to be able to make decisions based on intelligence that is unbiased.

The Libby trial and the events leading to the Iraq War highlight the urgent need to restore the highest professional standards of intelligence collection and analysis and protection of our officers and operations. The Congress has a constitutional duty to defend our national security that includes safeguarding our intelligence. That is why I am grateful for this opportunity to appear before this committee to assist it in its important work. Thank you and I welcome any questions.

I felt confident and focused. I also thought I had prepared for every possible question, even vicious or overtly political ones

from Republican committee members. What I had not anticipated was a foolish question, which is what came from Georgia
congressman Lynn Westmoreland. He started off cute: "Well, if
ah seem a little nervous, ah've never interviewed ah spy before,"
he said in his Georgia drawl. I smiled and responded, "Well,
Congressman, I've never testified before Congress under oath
before." In the second round of questions he let his zinger fly:
"Just to kinda keep score—not that you would put yourself in
any political category—but would you say you are Democrat or a
Republican?" Westmoreland asked this with the hint of a smirk.
I was taken aback and looked quickly to Congressman Waxman
for some guidance. Wasn't that an illegal question, like asking
someone his or her religion? But Waxman made no movement. I
wish I had had the presence of mind to reply, "Congressman,
first and foremost, I am a proud and loyal American." Alas.
Then, after a few more questions, it was over. The entire hearing
had taken two and a half hours. My head ached from concentrating so intently, but I was pleased—I finally had been able to tell a
piece of my story publicly.

As soon as I could, I called Joe in Utah to get his take. He
was proud and satisfied with the hearing. When I asked if the
children had seen it, he said they watched about five minutes
and then scampered off to play. That was fine with me: if they
care, they can watch it again on DVD in ten years. As for me, I
couldn't wait to get back to Ellen's quiet home, take off my shoes,
and rest for a bit. It was time to leave town, and that's just what I
intended to do.

As the plane circled lower over watermelon-colored Sandia
Mountain, which hovers over Albuquerque, tears welled up. I
couldn't wait to hug Joe, Joe's oldest son, Joe V, and our children, Trevor and Samantha. They would all meet me at the air-

port and we planned to drive up together to our new home in Santa Fe. As I rushed into their arms I felt a huge sense of relief. We had lived through an incredibly tumultuous period in our lives with the best grace and humor we could muster. We had told the truth, and had tried to live honorably. As we drove through the arid but stunningly beautiful landscape north of Albuquerque, we passed through several Indian reservations. I pointed out the ancient, extinct volcanoes dotting the horizon to the children, who were so excited to see their new house that they could barely stay in their seats. When we finally got out of the car in Santa Fe and took in the vistas in all directions, the only sound was the gentle wind. We were home.

Epilogue

On May 17, 2007, oral arguments were heard in our civil suit against Vice President Dick Cheney, I. Lewis "Scooter" Libby, Karl Rove, and Richard Armitage in a federal district court in Washington, D.C. On July 19, the case was dismissed. Judge John D. Bates wrote that "the alleged means by which defendants chose to rebut Mr. Wilson's comments and attack his credibility may have been highly unsavory." However, he further commented that there was no constitutional remedy for our claims. The court's decision stressed that our allegations posed "... important questions relating to the propriety of actions undertaken by our highest government officials," but that the claims would be dismissed for jurisdictional reasons. The court did not express an opinion on the claims' merits. We immediately filed a notice of appeal, and the case will continue through the court system.

On May 31, 2007, I, along with co-plaintiff publisher Simon & Schuster, Inc., filed suit in a federal district court in New York against Director of National Intelligence J. Michael McConnell, the Central Intelligence Agency, and the Director of the Central Intelligence Agency, General Michael V. Hayden. The suit alleged, among other things, that the government defendants unconstitutionally interfered with the publication of this book "by classifying public domain information." The case was assigned to federal district judge Barbara S. Jones, who was formerly a prosecutor in the United States Attorney's New York office. On August 1, 2007, Judge Jones ruled in the government's favor. The court's decision stated that "information concerning Wilson's pre-2002 employment for the CIA (if any) is properly classified, has never been declassified, and was not otherwise officially acknowledged by the CIA." The ruling was based, in part, upon a secret and classified declaration by Deputy CIA Director Stephen Kappes (that my lawyers were not allowed to see or respond to) and also upon "considerations of the CIA's commitment to secrecy and matters of foreign relations." The court's decision stated that "[T]o be sure, the public may draw whatever conclusions it might from the fact that the information at issue was sent on CIA letterhead by the Chief of Retirement and Insurance Services." The court further stated that information about "Wilson's pre-2002 service dates [is] in the public domain," and that, "as part of the legislative process" the information "entered the *Congressional Record* and has since been publicly accessible on the Internet through the Library of Congress's website." An appeal of this decision to the United States Court of Appeals for the Second Circuit is under consideration.

On July 2, 2007, President Bush commuted Scooter Libby's thirty-month prison sentence. Libby must still pay the $250,000 fine, but will serve no jail time.

Afterword

Laura Rozen

1. THE PATH TO THE CIA

It was early spring in 1985. President Ronald Reagan had recently been sworn in for his second term, and Diane Plame, a former schoolteacher in the prosperous Philadelphia suburb of Huntington Valley, Pennsylvania, was drinking coffee and reading the *Philadelphia Inquirer* when she cut out an ad and put it aside to send to her daughter, a senior at Pennsylvania State University. "I saw an ad one day in the paper that the CIA was interviewing," Diane Plame remembers. "I cut it out and mailed it to her."

When Mrs. Plame recounted the story in the summer of 2007, her daughter, Valerie Plame Wilson, had become the most famous CIA clandestine officer ever exposed by her own government. Past eras had seen explosive scandals involving the CIA. In the 1970s, former CIA officer Philip Agee published lists of names of alleged CIA officers in a deliberate campaign to thwart U.S. foreign policy. In the Nixon era, it was revealed that former CIA officers had conducted the Watergate break-in. Indeed, in the summer of 2007, the CIA released 702 pages of internal documents—the "family jewels"—detailing the clandestine intelligence agency's Cold War role in spying on American journalists, infiltrating anti–Vietnam War student groups, plotting assassinations of foreign leaders, withholding evidence from the FBI of the CIA's links to the Watergate break-in, and training the police forces of authoritarian regimes in how to suppress left-leaning civil society movements.[1]

But the events surrounding the exposure of Plame's daughter as a CIA operative in the summer of 2003 in a nationally syndicated newspaper column had not followed the arc of these other scandals. The outing of Valerie Plame was not the result of CIA assassination plots, covert arms deals, or other CIA misdeeds. It came amid a subterranean political battle between the White House and the CIA over who would take the blame for the faulty evidence cited as justification for the invasion and occupation of Iraq. The Bush White House expected the CIA to take the blame, and the vice president's office even drafted a speech for the CIA Director to make doing just that. The Republican-controlled congressional intelligence committees were willing to help the White House promote the narrative: any faulty prewar intelligence statements made by the White House were the CIA's fault. And then a former diplomat emerged who had a different story. Joseph Wilson said the White House should have known that its prewar claims that Iraq's Saddam Hussein was seeking five hundred tons of yellowcake uranium from the tiny African nation of Niger were bogus. Why? Because he had gone to Niger at the behest of the CIA, which had been tasked by the vice president with investigating the Niger yellowcake report, and reported back that there was good reason to think there was nothing to the story. In March 2003, the United Nations' nuclear watchdog agency would agree that the documents from which the United States and British government had drawn the evidence of the alleged transaction were crude forgeries. The United States proceeded with its invasion anyway, and by the summer of 2003 the White House was seized with growing panic: there were no weap-

---

1 See the CIA "family jewels" collection at the National Security Archives, released June 26, 2007.

ons of mass destruction in Iraq. Its main pretext for war was crumbling, an anti-American insurgency was emerging, and the presidential election was only one year away.

Wilson's accusations, made in a July 6, 2003, op-ed in the *New York Times* and titled, "What I Did Not Find in Africa," focused the White House's rising panic. How could it undermine the credibility of Joseph Wilson, who was suggesting that the Bush administration had hyped the prewar intelligence to sell the war to the American public? And so Vice President Dick Cheney and his aides quietly inquired about Wilson with top government officials at the CIA and State Department and discovered a detail they thought useful to redirecting the story. They learned that Wilson's wife, Valerie Plame Wilson, worked at the CIA. Indeed, she worked in a special division devoted to countering the proliferation of unconventional weapons.

So began a White House campaign to whisper in reporters' ears: don't get too far out on the Wilson story because the reason he was sent to Niger was because his wife was a weapons of mass destruction operative at the CIA, and she had helped him get the (unpaid) gig. "Did his wife send him on a junket?" Vice President Cheney wrote on the margins of his copy of Wilson's op-ed. "Valerie Flame," *New York Times* reporter Judith Miller wrote in her notebook shortly after a two-hour meeting with the vice president's Chief of staff, I. Lewis "Scooter" Libby, at a Washington hotel, a meeting Libby kept off his calendar. "Wilson never worked for the CIA, but his wife, Valerie Plame, is an Agency operative on weapons of mass destruction," Robert Novak published in his syndicated column on July 14, 2003.[2] Joseph Wilson's wife is "fair game," White House political operative Karl Rove told television host Chris Matthews.

---

2   Robert Novak, "Mission to Niger," Townhall.com, July 14, 2003.

. . .

As Richard Nixon managed to cover up his knowledge of the Watergate break-in until after his reelection, when its exposure would force his resignation, so the Bush White House largely successfully managed to control the public narrative about the increasingly controversial road to war in Iraq long enough to win reelection in 2004. It was not until a year after that, in October 2005, that the vice president's Chief of staff, Scooter Libby, was indicted, and in 2007, convicted and sentenced to thirty months in prison, $250,000 in fines, and two years probation for lying about and obstructing the investigation of White House officials' role in outing Valerie Plame.[3] On July 2, 2007, President Bush ordered the commutation of Libby's jail sentence, preserving the jury's guilty verdicts but sparing Libby the imminent prospect of becoming the first White House official to go to prison since the Nixon era.

On that early spring morning in 1985, while flipping through the *Philadelphia Inquirer,* Diane Plame only knew that Valerie, unlike her daughter's close friends, was still unsure of what she wanted to do with her life. "All her friends knew exactly what they wanted to do," Diane Plame said. "She was supposed to go with some friends one Easter break to Florida, but the trip fell through, and she came home and said, 'I might as well go back and take that test' " the CIA had advertised.

Diane Plame says of her and her husband, "We were blessed. With both our son"—Valerie's older half brother, Robert Plame—

---

3 For an excellent summary and analysis of the Libby trial proceedings, see Murray Waas and Jeff Lomonaco, *The United States v. I. Lewis Libby* (New York: Union Square Press, 2007).

"and our daughter. They were very easy to raise." Valerie was "always very responsible, and fun, just a neat, well-rounded human being." She played hockey in junior high, ran varsity track in high school, and had a close-knit circle of friends—of whom her mother says, "They were the achievers." And the good kids.

Valerie's brother, Robert sixteen years her senior, her father's son from his first marriage, followed in the family tradition of military service and became a Marine. In 1967, while serving in Vietnam, Robert was badly wounded, a trauma that seared the family and was made all the more harrowing by learning one day that two Marines had been to their home when they were out. "I ran down and knocked on the neighbors' doors," Diane Plame recalls of that awful day. Had they seen the Marines knocking on their door? "Yes, they did. My husband collapsed in the chair." When the Marines returned later, "I opened the door and asked, 'Is he dead or alive?' " He was alive, but badly wounded on a reconnaissance patrol. A gunshot had severed the artery in his right arm. He was transported to a medical outpost, Diane Plame recounts, where a surgeon touring U.S. military medical facilities in Vietnam saw Robert's injuries and told him, "I am going to save your arm." Three years and fourteen operations later, Robert had recovered.

But the experience contributed to a quiet change in Valerie's parents, particularly her father, Samuel Plame, a retired Air Force colonel and squadron commander. "We were registered Republicans," Diane Plame says, although "not 'card-carrying.' . . . But my husband grew disillusioned with Vietnam," including the fact that the United States was fighting there without the president having declared a war.

Diane and Sam Plame loved to travel, especially in Europe, as Valerie would, too. In her late twenties, Diane Plame spent two years teaching the children of the Third Armored Division at the American School in Frankfurt, Germany. "I went over there to stay single," she laughs. She came home with Sam. "In Germany, I was living in the nurses' quarters, which was not on the main base, and it had an officers' club there next to the hospital." She was there one night with her friends, "and a person comes up and says, 'Can I buy you a drink?' " She later agreed to follow Sam to the Chicago area, got married, and on August 13, 1963, gave birth to Valerie, in Anchorage, Alaska, where Sam was serving as a squadron commander at the local Air Force base. "My brother had been a pilot in the Air Force, and my husband is retired Air Force," she says.

In 1966, when Valerie was a toddler, the family moved to the suburbs of Philadelphia, where Diane McClintock Plame had grown up. Valerie attended Pine Road Elementary School and Lower Moreland High School in the prosperous Montgomery County suburbs, and her mother taught in the neighboring town of Abington.

As Plame describes in her memoir, she and her parents would frequently pack their bags and show up at the airport to fly on earlier incarnations of budget airlines to Europe. Diane Plame fondly recalls them renting a villa in Porto Santo Stefano, Tuscany, Italy, in 1973. The villa she picked out "overlooked the Tyrrhenian Sea. All our rooms opened out onto a terrace." Valerie's parents would later visit her on her foreign assignments, to Athens, London, and Brussels.

Valerie studied German and business at Penn State and was a member of a sorority. After freshman year, Diane Plame recalls, Valerie and a college girlfriend went to work at dude ranches in Wyoming, near Yellowstone National Park. In her junior year, she did a semester abroad studying in Cologne, Germany. So, knowing her daughter's interest in travel, foreign affairs, and history, and the family's tradition of public service, when Diane Plame saw the ad in the *Inquirer* that the CIA was interviewing, she sent it to her daughter. And Valerie found a career in which she thrived.

Becoming "Val P."

While waiting for her security clearance to come through, Valerie took an apartment in the Glover Park area of Washington, D.C., and worked at the historic Woodward & Lothrop department store downtown. According to *Vanity Fair*, Plame was engaged and briefly married to her college boyfriend, Todd Sesler, who reportedly started to pursue a career in the Agency with her before deciding against it.[4] The marriage was brief.

The Agency that Plame joined as a new recruit in 1985 was in the midst of rapid growth and exciting transformation. William Casey, a hard-charging, committed anticommunist and Reagan confidant, was CIA Director, and to this day many in the Agency consider him the best director the Agency has ever had, despite the fact that several Agency officials later faced legal jeopardy for their role in the Iran-Contra operation, which Reagan and Casey had authorized but which violated the Boland amendment prohibiting U.S. military aid to the anticommunist Contra rebels of Nicaragua.

Valerie Plame was accepted into the elite Career Trainee program, an innovation of Casey and future CIA Director Robert Gates. In classes of fifty or so, future intelligence analysts and operational case officers were mixed together for an intense academic grounding in the ways of the Agency and on government and political systems before they were sent to the "Farm" for paramilitary-style operational training and corps-building.

---

4 Vicky Ward, "Double Exposure," *Vanity Fair*, January 2004.

No more than 250 elite recruits were accepted into the Career Trainee program each year, classmates said. Valerie's classmates in the fall of 1985 knew her only as "Val P."

"It was the Reagan years, and they did everything with us," remembers Brent Cavan. "They told us that they were investing a quarter of a million dollars on each of us, beyond our salary."

The Career Trainee program offered "a broad exposure to everything the CIA does," Cavan recalls. "How the government works, how the communist systems don't work, how the Agency works, political economy." It was a "horrendous process" to get accepted—involving physical and psychological tests and a polygraph.

But the Agency was also in the midst of a democratizing revolution in terms of whom it was looking to recruit. In past generations, the CIA had tended to hire the proverbial "guys who went to Yale who were the sons of the guys who went to Yale who were the sons of guys who went to Yale," as former CIA East Europe/Soviet division Chief Milt Bearden says. This was a legacy of the CIA's World War II–era predecessor organization, the Office of Strategic Services. But in the midst of the Reagan/Casey expansion of the 1980s, the Agency was looking for a different type of elite officer, and the selection process was becoming more meritocratic than upper-class and Ivy League.

"At that point, they were expanding the military, they were expanding the Agency, we were fighting the Soviet Union, we were fighting the proxies," Cavan explains. The CIA in 1985 was "looking for bright, young, well-rounded people. In the interviews, they didn't just ask about academic credentials. They were looking for Renaissance men, people who had varied backgrounds, who knew the outdoors. They wanted some diversity, people who had a bit of savvy."

The democratization of CIA recruiting in the era when Plame

arrived included more opportunities for women. "For case officers, it was still a man's world," remembers Larry Johnson, another member of the September 1985 class. "She was there at the start of the transition. . . . It was the social change at the time, starting under Reagan, which is terribly ironic. Bill Casey, as much despised as he was by some, was the best CIA Director in the last fifty years. He stood by his people. He had some bad ideas, but ultimately he understood the business of intelligence.

"Valerie was one of the 'kids,'" Johnson says. "I was thirty years old, she was twenty-two." He says that he and some of the slightly older members of the class were "older brothers" to the few members of their Career Trainee class who were straight out of college.

"She was quiet and kept to herself. . . . She didn't try to pretend to be something that she was not. She didn't shoot her mouth off," Johnson recalls with admiration. "Looking back, for her age, how so damn young she was, she was remarkably mature, and very serious," Johnson adds. "It was clear she wanted to be taken seriously."

Johnson says only three people from their Career Trainee class of fifty were destined, like Valerie, to be NOCs—Nonofficial Covered Officers, the most clandestine in the Agency. After she was exposed in 2003, several of her classmates who had known her only as "Val P." almost twenty years earlier were outraged and came out of their quiet lives in business, government, and, one in disguise, from the Agency, to stand up and protest what had happened to her.

Diane Plame confesses that when Valerie called to tell her that Novak had outed her in his column, one thing she felt was relief. "I knew her heart was broken. But I also was so relieved that I didn't have to worry about her so much anymore." Diane Plame says there was "a lot she didn't know" about her daughter's CIA career. "I did not know she was a NOC. She never told me that," she said, adding that that was probably a good thing.

2. ATHENS TOUR

In the fall of 1989, Valerie Plame moved to Athens, Greece, to serve as a CIA Case Officer on her first foreign tour. She was twenty-six and would serve in Athens for three years. With its businessmen, foreign diplomats, communists, offices of Palestinian and Middle Eastern groups, historical and geographical links to Egypt and the Middle East, its soft targets for terrorism, and its extensive seacoast and islands, Greece was an important listening post for the Agency. According to family, friends, and associates, Valerie settled in a northern suburb of Athens, in a family neighborhood on the second floor of a house that had a pretty garden and several terraces. She learned Greek, cultivated and recruited foreign agents and polished her tradecraft, and fell in love with the Mediterranean country. "I loved the climate, the landscape, the villages, the culture, and after a while, even the people themselves," Plame writes. But it was also a time of significant danger for U.S. officials in Greece, with the Greek leftist terrorist group 17 November having killed several U.S. officials beginning with CIA Station Chief Richard Welch in Athens in 1975. Indeed, it was the killing of Welch and the exposure of the names of hundreds of alleged CIA personnel by former CIA officer Philip Agee and by the magazine *CounterSpy* that prompted Congress in 1982 to pass the Intelligence Identities Protection Act—the federal law that would later be mulled after Plame's own identity was exposed by Bush administration officials to journalists in the summer of 2003.

While serving as a Case Officer in Athens, Valerie had official "cover" as a junior political officer at the U.S. Embassy. She worked a full day job as a State Department political officer and consular official, interviewing those applying at the embassy for visas, and performed her actual covert CIA duties—identifying, cultivating, and recruiting foreign spies—often after normal business hours.

Having official cover—and a diplomatic passport—gave Plame a degree of protection: if she were discovered or arrested by Greek authorities, she would have enjoyed full diplomatic immunity. (Such diplomatic protection proved useful to two of Plame's apparent successors in Athens in November 1993, when Greek authorities detained two U.S. "diplomats" after finding guns, radio transmitters, and blond wigs in the Volkswagen van from which they had apparently been conducting covert surveillance. Soon after, the U.S. Embassy quietly withdrew the two "diplomats" to avoid the embarrassment of Greece expelling them for conducting "activities incompatible with their diplomatic duties"—diplomatic-speak for spying.) Plame's job as a Case Officer was in essence to recruit local foreign agents to report to her with inside information, political machinations and motivations, and insights about which they had special knowledge and access.

At the time, the CIA Station in Athens was divided into three sections: one focused on Greek internal political developments—"the Greek scene"; a second focused on the Soviet threat; and a third on the group 17 November, which after Welch in 1975 had killed several other American, British, Turkish, and Greek officials. According to associates, Plame worked in the internal politics section, so in effect her official "cover" job as a political officer for the State Department greatly resembled her actual, albeit covert CIA job, which was to develop and recruit agent sources who could help the U.S. government better understand, predict, and influence Greek internal political developments. The job is "to go out and meet everyone [one] can and figure out their weaknesses and whether they can be recruited," one embassy associate of Plame's said.

The CIA Station Chief during Valerie's tenure was Doug Smith, a veteran Operations Officer who had served in several foreign assignments. Valerie "was certainly ambitious, and worked hard," Smith, now retired, recalls. "It's a matter of luck and skill—how people react to you, whether people like you, want to see you, and want to tell you things," he adds, describing the qualities that make a successful Case Officer. "It's rare that someone on a first tour does a really wonderful job. She did well."

Plame's former Deputy Chief in Athens, whom she calls "Jim" in her memoir, and who is still serving in the Agency, conveyed through associates that he, too, has "a very high opinion of Valerie" and the caliber of her work.

The Greek Scene

The Greece in which Valerie arrived in 1989 was in a state of uneasiness and receding political turmoil—along with lingering wrath directed against Washington and those believed to be colluding with it. Invaded first by the Italians and then by the German Nazis during World War II, Greece after the war became a central front in the Cold War and suffered through a traumatic civil war from 1946 to 1949. By the 1960s, the Cold War fault lines were between the leftist pan-Hellenic Socialist movement officially hostile to Washington, and the liberal-conservative New Democracy Party. In 1967, concerned that Socialist candidate

Andreas Papandreou was going to win the presidential elections, a group of anticommunist Greek military officers led by Colonel George Papadopoulos staged a military coup and set up the dictatorial "Colonel's Regime." Though the CIA reportedly had no role in the junta and the Lyndon Johnson administration condemned the coup, the Agency was familiar with some of the officers involved and maintained relations with them.[5]

Constitutional democracy was restored in 1974, making way for the Third Hellenic Republic, which has prevailed through today. But tension remained. The Turkish invasion of Cyprus in 1974 prompted Greece to temporarily withdraw from NATO, and in 1973 the Marxist terrorist group 17 November (or N17, as it

---

5 George Crile describes CIA officer Gust Avrokotos's relationship to the colonels who staged the junta in *Charlie Wilson's War:* "On April 21, 1967, [Avrokotos] got one of those breaks that can make a career, when a military junta seized power in Athens and suspended democratic and constitutional government. Liberals in the United States and around the world were outraged, but overnight 'the colonels' coup' turned Avrokotos into one of the CIA's indispensable, frontline players. Well before this, he had made it his business to get to know the colonels. They had all started off life as peasants before joining the army, and they felt a kinship with this charismatic, working-class American whose parents had come from Lemnos [Greece]. They could speak Greek with him. He drank and whored with them, and they knew from the heart that he shared their ferocious anti-Communism. Avrokotos understood that the colonels had expected the United States to thank them, however discreetly, for preventing the anti-American candidate, Andreas Papandreou, from taking power. The polls had indicated that Papandreou would win the election, and the colonels suspected that the CIA itself was trying to sabotage Papandreou's campaign. But world reaction was so bitter and the move so brutally antidemocratic that the [Lyndon] Johnson administration took to verbally attacking the junta and threatening to cut off U.S. assistance. After the colonels arrested Papandreou, who had lived in the United States for years, the embassy sent Avrokotos to deliver a message to them. The United States had taken the unusual step of issuing the Greek leader an American passport, and the embassy wanted the junta to permit him to leave the country. 'That's the official position. You should let him go,' the young CIA man told the colonels. 'But unofficially, as your friend, my advice is to shoot the motherfucker because he's going to come back to haunt you.'" George Crile, *Charlie Wilson's War* (New York: Grove, 2003), pp. 51–52.

was sometimes known) emerged and over the next three decades carried out the assassination of twenty-three people in over one hundred attacks, beginning with the CIA's Welch. The terror group took its name from the tumultuous last day of the 1973 student uprisings at Athens Polytechnic University against the Greek military dictatorship established by the colonels.

17 November

From its inception, one of N17's prime targets was the CIA and the U.S. presence in Greece. Welch was shot to death on December 23, 1975, outside his Athens residence in front of his wife and driver. In its manifestos, communiqués, and letters claiming responsibility for assassinations, N17 demanded that the American "imperialists" withdraw from air bases in Greece, that Turkey abandon Cyprus, and that Greece pull out of NATO and the European Commission. Though the group claimed responsibility for the Welch killing in a manifesto delivered to the French newspaper *Libération* via the offices of French existentialist writer Jean-Paul Sartre, at the time few in the CIA or the Greek security services could quite believe that a local group acting alone had the ability to carry out such brazen attacks. "These were guys we had never heard of," says Smith. "Neither the Agency or the Greek police had heard of 17 November."

How exactly Welch had been exposed to a degree that 17 November could target him was a matter of some dispute. In 1975, a former CIA officer, Philip Agee, who had grown disillusioned with the Agency's support for authoritarian regimes in Latin America, published a book, *Inside the Company: CIA Diary*, whose appendix included thirty pages of names of alleged CIA personnel. Many of the names he apparently deduced from State Department and embassy telephone directories. That same year, other names—including Welch's—were listed in *CounterSpy*. And after Welch's assassination, many in the Agency and in the United States blamed Agee's and *CounterSpy*'s acts for getting Welch killed.

Today, however, most believe Welch's exposure, including his address, by local Greek media was more instrumental. "Agee exposed a lot of names," says Smith. "Then other people caught on to this . . . . But Welch's name and a number of names were published in the local press. And that is how we think they [N17] got on to Welch's name."

Agee has always vehemently denied any responsibility for Welch's death, noting that the name did not appear in his book. Indeed, according to a 1997 story by James Risen in the *Los Angeles Times*, Agee, by then living in exile in Cuba, filed a libel suit against former First Lady Barbara Bush for writing in her autobiography "that Agee [was] responsible for revealing the identity of the CIA's Athens Station Chief . . . just before the Station Chief was killed. The former first lady ultimately agreed to remove the allegation from her book." Today, Agee reportedly runs a travel agency and Web site in Cuba.

In any event, Agee's actions appalled Congress, and contributed to its adoption in 1982 of the Intelligence Identities Protection Act, which would later become the subject of so much attention following Plame's exposure by her own government. This would have been impossible to imagine for the ambitious young government officer on her first foreign tour.

In June 1988, just a year before Plame arrived in Athens, 17 November had killed the U.S. Embassy's naval attaché, Navy Captain William Nordeen, pulling a booby-trapped car alongside his armored car only a few minutes away from his Athens home. "It was a scary thing," John Brady Kiesling, a political officer at the embassy at the time of Plame's tour, recalls. "We were nervous and we were angry. And everybody driving to work was looking in their rearview mirrors. We had instructions never to leave from home at the same time. Always take a different route. Know your escape route. . . . We were exhorted."

Plame, like some other U.S. officials, was inexplicably assigned to housing in the northern suburbs of Athens, accessible to the capital and their embassy by a single road that had a bottleneck that made drivers vulnerable to attack. "It was on that road that [British brigadier] Stephen Saunders was murdered in 2000," recalls Kiesling. "For some reason, that's where we put people."

The deadly 17N group was, not surprising, the major preoccupation of Plame's boss, Station Chief Smith. "They had just killed our naval attaché when I got there in the summer of '88," he says. The terrorists struck again in 1991, killing U.S. Air Force Sergeant Ronald Stewart, assigned to the Hellinikon Air Base near Athens, on March 12 with a remote-controlled bombing device. One of N17's demands was that the United States abandon Hellinikon base, which it ultimately did in 1991.

At the time of Plame's tour, the Greek police had not managed to arrest a single member of the group. Indeed, from the time of N17's inception, some had speculated, including at the Agency, that N17 might have ties to Middle Eastern terrorist groups or be a front for other anti-American forces. The group claimed responsibility for killing the CIA's Welch, but says Smith, "We really didn't believe their first claim. Not until they killed another guy and sent a letter to [the French newspaper] *Libération*, explaining how they had done it. Then we realized, these people do exist."

When N17 was finally wrapped up in 2002, "by and large, the group was exactly what they said they were," says Kiesling, who is writing a book about N17. "Urban revolutionaries who hoped through armed propaganda to show that the system was vulnerable, the masses could rise up, and create a more just world based on workers' self-management." What's more, U.S. sources acknowledge, the CIA ultimately had very little to do with taking down the group. "The CIA barked up many wrong trees," says Kiesling. What finally brought N17 down was an accident. In June 2002, a bomb blew up in the hands of a N17 terrorist, wounding him. He was picked up by the Greek police and taken to the hospital, and when he came to, he said he wanted to talk to a priest and a police officer, recalls Smith. "So they obliged him, he confessed to what he'd been doing, and then, over the next few weeks, he gave out hints, people's aliases; he was responsible for [several] arrests. The cops had volumes about the Greek suspects, but most of these were not known." The police were able to arrest and prosecute many of the group's members. One of Europe's most dangerous terrorist groups had been defeated by local law enforcement and its own mistakes, and basically had ceased to exist.

Life at the Embassy

As a junior Case Officer, Plame was responsible for cultivating sources who could provide information on internal Greek political developments. "She was doing internal Greek stuff," a colleague recalls. "There was always interesting stuff going on—a kind of holdover from the civil war, because of the sort of basic anti-American undertones."

While Plame told people—if she told them anything—that she was a political officer at the U.S. Embassy, Kiesling really was a political officer at the embassy in Athens, from 1988 until 1992. (Two decades later, in 2003, Kiesling would make international headlines when, as a senior diplomat in Athens, he resigned from the State Department over the Iraq War, a decision he describes in his diplomatic memoir, *Diplomacy Lessons.*)[6] Their jobs overlapped and they both worked out of the classified section of the third floor of the white marble embassy designed by Walter Gropius to echo the Parthenon.

Ironically enough, it was sometimes Kiesling's job to help promote the CIA officers' cover. "Part of my job was to provide cover for them to go to diplomatic receptions. Let's say it's some country's national day. Normally you want to send the ambassador, but the ambassador doesn't want to go, so it gets dumped on some political councilor and you farm out the invitation." Such receptions were useful opportunities for source cultivation for CIA officers such as Plame. "Here's a guy who's friendly and might be willing to talk," Kiesling describes. "And of course, the funny thing is, many of the people who go to these receptions are spies looking for other spies. A huge amount of what the CIA ended up doing back then was tail chasing," he says with the barest hint of disdain.

As a political officer, Kiesling's own job wasn't so different from Valerie's, in some respects. "You find people who know what they are talking about, and meet as many people as you can," he said. "Politicians. [People who] are really smart and analytical. Opposition members of Parliament and the like. I used to go every few months to the Communist Party to meet with the Politburo and have a Greek coffee." And as he points out, the best way to protect your cover as a spy is to inhabit your cover identity as much as possible.

The political section had about a dozen officers, "and we had people like Valerie," Kiesling says, referring to those who were officially in their section but reporting to the Agency. "She was in the consular section and was supposed to do a rotation." He

6   John Brady Kiesling, *Diplomacy Lessons: Realism for an Unloved Superpower* (Dulles, Va.: Potomac Books, 2006).

recalls Plame, ostensibly then a Third Secretary Consular officer, as blond, well-dressed, demure—and with a bit of the CIA young Turks' cockiness. "I think she was ambitious. In my perception, she had a bit of the CIA snobbery."

In her own preceding account, Plame readily acknowledges that she and other junior CIA officers were at times "impossibly arrogant." Her account also echoes the sense of institutional tension and mistrust between embassy diplomats and spooks. "John . . . had nothing but disgust for the CIA, and considered . . . dirty rotten . . . ," she writes in her second chapter. "John's opinion was shared by many, although not all, of his colleagues who saw in the CIA the cowboy behavior that gave the United States a bad name and made their job . . . that much harder. . . . These feelings were strongly reciprocated by the CIA, who viewed State Department officers as feckless, ineffective whiners who worked strictly bankers' hours."

"It's a competitive relationship," Kiesling agrees, describing tensions between diplomats and embassy spooks. "As if they think, they are the ones doing all the real stuff, and we are wimps. I guess it's a necessary part of morale building." [7]

A Twist

Valerie Plame's Athens tour coincided with another minor embassy scandal that would later resonate in a major Washington investigation that touched the CIA during the George W. Bush administration.

As Plame describes her duties as a consular officer, interview-

---

[7] "Most of the real diplomats at the embassy treated their spy colleagues as if they were untouchables," George Criles describes in *Charlie Wilson's War*. " 'They called us 'spooks,' [former CIA case officer in Athens Gust] Avrokotos recalls. . . . 'In the big embassies . . . It's a real caste system.' . . . The 'spooks' themselves considered case officers green for their first two tours."

ing applicants for U.S. visas, "I was assisted in this endeavor by 'Peter,' a foreign national who had worked in the consular section for years. . . . His language fluency came in handy all the time and I came to rely upon his judgment in questionable cases. I was saddened and surprised several years later when I heard that he had been arrested and ultimately convicted on the charge of visa fraud. He was selling visas and probably to the very people about whom I had expressed my doubts. I have to say I never suspected him."

Some twenty plus years later, in 2005, reporters learned of an Agency link to a burgeoning Washington corruption scandal involving Congressman Randy "Duke" Cunningham (R-California), who pled guilty to bribery-related charges in November 2005 and was sentenced to eight years in prison.[8] Among the defense contractors and others who were identified in plea documents as Cunningham's alleged co-conspirators was a mysterious Greek-American, Long Island-based businessman and real estate developer, Thomas Theodore Kontogiannis. As it turned out, Kontogiannis, who secretly pled guilty in the Cunningham case in 2007,[9] had pled guilty in 1994 to visa fraud along with a Greek national working at the U.S. Embassy in Greece.[10] According to sources, Kontogiannis's embassy collaborator in Athens was almost certainly Valerie's colleague "Peter."

---

8   See Laura Rozen, " 'Duke' of Deception," *The American Prospect*, January 13, 2006.

9   Dean Calbreath, "Cunningham financier admits role in scandal," *San Diego Union-Tribune*, June 15, 2007.

10 Court documents identify Kontogiannis's 1994 co-defendant as Pantelis Papazachariou. See *USA v. Papazachariou, et al.*, filed March 25, 1993. See also Murray Weiss, "Bidder Pill: Board of Ed Had Chances to Halt 'Scam'," *New York Post*, October 2, 2000. "About the time of Miller's appointment, Kontogiannis ran afoul of the law. He and an official at the U.S. Embassy in Athens were arrested by the FBI for taking bribes to provide phony U.S. visas. Both pleaded guilty, and Kontogiannis was sentenced to five years' probation. He told The Post recently he was only trying to help a Greek national visit his dying mother in the U.S. Sources said his motive was pure greed."

In the spring of 2006, the wider Cunningham investigation factored in the resignations of both CIA Director Porter Goss and his controversial choice to be CIA Executive Director, Kyle Dustin "Dusty" Foggo, when the latter was implicated in a related case.[11]

Official Cover

While Plame was pursuing potential foreign recruits in Greece, she enjoyed the protection of diplomatic cover and the knowledge that, should her espionage activities be detected or exposed, the United States would whisk her away to safety. There is no sign that she ever required such drastic measures while in Greece, but two of her apparent successors did. In November 1993, a year after Plame had returned to Washington, international media reported on a strange arrest in Athens. "Greece reacted cautiously Wednesday to the bizarre case of two U.S. diplomats arrested Tuesday near a school that was at the center of celebrations of the 20th anniversary of the overthrow of a right-wing dictatorship," Agence France-Presse reported with a wink:

> In the diplomats' car, police found two firearms, two walkie-talkies and a pair of blond wigs. U.S. Ambassador Thomas Niles reportedly expressed his "sadness" over the incident to Foreign Minister Carolos Papoulias and said the embassy was investigating. The embassy has refused all comment. . . .
>
> The two diplomats, one of them identified as second Secretary Charles Faddis, the other unidentified, were arrested at dusk Tuesday in the vicinity of Athens Polytechnic Col-

---

11 See for instance, Ken Silverstein, "The Loss of Goss," *Harpers.com*, May 8, 2006, and Dean Calbreath, "Foggo is indicted on new charges," *San Diego Union-Tribune*, May 12, 2007.

lege, in Kypseli neighborhood. They tried to flee but were arrested anyway. . . . They were held for about five hours and released after showing their diplomatic passports.

Athens newspapers ran banner headlines on the case, with one suggesting the pair were tagging Palestinians hostile to Palestine Liberation Organization Chairman Yasser Arafat, who is due in Athens early next week.

Shortly thereafter, the two "diplomats," now identified all over the Greek media, were withdrawn by the U.S. Embassy, their covers blown, but were spared harsher punishment by their diplomatic status.

It was protection that Plame would willingly forgo at great personal risk in her future assignments.

3. BECOMING A NOC

In the fall of 1992, Valerie Plame moved back to Washington, D.C., from Greece, collected her Headquarters building access pass, and, while working a desk job for a branch in the Directorate of Operations Europe Division, began to contemplate a risky proposition: turning in her diplomatic passport and becoming a whole new class of clandestine CIA officer—a "NOC" (pronounced "knock"), or Nonofficial Covered Officer. Becoming a NOC would require Plame to erase all visible connections to the U.S. government, while, with the help of the Agency's Office of Central Cover, developing and inhabiting a plausible new private sector career and professional identity that would serve as useful cover for her to meet and develop potential sources of intelligence value to the Agency without revealing herself as an agent of the U.S. government. It also meant giving up the protection of diplomatic status should her covert activities be discovered. "A NOC had no overt affiliation with the U.S. government," Plame writes. "If he was caught, the United States would deny any connection."

As part of the process of visibly distancing herself from her association with the U.S. government and her former "cover" career as a junior State Department officer in Greece, and in order to develop the credentials and the knowledge to plausibly inhabit a private-sector cover career and identity, Plame pursued two graduate degrees in international affairs and European studies, first at the London School of Economics from 1993 to 1994, and, after a year of learning French, at the College of Europe in Bruges, Belgium, from 1995 to 1996.

In 1996, Plame settled in an apartment in Brussels and began her public career as an energy executive (her business card while based in Brussels described her as "Vice President, International" for a small petroleum-related company), and her covert career as a NOC. Her cover allowed her to travel widely, attend conferences, and meet and interact with a broader range of people who might have intelligence value to the Agency than case officers operating within the embassy would have when circulating on the diplomatic and cocktail circuit. Such access to a deeper and more diverse pool of potential information sources, including from the foreign corporate world, without the formality and obstacles presented by ostensibly being from the U.S. government, was growing increasingly useful to the Agency as its concerns turned to countering the more diffuse and transnational challenges of the post–Cold War world. These challenges included tracking and countering the proliferation of weapons, including weapons of mass destruction; counternarcotics; economic intelligence-gathering; tracking high-tech technology developments; and counterterrorism.

History and Background of the NOC program

The CIA has cooperated with—and in turn relied on the cooperation of—corporate America from its inception. Several of the Agency's directors and top management came from Wall Street, law firms, and the corporate world. "Wild Bill" Donovan, the director of the CIA's predecessor organization, the Office of

Strategic Services, had worked as a lawyer in New York, and Reagan's DCI, William Casey, had served as a corporate lawyer and Nixon's chairman of the Securities and Exchange Commission.

Casey in turn brought in a member of Reagan's "Kitchen Cabinet," California businessman Peter Daley, chairman of the World Business Council, to broker links between the Agency and some of America's Fortune 100 companies, according to a former intelligence officer familiar with the setup. The outreach to corporate America was partly motivated by the CIA Director's desire not to be blindsided when, for example, a prominent CEO would telephone the president to tell him what his rep in Mexico was hearing, leading the president to ask the CIA Director about the details. Indeed, according to Agency veterans, the CIA had a whole division, Domestic Collection, that later morphed into the National Resources Division, to interface with businesspeople who cooperated with it from time to time.

Such close ties between American businesses and the Agency also involved providing "cover." As journalist Jim Hougan described in his 1978 book, *Spooks*, "Besides sharing 'intelligence' with the oil companies—a part of the Agency's 'mission'—the CIA also found itself having to prevail upon the larger companies both for the creation of 'cover' slots and for the loan of oil company executives who could assist the Agency in oil-related matters on a day-to-day basis." [12]

In 1995, an exposé in the investigative magazine *Mother Jones* by Robert Dreyfuss revealed that cooperation between American business and the CIA was far more extensive than had been previously known. And at the heart of that cooperation was something called the "nonofficial cover" program:

---

[12] Jim Hougan, *Spooks* (New York: Bantam, 1979).

. . . A Central Intelligence Agency program revived by the late director [William Casey] in the 1980s marries the spy agency to corporate America in order to gather intelligence on economics, trade, and technology. . . . And dozens of U.S. corporations—from Fortune 500 companies to small, high-tech firms—are secretly assisting the CIA, allowing the agency to place full-time officers from its operations divisions into corporate offices abroad.

Serving under what is referred to as "nonofficial cover" (NOC), CIA officers pose as American businessmen in friendly countries, from Asia to Central America to Western Europe. There, they recruit agents from the ranks of foreign officials and business leaders, pilfer secrets, and even conduct special operations and paramilitary activities. . . .

In recent years, according to several CIA sources, NOCs have increasingly turned their attention to economics. Using their business covers, they seek to recruit agents in foreign government economic ministries or gain intelligence about high-tech firms in computer, electronics, and aerospace industries. They also help track the development of critical technologies, both military and civilian.[13]

As Dreyfuss's reporting indicates, the NOC program waxed and waned depending on the political mood and moment, experiencing a revival during the freewheeling, high-risk Reagan years when Casey led the CIA, and again in the mid-1990s, after the Cold War, as the Agency's concerns turned to the more transnational less suited to pursuit under State Department cover.

NOCs are case officers, as Plame was in Athens, but minus the

---

13 Robert Dreyfuss, "The CIA Crosses Over," *Mother Jones*, January/February 1995.

embassy cover. They report to a special division inside the Directorate of Operations called the Office of External Development. As case officers, NOCs identify and assess possible foreign agents the CIA might recruit, and handle agents. But because they lack diplomatic protection, NOCs identify and scout out potential recruits only up to the point of actually signing them up, since doing so would require them to "break cover"—reveal their true affiliation with the CIA. Instead, when the NOC believes a target is ready for the recruiting pitch, he or she generally coordinates through Agency channels, and the CIA sends a covered officer to make the pitch. The reason is obvious: if the recruitment goes wrong and the target makes a fuss about the CIA trying to lure him to betray his country's or company's secrets to the Agency, the covered CIA officer has diplomatic protection, whereas the NOC does not.[14]

According to its devotees, among them Casey, NOC status was thought to provide various forms of access and cover less available to "covered" officers, a veteran former senior intelligence official familiar with the program explained. These include "cover for status"—an excuse for an American to go live in Damascus, Syria, say, posing as an American telecommunications rep posted there; "cover for action"—a midnight meeting with a foreign target in a downtown city and "cover for access." But according to this veteran officer, the whole idea that nonofficial cover could provide substantially more access to a degree that justified the risk was a bit overblown. "Wouldn't it be wonderful if one arrangement actually got you all of it," he said.

In actuality, the former officer argued, NOCs did not always have great advantages of access in some situations. One reason is that in many countries of the world—say Syria—American busi-

---

14 See Louis Boifeuillette, "A Staff Agent's Second Thoughts," *Journal of the Study of Intelligence* 11 (Winter 1967): 61–65.

nesspeople are scrutinized as closely as American government officials. And the private businessperson lacks the benefit of diplomatic status or protection should the foreign government grow suspicious or its internal revenue service take a fine-toothed comb to his or her financial details.

Another is the work required to plausibly maintain and perform one's cover, nongovernmental job. Says a former NOC:

> I have said that toward the end of my tour I had rather too much time on my hands as my cover job petered out. Now this needs some explanation; you may well ask why, if the guy had so little to do in the Hefner office, he didn't go out and develop some agents. The answer is that by and large you cannot do much unless you have a valid reason for seeing a potential agent at his place of work, and this depends on your cover activity. You cannot simply barge into a man's office and start developing him. If you are in the embassy, your chances of manufacturing a valid reason for doing this with respect to a worth-while prospect are much better. But a beer salesman cannot just drop in on a police official, or on someone in the foreign ministry, or on an army officer.[15]

Nevertheless, the program had a bureaucratic momentum, and was beloved by certain Directors and congressmen. "What happened over the years is that these things become bureaucratically optimized," said the veteran intelligence officer. "Over the years, organizations develop methodologies that turn into philosophy."

According to media reports, by the mid-1990s, when Plame was becoming a Nonofficial Cover CIA Officer, the NOC program had several hundred officers around the world, and was growing

---

15 Boifeuillete, "A Staff Agent's Second Thoughts," p. 63.

with the cooperation and recruitment of American companies. "Senior officials from the agency's National Collections Branch have been quietly approaching businesses doing overseas work to ask if they will provide covers for CIA case officers," *Time* magazine reported.[16] "Energy companies, import-export firms, multinational concerns, banks with foreign branches and high-tech corporations are among those being approached. Usually the company president and perhaps another senior officer, such as the general counsel, are the only ones who know of the arrangement. 'The CEOs do it out of a sense of patriotism,' says former deputy CIA Director Bobby Inman."

Robert Dreyfuss wrote, "The Office of External Development also helps identify and recruit U.S. corporations to participate in the NOC program. . . . The CIA first—without the knowledge of the target firm—prepares a detailed profile of the company and its Chief executives. Then the CIA extends quiet feelers to the company's CEO, to gauge the company's willingness to lend its overseas offices to a NOC. Finally, when the CIA is satisfied that the company will be receptive, it makes the pitch."[17] According to the media reports, the companies that agreed to provide covers for NOCs actually got free employees. The NOCs received their usually modest government wages and had to pass their sometimes considerable cover-company salaries to the CIA, which returned them to the companies. The CIA even handled NOCs' tax returns to avoid the complications such dual careers entailed.

Even though the NOC program was seen as increasingly useful to intelligence gathering on the more unconventional threats the Agency found itself facing in the post–Cold War, it also generated a degree of controversy both within and outside the Agency. For

---

16 Elaine Shannon and Douglas Waller, "Spies for the New World Disorder," *Time*, February 20, 1995.
17 Robert Dreyfuss, "Office of Central Cover," *Mother Jones*, January/February 1995.

one, it was significantly more risky, both for the companies whose reputations could be damaged if their employees were exposed as conducting espionage, and for those officers serving as NOCs without diplomatic protection.

NOC officers were far more expensive and logistically complicated to support. "Intelligence officials say that placing NOC officers overseas can be four times as expensive as assigning officers under an embassy cover," *Time* reported. "It can cost the agency as much as $3 million to set up a CIA officer as a corporate exec in Tokyo. Elaborate clandestine communications must be established so the NOC officer can pass his intelligence on to special handlers, who are often based in another country."

The NOC program also generated headaches and controversy within the CIA Division of Operations—and was not always appreciated by Station Chiefs who had to manage dangerous operations while worrying about risk-averse managers and politicians back in Washington. NOCs "require more support than inside operations officers and have different kinds of problems that need solving," writes former CIA officer Melissa Boyle Mahle, in her memoir, *Denial and Deception*.[18] "Because of the high risks the types of activities in which they are involved are more limited. Given the choice between having a full-service operations officer or a super-secret NOC with a limited playbook, Directorate of Operations division managers too frequently choose the easy path. The end result was a lot of underutilized and unhappy NOCs."

Such risk aversion was not unwarranted. In 1995, a Paris operation involving a NOC trying to gather economic intelligence went awry. "The CIA's Paris Station had at least five operatives—four officers posing as diplomats and a woman posing as the Paris representative of a private American foundation working on a two-

---

18 Melissa Boyle Mahle, *Denial and Deception: An Insider's View of the CIA from Iran-Contra to 9/11* (New York: Nation Books, 2004), p. 75.

pronged project," the *New York Times*'s Tim Weiner reported.[19] "They were assigned to uncover French positions on world trade talks and to counter French economic espionage against American companies. The undercover operative posing as a foundation representative made fundamental mistakes: communicating too openly with the CIA Station and communing too secretly with her target, a French official. [Dick] Holm, the Station Chief, found out about the love affair she was conducting with the official. It was clear that the romance could compromise the operation. He and [Joe] DeTrani, his boss as Chief of the Europe division, agonized over whether to abort it. Mr. Holm wanted to carry on, and he convinced his boss. . . . But French counterintelligence officials soon knew that a network of CIA officers was operating against them . . . The operation quickly unraveled." The Paris Station Chief retired while undergoing investigation by the CIA Inspector General.

Plame's Cover

While many of those brought into the NOC program in the mid-1990s were recruited from the outside, including business schools (and were trained in operations elsewhere than at the "Farm," in order to try to protect them from any association with the U.S. government), Plame had a different path. She of course had already served as an embassy-covered CIA case officer in Greece, albeit with a few years of graduate study separating her past from her future.

In an earlier era, CIA operations officers were frequently assigned to pose as businessmen in foreign locales, often with

---

19 Tim Weiner, "CIA Confirms Blunders During Economic Spying on France," *New York Times*, March 3, 1996.

very little time invested in training them for their cover career. "That's the way we used to do it," says one former senior officer. " 'Now you are the rep of a shipping company.' They put you through training and you go. But just because that's the way it used to be doesn't mean it's right."

In Plame's case, proper training was extensive. In October 1993, Plame moved to England to pursue a one-year master's degree at the London School of Economics, studying international politics, finance, and monetary policy. She lived in a furnished one-bedroom apartment in the London neighborhood of Chelsea. "It was beautiful—modest, but lovely," recalls Plame's childhood friend Janet Angstadt, who visited her there. "It was just a lovely setting, with a little flower market to the side. She had a list of things to see in the city, and she had these amazing ideas about what would be fun—open-air markets, untraditional stuff, off the beaten path."

Whether Plame was vetting people she came into contact with in graduate school as possible information-gathering targets, or was just gaining academic training she would need for her future cover, putting time and distance between her past cover work for the U.S. government, isn't totally clear. Former operations officers say the CIA does not send covert agents to gather intelligence on U.S. persons at American universities (although clearly the CIA has helpers at universities who spot potential recruits), but seem to indicate that foreign universities are another matter. One former veteran senior CIA official said that if it had been his call, Plame would have been working as a NOC while attending graduate school, although he does not know if it was the case with Valerie. Diane Plame said she did not know if Valerie was working as a NOC, only that she was in graduate school.

In 1994, after completing her master's degree, Plame returned home to the Philadelphia suburbs to learn French in preparation for studying at the French-language College of Europe in Bruges, Belgium, the following year. To her friend Angstadt, Plame's year at her parents' house seemed like a point of career confusion: "I worried that she had lost her way," Angstadt says. At the time, Angstadt had understood that Plame was on leave from the State Department. "She was saying, 'Everything has changed so much.' She was still talking to the State Department at the time, wondering if she might get something else with them. She kept saying she was waiting for the right assignment, things might come together."

"Actually, I didn't realize it at the time, but she wouldn't always use the name 'State Department'," Angstadt recalls. "She was trying as hard as she could to bring the worlds"—her actual world and her cover world—"together where possible, but there was always this narrow band" where things didn't quite fit, Angstadt says. Sensing occasional discrepancies, Angstadt would sometimes probe, but Plame would deflect such inquiries. "Mostly I was just motivated out of concern," Angstadt says.

Plame moved to Belgium, to study European affairs at the College of Europe for the 1995–1996 school year, and as required she lived in the dorm. In 1996, she moved to nearby Brussels, settling in the second floor of a "stately house on a lovely street," her mother recalls. Her parents came over to help her move in; her father Sam helped her hang her eclectic art collection: watercolors, old maps, architects' drawings of historical places. It was in Brussels that Plame would finally get set on a full-fledged career as a NOC.

It got off to a somewhat comical start. Explaining her new cover position to her friend Angstadt, Plame said she had gotten a job in Brussels with a small North Carolina–based company that sold oil partnerships to people in the United States. Angstadt, a securities lawyer formerly with the Securities and Exchange Commission, thought that what her friend said she would be doing may not be legal. "I told her that I thought she might have to take the Series 7"—a licensing exam for those who sell securities in the United States—"because what she described was possibly, arguably a securities sale." Describing Plame's reaction, Angstadt said, "Miraculously, she just backed away. It was clear that this was not an area where she wanted to go. I always thought that she trained us to be okay with just not asking her questions. She was so private about those things."

"As an energy consultant, her work would have involved attending energy conferences, making contacts with people, identifying folks who may want to provide information," a former CIA colleague of Plame's suggests. "It would have involved spotting and assessing and identifying folks, and then turning them over to someone under official cover who would make the pitch. By establishing that cover in that industry, it would have allowed her to move into a whole arena without the specter of the government hanging over you." Those who say it wasn't useful cover "probably didn't know what she was doing," he added.

"I will say this," former CIA and National Security Council official Bruce Riedel observes. "I have looked at the part of her CV that is in the open domain. The Agency spent an awful lot of effort building a really good cover for this person. A lot of effort. People who say this was not a covert operative don't understand what they're saying. This was intended to be a nonofficial-cover person who would have the credentials to be a very serious operative. The damage done to the mission of the organization by exposing her, and how cover is built, is pretty serious."

After Plame's cover was blown six years later, media reports indicated that she had identified her employer in a campaign donation filing as Brewster-Jennings & Associates, an apparent front company. Its address was a twenty-one-story downtown Boston office building, but a company by that name had no visible presence there. "A spokeswoman for Dun & Bradstreet Inc., a New Jersey operator of commercial databases, said Brewster-Jennings was first entered into its records on May 22, 1994, but wouldn't discuss the source of the filing," the *Boston Globe* reported.[20] "Its records list the company at 101 Arch St. as a 'legal services office,' which could mean a law firm, with annual sales of $60,000, one employee, and a Chief executive listed as 'Victor Brewster, Partner."

In fact, according to later reports, Brewster-Jennings may have had its own front company at that location. "Although this has been erased from almost all databases, Brewster-Jennings once did share an address and phone number with the accounting firm Burke Dennehy in the same building," *Indy Media* reported.

Real estate developer Brewster Jennings, of Durango, Colorado, the grandson of the president of a predecessor company to Exxon Mobil Corporation, denied to the *Globe* any connection to any CIA front company. "Since the firm was named as a CIA front, he's heard from many friends and family members who 'find tremendous humor in all of this,' " the *Globe* reported.

More telling, former CIA counterterrorism Chief Vince Cannistraro explained to the *Globe*, "When operating undercover outside the United States, Plame would have had a real job with a more legitimate company. The Boston company 'is not an indicator of what she did overseas,' [Cannistraro] said."

In other words, though Plame listed herself as an analyst at Brewster-Jennings & Associates for U.S. legal filing purposes, and

---

20 Ross Kerber and Bryan Bender, "Apparent CIA Front Didn't Offer Much Cover," *Boston Globe*, October 10, 2003.

told her friend Angstadt, for instance, that that was the name of the company she was working for, the company Plame worked for while in Europe was likely a different and a real company.

On a visit to see Plame in Brussels in 1997, Angstadt recalls sitting in Plame's apartment, talking about the future. "What I remember so vividly . . . is talking about who we want to meet, what we wanted our lives to look like. I had never heard her speak so clearly about who she was looking for. She said, 'I would like him to be older, having had some success in life, and very worldly, having lived in Europe.' I said, 'Okay,' " Angstadt laughs. "Okay. All this is possible for you. For the whole trip, we were joking about it. 'How about that guy over there?' It's a little spooky to have such a strong memory."

By all accounts, Plame enjoyed living in Brussels and Europe, but was growing disillusioned with an increasingly distracted Agency.

A Post–Cold War CIA Adrift

Plame's career doubts came as a deepening malaise gripped the Agency in the wake of the Cold War. The CIA was struggling to re-define its purpose in the new era. Former CIA officer Mahle describes the mood in her memoir. "Now that the Cold War mission had been removed, what was the CIA to do? . . . Everyday when CIA officers got up and went to work . . . they asked this million-dollar question: What is the mission? What am I supposed to do today, tomorrow, for the duration of the assignment? And does anybody out there really care?"[21]

---

21 Mahle, *Denial and Deception: An Insider's View of the CIA from Iran-Contra to 9/11* (New York: Nation Books, 2004), p. 75.

The Langley, Virginia, CIA Headquarters that Plame had returned to from Greece in 1992 was under the helm of Robert Gates. Despite the fact that he was the only CIA analyst to rise through the ranks to become its Director,[22] he was not widely admired by Agency hands at the time, according to some former CIA officers, in part because of the perception that he was willing to shape intelligence analysis—in particular regarding the Soviet threat—to please his client in the White House.[23] It is perhaps testament to the profound drift and disillusion that gripped the post–Cold War Agency at the time of Plame's return from Greece that in Gates's memoir, *From the Shadows*, his chapter on winning the epic struggle with the Soviet Union is titled "A Joyless Victory."

"Because the Cold War itself had been waged in shades of gray, there was little definition or sharpness to its conclusion," Gates wrote. "Did we win or did the Soviets just lose? Or was it both? . . . And so the greatest of American triumphs . . . became a peculiarly joyless victory. We had won the Cold War, but there would be no parade."

America's first baby boomer president, Bill Clinton, appointed James Woolsey, a hawkish arms control negotiator, to be CIA

---

22 Former CIA case officer Porter Goss, who served in Latin America, the Caribbean, Mexico, Miami, and London in the 1960s, would become George W. Bush's CIA Director from 2004 until 2006. But he left the CIA in the early 1970s and went into politics, serving as mayor of Sanibel, Florida, and from 1988 until 2004, in the House of Representatives. From 1997 until 2004, he served as chairman of the House Permanent Select Committee on Intelligence. Goss brought over a staff, described by many as highly partisan, with him from Congress to Langley, who got into disputes that caused several senior operations officers to quit, and few serving CIA officers described Goss as one of them.

23 See Daniel Schulman, "CIA Veteran: How Robert Gates Cooked the Intelligence," *Mother Jones*, December 4, 2006.

Director. By all accounts, it was a terrible fit. According to Woolsey, he had only two private face-to-face meetings with Clinton for the two years he served as DCI until he resigned in 1995.[24] (Over the next several years, Woolsey became among the most ardent, high-profile advocates for toppling Saddam Hussein, and a champion of Iraqi exile leader Ahmad Chalabi, who, with his stable of defectors, made fantastic and later discredited claims about Iraq weapons of mass destruction and Hussein's ties to Al Qaeda.)

Woolsey's successor, former MIT chemical engineering professor John Deutsch, would only last a year and a half at the helm. While credited with instituting task forces and reforms to make the Agency less of a boys' club where it was difficult for women and minorities to advance,[25] Deutsch's term would end grimly in 1996, amid a security investigation probing allegations that he mishandled classified information by storing it on a home computer. He reportedly surfed the Internet from the same computer, potentially making the information vulnerable to foreign intelligence services. Clinton pardoned Deutsch, sparing him from possible criminal charges.

Some measure of stability at the top of the Agency would only be restored with the 1997 confirmation of George Tenet, an affable, Queens-born Greek-American. A former Senate Intelligence Committee staffer, he would serve until 2004, becoming the second-longest-serving DCI after Allen Dulles.

•   •   •

---

24 See James Risen, *State of War* (New York: Free Press, 2006), pp. 5–7.
25 See Stan Crock, "Nora Slatkin's Mission Impossible," *BusinessWeek*, September 1996.

For officers such as Plame working at Headquarters and in the field, the revolving door of DCIs, the perception of neglect by the White House, and institutional malaise and doubts about its core mission were felt in slashed budgets, reduced staff, managerial distractedness, and plummeting morale. As Plame writes, "We were knocking, but no one was home."

4. WORKING IN THE "ISLAND OF MISFIT TOYS" (1997–2000)

As the Agency struggled to right itself in the midst of a revolving door of directors, low morale, and changing national security challenges, Plame was ordered home from Brussels for meetings.

In 1997, only a year into the job, she was called back to the United States and invited to work in a new Counterproliferation Division in the Directorate of Operations, and, according to associates, it is true that she was one of the recruits handpicked by the Division Chief. But according to her mother, a more immediate reason, or at least the one that she was told at the time, was concern that Plame might be among the officers betrayed to the Russians by traitor Aldrich Ames, a senior CIA official who spied for the Russians for nine years before he was finally caught in 1994. "She had been brought back by the Agency," remembered Diane Plame. "They were afraid her name was on the list. She was so crushed, so down, that after all she had been trained for and loved, now they were bringing her back."

Whether Plame's profile was actually among those Ames betrayed to the Russians does not seem to have ever been determined. According to former intelligence officials, before Ames was caught, he sat on a CIA promotions board and had access to the files, although not the real names, of all the Nonofficial Covered Officers working at the civil service rank of General Service-12 ["GS-12"] who were being considered for promotion to the GS-13 level.[26] "He didn't have their real names, but he had the files, and where they were," said a former intelligence officer. The Chief of the Office of External Development, which ran the NOC program, "could never establish what [Ames] gave to the Russians. He never told, or couldn't remember."

CNN reported that in 1995 closed testimony to Congress, then CIA Director John Deutsch acknowledged that "Ames compromised more than 100 U.S. spies. Ten were executed. Others fell under the control of the KGB. The controlled agents were used by the Soviets to feed selective information to the CIA, which then went to key policy members, including the president."[27] In addition, "weird stuff," according to a former Operations Officer, turned up in places for years that caused consternation at the Agency that it might have been information passed from Ames to the Russians that was only later being digested or acted upon. "It's like that warehouse at the end of *Raiders of the Lost Ark,*" the former officer said of the information Ames had given to the Russians. It sometimes took years for evidence of something Ames had turned over to the Russians to channel its way to some Agency liaison and cause the CIA embarrassment, if not worse.

• • •

---

26 The "General Service" rankings outline the experience, qualifications, and education required, and salary range for federal civil servants, as determined by the U.S. Office of Personnel Management.

27 James McIntyre, "Ames' damage to U.S. said 'mind-boggling,' " CNN, October 31, 1995.

The trip home for Plame led to one fateful and happy development. "The weekend she had come back," Diane Plame recalls, "a friend of hers she had met over there, a Turkish girl, got her to go to the Turkish embassy for some big affair. And she and Joe spotted each other."

Joseph C. Wilson IV was a former U.S. ambassador to Gabon, and, as acting U.S. ambassador in Iraq, was the last American diplomat to have met with Saddam Hussein. At the time he met Valerie, he was working as a political adviser to General George Joulwan, the commander of U.S. European Command forces stationed in Stuttgart, Germany.[28] He was in Washington to attend an American Turkish Council reception being held at the Turkish ambassador's residence, one of the most splendid buildings in Washington, in advance of an awards ceremony the next day to honor U.S. troops serving in Bosnia.

Wilson recalls the night he met Plame at the reception as almost surreally enchanting. "There's this ornate center staircase that goes upstairs to the reception area. I am standing on one side of the room, and I am literally making my last run around the room . . . and I looked across the room, and saw this beautiful blond. And quite literally, the noise of 300 people around me went dead. All the people disappeared. All I could see was this great big smile, and she kind of floated across the room. I was thinking, I must know her, where do I know her from? She gets right up next to me, and I realize, I don't know her," but by then, he had literally fallen in love.

At the time, Wilson was forty-seven and in the process of divorcing his French wife, and Plame was thirty-three. They exchanged business cards—he won't reveal the name of the company on her card, except to say she was listed on it as a "vice

---

28 See Joseph Wilson, *The Politics of Truth: Inside the Lies That Led to War and Betrayed My Wife's CIA Identity* (New York: Carroll & Graf, 2004).

president" with international responsibilities. "She told me she was an energy executive living in Brussels," he says.

Plame returned to Brussels to "finish up and get her things straightened away," her mother recalls. Wilson returned to Stuttgart.

A few weeks later after, she e-mailed him with the subject line, "Mr. Ambassador." And they arranged to go out to dinner when he had NATO business in Brussels. As their relationship quickly progressed, Plame and Wilson soon realized that the relationship was serious and they had a future together. "We thought we were meant for each other," Wilson says. "Valerie was something of a prude, and before she was prepared to move the relationship to another level, she wanted to make sure I wouldn't be freaked out and scared away by what she really did. She said, 'I have to tell you something.' And she was really nervous about it," he recalls. " 'I work for the CIA.' "

She had never told anyone whom she really worked for except her immediate family.

"My response was, 'All I really care about: is your name really Valerie?' " She affirmed that it was.

Later in 1997, both Plame and Wilson moved to Washington, Wilson to serve as Clinton's senior Africa adviser at the National Security Council, and Plame to take up her job at the Agency's Counterproliferation Division. Together they moved into an apartment at the Watergate, and were married April 3, 1998, at the District of Columbia courthouse, with her mother and father as witnesses.

CPD

Plame aptly describes the CIA Counterproliferation Division as an "island of misfit toys." According to a former senior CIA manager, other Directorate of Operations officers viewed the new functional centers such as the Counterproliferation Division (CPD) and its counterpart, the Counterterrorism Center (CTC), which were created in the 1990s to deal with emerging unconventional threats, as bureaucratic upstarts that upset the traditional geographical-based division structure they were accustomed to. According to the former senior CIA manager, those who worked in CPD were "a group of zealots" whose international operations caused complications for far-flung CIA officers. CPD officers' missions interloped into their territories on occasion. Plame readily acknowledged such tensions. "The older divisions eyed CPD with deep suspicion and distrust," she writes.

The CPD's founder and first Chief was James Pavitt, a nattily dressed St. Louis–born CIA Operations Officer who had been a Station Chief in Luxembourg, Branch Chief in the Africa Division, and had worked at the NSC under Brent Scowcroft, who was George H. W. Bush's national security adviser. Pavitt had a reputation as something of a ladies' man who liked to be surrounded with beautiful women, associates recall. After his tour in the first Bush White House, Pavitt was assigned in 1993 to work across the agency operational/analytical divide, in the Non-Proliferation Center in the Directorate of Intelligence—the CIA's analytical side. President Clinton was increasingly pushing the Agency to make tracking and countering the threat of nuclear, chemical, and biological weapons proliferation a top priority. While working at the DI's Non-Proliferation Center, Pavitt got the idea of starting his own nonproliferation center in the Directorate of Operations— a concept vigorously opposed by the then Chief of the DI's center, Gordon Oehler, as redundant and stepping on his turf. But the idea drew support from Tenet, who had preceded Pavitt as an intelligence adviser on the National Security Council.

Clinton believed that "we needed to be doing more covert action to be more aggressive on counterproliferation," said the former agency manager. "He was rightly very worried about proliferation. Jim made the case to Tenet. . . . And Gordon Oehler was furious. The DI guys fought it." But Pavitt prevailed.

So with the go-ahead of his bosses, Pavitt set to work hand-picking operations officers, some of whom had been unhappy in their previous assignments for various reasons. And not uncontroversially, he decided to include Nonofficial Covered Officers (NOCs) such as Plame.

"Jim knew Valerie because he was in the Europe office and she was in the Europe office," the former officer said. "He brought over a whole crew of people, some of whom had been unhappy in their jobs, and gave them jobs and they were super loyal to him. They were raring to go and wanted to show the rest of the people [at the Agency] that they were just as good as they were. . . . He created a corps of people."

From the outset, one of Pavitt's first decisions provoked consternation among senior Agency management. "There was a big debate in 1996 about the use of NOCs in CPD," the former officer said. Until then, NOCs had been controlled by their own division, the Office of External Development. "But Jim didn't want to have to deal with [the Chief of OED], he wanted to have his own NOCs. And there was this huge bitter bureaucratic fight, and again, Jim carried the day because of his relationship with Tenet."

The CPD "cooked up all these odd ideas," the former officer said. "Occasionally, one of them would work."

Despite upsetting the standard ways of doing business at the Agency Directorate of Operations, the CPD would have at least one spectacular success—in 2003, it took down the nuclear black market network of A. Q. Khan.

Taking Down A. Q. Khan

Abdul Qadeer Khan, a European-educated, Pakistani metallurgist with a Ph.D., took a job in the 1970s with a Dutch subsidiary of

URENCO, an international consortium that developed advanced centrifuge technology for nuclear energy programs. "Almost immediately after starting to work [at URENCO, Khan] began making trips inside the secret centrifuge plant by himself, acquiring an inside understanding of the secret technology," writes Gordon Corera in his book on the Khan network, *Shopping for Bombs*. By 1974, he was offering himself as a nuclear spy to the Pakistani prime minister:

> Khan embarked on his life as a spy in the autumn on 1974. . . . He wrote a letter . . . to [Pakistan's] Prime Minister Zulfikar Ali Bhutto . . . that he should consider the enrichment route to developing fissile nuclear material for a bomb, that he had the know-how to accomplish it, and that he wanted to return [to Pakistan] to help. . . . Back in the Netherlands by the end of 1974, Khan's work as a stealer of secrets became increasingly bold. . . . By 1975 Khan had access to the information that would become the basis of his career as . . . an international proliferator. He stole the designs for almost every centrifuge on the drawing board.[29]

By 1976, Khan had become the head of Pakistan's secret nuclear weapons program, working out of a secret facility in Kahuta, which Pakistan later named in honor of him. Meantime, a variety of events was contributing to the rapid proliferation of covert nuclear programs in several countries, and demand grew for a black market supplier willing to sell designs for uranium enrichment and centrifuge technology, and for someone to serve as a middleman on the necessary components and equipment.

---

29 Gordon Corera, *Shopping for Bombs* (New York: Oxford University Press, 2006), pp. 8–15.

After leading Pakistan's efforts to get a bomb, Khan would serve as a "one-man proliferator. . . . For decades he had made a personal fortune by selling high-tech nuclear components to Libya and North Korea, among others," Plame writes. But it would take decades for the CIA to understand fully the extent of his activities.

Although by 1979, Khan was on the CIA's radar as a top official in Pakistan's covert nuclear weapons program, anticommunism trumped antiproliferation in the Reagan era, Corera reports, as the United States and the CIA worked closely with the Pakistani leadership and security and intelligence services to supply arms covertly to mujahideen forces fighting the Soviets in Afghanistan.

It was only in the "latter half of the 1990s," Corera writes, that "the CIA and [British security agency] MI6 decided to aggressively target the Khan network and see what could be discovered. . . . The small trans-Atlantic team working on Khan centered its strategy on firstly identifying the key members of his business network and then gaining as much intelligence on their activities as possible. . . . The old fashioned recruitment of spies was at the heart of the breaking of the A. Q. Khan network. According to a former head of the CIA's clandestine service, it took a 'patient, decade-long operation involving multimillion dollar recruitment pitches, covert entries, ballet-like sophistication and a level of patience we are often accused of not possessing' to first track and then break Khan."[30]

This is confirmed by Tenet's account:

> . . . A.Q. Khan's nuclear proliferation network was a project we focused on during my entire seven-year tenure as

---

30 Corera, *Shopping for Bombs*, pp. 155–56.

DCI. Our efforts against this organization were among the closest held secrets within the Agency. . . .

In the late 1900s, the section within CIA's Counterproliferation Division (CPD) in charge of this effort was run by a career intelligence officer who once told me that as a child, the officer read a book on the bombing of Hiroshima and was awestruck by the devastation that a nuclear bomb could deliver. . . .

The small unit working this effort recognized that it would be impossible to penetrate proliferation networks using conventional intelligence-gathering tactics. Security considerations do not permit to describe the techniques we used.

Patiently, we put ourselves in a position to come into contact with individuals and organizations that we believed were part of the overall proliferation problem. As is so often the case, our colleagues in British intelligence joined us in our efforts and were critically important in working against this target.

We discovered the extent of Khan's hidden network, which stretched from Pakistan, to Europe, to Middle East, to Asia. We pieced together a picture of the organization, revealing its subsidiaries, scientists, front companies, agents, finances and manufacturing plants. Our spies gained access through a series of daring operations over several years.

What we learned from our operations was extraordinary. We confirmed that Khan was delivering to his customers such things as illicit uranium centrifuges.[31]

---

31 George Tenet with Bill Harlow, *At the Center of the Storm* (New York: HarperCollins, 2007), p. 283.

Amid the investigation of Khan's global activities, the CIA learned of reports in the late 1990s that Khan had, among his world travels, made three visits to Africa, including to the tiny impoverished nation of Niger—whose biggest export is uranium. As Corera reported:

> The details of three trips to Africa between 1998 and 2000 have emerged in an unusual way. Before his proliferation activities were well known, one of Khan's friends, Abdul Siddiqui, a London-based accountant, wrote a memoir-cum travelogue that reveals unique details of where Khan went and who accompanied him. . . . The only hint that Siddiqui gives of a nuclear aspect to the trips comes in a single line. "Niger has big uranium deposits." . . . Could Khan have been looking for supplies for the network as part of his plans to offer a full-spectrum service?[32]

The CIA wanted to find out. And as Plame alludes in her chapter, she shared an office with the group leading the effort. "I shared my quarters, dubbed the 'secret squirrel den'—complete with the rare and much coveted windows—with a small group of people devoted to tracking and bringing down the A. Q. Khan nuclear proliferation network." At the time, Plame's husband Wilson had recently set up his own consulting business, with a focus on advising clients interested in investing in Africa, his foreign policy specialty after having served as a diplomat in Africa for years, and most recently, as Clinton's senior director of African affairs at the National Security Council. Wilson was planning to make a business trip to Africa. So the CIA asked Wilson, as they occasionally do of businessmen, and Wilson agreed, to report back to them what he could find out about Khan's trip to Niger.

---

32 Corera, *Shopping for Bombs*, pp. 132–34.

Wilson's 1999 trip to Niger on behalf of the CIA was first revealed by the Senate Select Committee on Intelligence in its 2004 report on prewar intelligence:

Wilson "had traveled previously to Niger on the CIA's behalf [redacted]. The former ambassador was selected for the 1999 trip after his wife mentioned to her supervisors that her husband was planning a business trip to Niger in the near future and might be willing to use his contacts in the region [redacted]. Because the former ambassador did not uncover any information about [redacted] during this visit to Niger, CPD did not distribute an intelligence report on the visit."[33]

It is most likely that the last redaction refers to Khan. Wilson himself did not reveal the 1999 trip to Niger in his diplomatic memoir—presumably, although he hasn't said this explicitly, because the CIA asked him to sign some sort of confidentiality agreement.

Even after the Senate Intelligence Committee released details of his 1999 trip for the first time, Wilson wouldn't speak about it, and referred to public accounts. Pierced together from those, the story is this: in 1999, the CIA asked Wilson in the context of another trip he was going to make to Africa to stop in Niger and look into a uranium-related question.

The CIA has a unit, the National Resources Division (NR), whose mission is to ask certain trusted, non-Agency employees— the CEO of an oil company, for instance, or, in the case of Wilson, a business consultant with frequent travel to and knowledge of West Africa—to brief the Agency on some matter or make a dis-

---

33 "Report of the Select Committee on Intelligence on the U.S. Intelligence Community's Prewar Intelligence Assessments on Iraq," Congressional Report, July 7, 2004, p. 39.

creet inquiry as part of a foreign business trip they are planning, as a kind of voluntary, patriotic courtesy. The NR Division handles such contacts and information requests and exchange. "This activity has been going on for a long time," a CIA official who requested that he not be named explained. "If an American businessman has visited another place or country, if they want to talk," they work through the National Resources Division, an outgrowth of the Cold War Domestic Collection Division.

Public reports detailed above show the Agency was concerned about Khan's trips to Niger and West Africa. "The concern was 'what was he up to? Where was he going?' " a source familiar with the Khan inquiry says.

But according to the Senate Intelligence Committee report and Gordon Corera, Wilson did not find evidence that Khan's trip to Niger had anything to do with uranium. "Wilson toured around the dusty streets and asked around the relatively small community of Niamey if anyone had seen a party traveling through," Corera writes.[34] "Wilson talked to local politicians, taxi drivers, and anyone else who might have spotted the group. But the trip turned up a blank and no CIA report was written based on it." The Senate Intelligence Committee report said something slightly different: not that the CIA hadn't produced a report about Wilson's trip, but that it hadn't distributed it. "Because the former ambassador did not uncover any information about" Khan "during this visit to Niger, CPD did not distribute an intelligence report on the visit," the Senate Intelligence Committee said.

In fact, apparently some sort of contract or documentation on Wilson's 1999 Niger trip did exist. And it had a detail that apparently later caught the eye of the office of Vice President Cheney.

CIA documents made public during the 2007 trial of former

---

34 Corera, *Shopping for Bombs*, p. 134.

vice presidential chief of staff I. Lewis "Scooter" Libby revealed something striking.[35] According to Jeff Lomonaco, co-editor of the collected proceedings of the Libby trial, *The United States v. I. Lewis Libby*, "In the spring of 2003, the CIA is saying there were two streams of reporting on Niger-Iraq, and one came from a sensitive source who had traveled to Niger in early 2002, i.e., Joseph Wilson." In June, the Office of the Vice President got this information and quickly identified the unnamed sensitive source as Wilson. But by July, Libby had also evidently learned of Wilson's 1999 trip to Niger, jotting down a note "Khan + Wilson" on the very same page as his note indicating the vice president was telling him to talk to Judith Miller of the *New York Times*— the very meeting at which he would disclose that Wilson's wife worked at the CIA.[36]

Indeed, Libby's notes from around July 8, 2003 indicated that Cheney asked him about an alleged attempted purchase of uranium from Niger by A. Q. Khan.[37] Court testimony indicated that around the time of the query and Libby's "Khan + Wilson" note, Libby consulted with the Office of the Vice President's then legal adviser David Addington about what kind of documentation would exist if the spouse of a CIA official performed a fact-finding mission for the Agency, and about whether the president had the right to automatically authorize the disclosure of classified in-

---

35 See Libby trial defense exhibit 64, declassified CIA background paper/notification to House Permanent Select Committee on Intelligence, "[redacted] Purported Iraqi Attempts to Get Uranium from Niger," April 3, 2003 (http://wid.ap.org/documents/libby trial/jan24/DX64.pdf).

36 See Libby trial Government Exhibit 2A, 178aT, p. 62, "Khan + Wilson," www.usdoj .gov/usao/iln/osc/exhibits/0207/GX2A.pdf.

37 See Libby's notes from July 8, 2003, and Libby grand jury testimony March 24, 2004, Government Exhibit 2A, p. 62, www.usdoj.gov/usao/iln/osc/exhibits/0207/ GX2A.pdf, and Libby defense exhibit 178A, www.gwu.edu/~nsarchiv/NSAEBB/NSAE BB215/def_ex/DX178A.pdf, and 178AT www.gwu.edu/~nsarchiv/NSAEBB/NSAEBB 215/def_ex/DX178AT.pdf.

formation. The implication is that the vice president and his aide may have been mulling the legal risk of leaking classified information including both Plame's identity and CIA documents concerning Wilson's 1999 trip to Niger concerning A. Q. Khan— presumably in order to suggest that Wilson's wife had a possible role in sending him on the earlier trip, and by extension, who she was, and where she worked. In other words, to bolster the Office of the Vice President's claim that Wilson was not credible because, as they alleged, the reason he got the mission was because his wife Plame was sending him on a CIA "junket."

It would appear that though Wilson would make at least two trips on behalf of the Agency to Niger, in 1999 and 2002, and would conclude both times that concerns about uranium getting into rogue hands were not supported by the evidence, elements of the CIA and the White House would draw a different conclusion: that details in at least one of the CIA reports based on Wilson's trips did provide hints that Iraq was seeking uranium in Niger. At the very least, the Office of the Vice President found ammunition in both episodes for pushing back against Wilson.

MERLIN

Although the CPD enjoyed such successes as the campaign to take down A. Q. Khan, it also appears to have had some spectacular disasters.

Valerie writes in her chapter on the Counterproliferation Division: "I found that I thrived amidst the patriotic zeal and a renewed sense of mission. . . . This effort was enormous and required a cast of sometimes bizarre agents called upon to play a specific role in hopes of luring our target closer to our objective. . . . Actually, it was just these sorts of sudden detours and reverses that made operations fascinating for me. Being able to think on your feet and acknowledge that Murphy's Law lurked everywhere were critical to success. Being prepared with Plan B was always a good idea, as was strictly adhering to security practices. . . . With such an ambitious mandate and strong support from management, CPD ops officers quickly developed several cunning operations designed to infiltrate procurement networks and wreak havoc. With high esprit de corps, there was plenty of good-natured competition to see who could come up with the most creative and effective operations." (pages 83–86)

One place where CPD's ambitious mandate, creative approach, and cast of "bizarre agents" may have met with Murphy's Law was described by journalist James Risen in his book, *State of War.* The startling operation Risen revealed was called Operation MERLIN and it involved the CPD having a former Russian nuclear engineer pose as an out-of-work former Russian nuclear engineer willing to sell nuclear secrets to the highest bidder. The plan was to have the scientist sell the Iranians blueprints for Russian nuclear weapons that had been altered by American nuclear scientists working at Sandia National Laboratories in New Mexico, Risen reported. The idea of MERLIN, according to *State of War,* was that the Iranians would spend years building a nuclear weapon from the flawed CIA-provided designs that, when tested, wouldn't work.

The problem, as Risen revealed it, is that the Russian scientist immediately recognized that the blueprints had flaws, but couldn't get his CIA handlers to explain why. And he was concerned about whether the CIA was trying to set him up. In a panic, he ended up writing a letter informing the Iranian Mission to the IAEA in Vienna that the enclosed blueprints he was delivering had a design flaw. In one stroke, he had not only undermined the whole point of the operation, but potentially solved Iran's technical difficulties with parts of its alleged weapons program.

Risen says the reckless operation was born out of frustration. "The Counterproliferation Division . . . came up with MERLIN and other clandestine operations as creative, if unorthodox, ways to try to penetrate Tehran's nuclear development program," Risen writes.[38] "None are known to have worked."

Further suggestions that during Valerie's tenure CPD operations targeted Iran emerged during the Libby investigation. On May 1, 2006, MSNBC correspondent David Shuster reported that "Intelligence sources say Valerie Wilson was part of an operation three years ago tracking the proliferation of nuclear weapons material into Iran. And the sources allege that when Mrs. Wilson's cover was blown, the administration's ability to track Iran's nuclear ambitions was damaged as well."[39]

---

38 Risen, *State of War,* p. 208.
39 "Hardball with Chris Matthews," NBC, May 1, 2006.

5. THE ROAD TO IRAQ (2001–2003)

Returning to the Agency in April 2001, after a year at home following the birth of her twin son and daughter, and now going by her married name, Valerie Wilson was one of two CIA operations officers assigned to work in the Iraq branch of the Counterproliferation Division (CPD). According to several published accounts and her own, Wilson's job involved a high degree of covert operational responsibility coordinating the CPD's operations, using NOC Case Officers to recruit Iraqi graduate students, scientists, and businessmen suspected of securing equipment for Iraq's suspected unconventional weapons programs. The CPD also attempted to recruit the occasional foreign agent from among Washington's liaison intelligence services who could help illuminate the larger picture. A parallel effort run by the CIA National Resources Division sought the cooperation of U.S.-based relatives of senior Iraqi officials and scientists, to collect information on suspected programs from their relatives in Iraq.

Valerie's task took on even greater urgency as the Bush White House determined to take the war on terror to Saddam Hussein's Iraq after the September 11, 2001, Al Qaeda attacks on the

World Trade Center and the Pentagon. Numerous published accounts detail that shortly after September 11, Valerie Wilson was made the Chief of Operations of the Iraq branch of the CIA's Counterproliferation Division. As the United States moved closer to war, Wilson's CPD Iraq branch was designated the "Joint Task Force on Iraq." As she writes, "I coordinated our approaches to ... scientists worldwide, scheduled polygraph exams to test the authenticity of some of the outlandish claims we heard, and continuously conferred with our targeting and reports officers as well as our resident experts."

As Valerie Wilson was consumed with overseeing operations to collect and ascertain intelligence on Iraq's suspected WMD programs, the CIA received reports in October 2001 and again in February 2002 from the Italian military intelligence service, SISMI, that it had evidence that Iraq had contracted to purchase five hundred tons of unprocessed raw "yellowcake" uranium from Niger. The Italian reports were later determined to be based on crude forgeries that had been circulated by a former Italian *carabinieri* turned intelligence peddler with close ties to the Italian intelligence service.[40] Though elements of the CIA and the State Department Intelligence and Research Bureau were skeptical of the Italian report from the outset—not least because Niger's uranium mines were controlled by a French consortium, because the procedure required to transport five hundred tons of uranium would be impossible to go undetected, and because Iraq did not have the ability to process the yellowcake at the time and already had 550 tons of uranium in storage under International Atomic

---

40 For a comprehensive account of the Niger forgeries, see Peter Eisner and Knut Royce, *The Italian Letter: How the Bush Administration Used a Fake Letter to Build the Case for War in Iraq* (New York: Rodale Press, 2007).

Energy Agency seal—the report caught the attention of the Office of the Vice President, which asked the CIA to check into what it thought might be evidence that Iraq was seeking to reconstitute its nuclear program. Indeed, Valerie Wilson describes the highly unusual degree to which the Office of the Vice President reached deep down into her Division to inquire about the report. As she writes:

> One dreary day in February 2002, a young and capable officer rushed into my office. Normally somewhat reserved and calm . . . looked unusually animated and alarmed. She hurriedly told me that "someone from the vice president's office" had called her green secure line. Apparently, the caller, a staffer, said they were intrigued by an intelligence report that the Italian . . . government had passed to the U.S. government. . . . I was momentarily nonplussed that someone from the vice president's office had reached down into the junior working levels of the Agency to discuss or find an answer to an intelligence report. In my experience, I had never known that to happen. There were strict protocols and procedures for funneling intelligence to policy-makers or fielding their questions. Whole offices within the Agency were set up and devoted to doing just that. A call to a random Desk Officer might get the policy-maker a quick answer in the heat of the moment, but it was also a recipe for trouble. . . .
>
> However, I quickly shook off my surprise and turned to solving the problem presented to us. . . .
>
> . . . A midlevel Reports Officer who had joined the discussion in the hallway enthusiastically suggested: "What about talking to Joe about it?" He knew of Joe's history and role in the first Gulf War, his extensive experience in Africa, and also that in 1999 the CIA had sent Joe on a sensitive

mission to Africa on uranium issues. . . . I was far from keen on the idea, but we needed to respond to the vice president's office with something other than a lame and obviously unacceptable "We don't know, sorry." The Reports Officer and I walked over to the office of the . . . Chief to discuss our available plans of action. Bob, our boss, listened carefully and then suggested we put together a meeting with Joe and the appropriate Agency and State officers.

As the Wilson account indicates, Joseph Wilson understood that his trip was prompted by the interest of the vice president. But according to documents released during the Libby trial, Cheney claims he was not aware at the time that the CIA had sent someone—or of whom they had sent—to follow up on his request for more information. However, according to the Senate Select Committee on Intelligence "Phase I" report on prewar intelligence, Cheney was told on February 14, 2002, that the CIA was looking to clarify the Niger information, and were working with their clandestine sources to do so.[41]

So, after agreeing to undertake the pro bono mission (only Wilson's travel expenses were paid by the CIA), and consulting with the State Department, Wilson flew to Niger in late February 2002, where he met with former Nigerois officials, businessmen, Western expatriates, and other contacts over the course of an eight-day fact-finding mission.[42] Within hours of his return, two

---

41 The SSCI Phase I report mentions a Senior Publish When Ready document that the CIA sent back to Cheney on February 14, 2002, after getting the tasking from the briefer the day before. Furthermore, Cheney followed up, at least once in early March, to ask if they had any more information, and was almost certainly told they were debriefing a source that very day. An update was sent to his briefer with that information, according to the SSCI Phase I report.

42 For a detailed account of Wilson's trip to Niger, see his diplomatic memoir, *The Politics of Truth* (New York: Carroll & Graf, 2004).

CIA officers, including the Reports Officer who had originally suggested Joe's name for the mission, came to his home to debrief him. Valerie ordered Chinese takeout for the group and then left them alone. Wilson told his CIA debriefers that it was highly doubtful that such a uranium transaction had taken place, and outlined the reasons why: the mines were controlled by a French consortium, the transfer and shipment of five hundred tons of uranium yellowcake through the Sahara desert would have been impossible to conceal, the French consortium would have had to be complicit, and Niger's uranium was under a high degree of oversight. He also mentioned that a former Niger official told him of a meeting with an Iraqi delegation that had taken place on the sidelines of an Organization of African Unity conference held in Algiers in 1999. Former Niger prime minister Ibrahim Mayaki was approached by a West African businessman, Baraka, who asked him if he would be willing to meet with the Iraqi group, and Mayaki told Wilson that he remembers being worried at the time that the Iraqi delegation's interest in meeting with him might possibly have to do with uranium. But when they met, the issue never came up in the meeting, so there was no story, Mayaki told Wilson, and Wilson conveyed this to the CIA.[43] Wilson additionally said that "while I was satisfied personally that there was nothing to support allegations either that Iraq had tried to obtain or had succeeded in purchasing uranium from Niger, if there was inter-

---

43 In January 2004, Wilson revealed in his The Politics of Truth, he and his Niger contact (Mayaki) had a conversation in which the Niger contact said he remembered who led the Iraqi delegation. "He told me that while he was watching coverage of press conferences in Baghdad prior to the second Gulf War, he recognized the Iraqi information minister, Mohammad Saeed al-Sahaf, known to Americans as 'Baghdad Bob,' as the person whom he had met in Algiers. He had not known the name of the Iraqi at the time he told me about the conversation in 2002, and so this had not been included in my report" (p. 28).

est in investigating the matter further, my suggestion was simple: approach the French uranium company, COGEMA."[44]

The CIA wrote a report based on Wilson's findings, and distributed it on March 8, 2002. As Valerie writes, "There is a standard procedure for distributing [such reports] to all the government departments that have intelligence components, such as the State Department [INR, NSA], the Pentagon, and the overseas military commands. All of us had every reason to believe that their finished report would indeed be sent to the vice president's office as part of the established protocol." Former CIA Director George Tenet has said that the report on the CIA's unnamed sensitive source's findings got normal and wide distribution in the intelligence and policy community, although Cheney was apparently traveling at the time it was distributed, and Cheney's CIA briefer did not apparently mention it directly to him.[45]

Nevertheless, the CIA firmly warned the White House against citing the Iraq-Niger claims at other points, and at the highest levels. In October 2002, Tenet himself urged Deputy National Security Adviser Stephen Hadley and then national security adviser Condoleezza Rice to remove from a planned October 7 speech by Bush in Cincinnati a reference to Iraq seeking uranium in Niger, saying the report wasn't credible. Tenet prevailed—then. But two months later, a National Security Council official, Robert Joseph, would go around Tenet to find a CIA department head, WINPAC Chief Alan Foley, willing to sign off on the president citing the Niger claim in his January 2003 State of the Union address. "We also know that [Saddam Hussein] has recently

---

44 Wilson, *The Politics of Truth*, p. 28.

45 See Libby trial defense exhibit DX420.1, Office of Inspector General memo on interview with CIA ADDO/PS and Iraq Mission Manager, Robert Grenier: "He, Grenier, believes that the VP was not made aware of the report and that the reporting was viewed to be Embassy-like reporting, and the answer was to be expected. No definitiveness could be assigned to the report. . . ." See http://wid.ap.org/documents/libbytrial/jan24/DX420.pdf.

sought to buy uranium in Africa," Joseph sought Foley's permission for Bush to assert. Foley only asked that Joseph attribute the claim to a recent British white paper, and Bush ultimately said, "The British government has learned that Saddam Hussein recently sought significant quantities of uranium from Africa." It was sixteen words the White House would soon come to regret.[46] When the United Nations nuclear watchdog agency, the International Atomic Energy Agency, got hold of the documents on which first the Italians, and then the British and President Bush had based their claims, it quickly determined they were crude forgeries. Shortly thereafter, the United States invaded Iraq and discovered there were no weapons of mass destruction there after all. And Joseph Wilson had good reason to believe the White House should have known that it was overstating the intelligence.

Valerie Wilson describes the nature of her responsibilities at this time in some detail, and of particular interest to her group "were Iraq's worldwide procurement networks."

Valerie described one complicated foreign operation she ran:

My job was to orchestrate a meeting between [a young woman from a middle-class family doing highly technical . . . work in a European country] . . . in such a way that she would never suspect she was being pursued by the CIA . . . we decided that he would pose as a . . . man who had read a paper of hers published in an obscure academic journal. . . . Probably a bit lonely in a foreign country, the target fell hard for the . . . flattery and perhaps, too, his ability to discuss her area of arcane study with some degree of sophistication and competency. . . . The idea was that

---

46 "Rice: 16 words dispute 'enormously overblown,'" CNN, July 14, 2003.

her "assignments" would become increasingly sensitive and we could begin to explore what she knew about what her . . . adviser . . . was working on.

While Valerie's unit targeted students and foreign business-men with possible knowledge of or suspected links to suspected Iraqi weapons programs, a separate CIA unit, the National Resources Division—the same one that had coordinated the trip her husband took in 1999—reached out to U.S.-based relatives of Iraqi scientists and officials to seek their cooperation in trying to secure information from their relatives back in Iraq.[47] The effort by the CIA to recruit one such individual, an Iraqi-born doctor then working at the Cleveland Clinic, Sawsan Alhaddad, whose brother worked as an Iraqi scientist, was detailed by James Risen in his book, *State of War:*

> Doctor Sawsan Alhaddad was very busy when she received the strange phone call. . . . A quiet, petite, olive-skinned woman in her fifties, Sawsan wondered why a CIA officer who said he was calling from Pittsburgh would want to talk to an anesthesiologist in Cleveland. . . . Chris [the CIA officer] stunned Sawsan when he explained why he had come to talk to her. He told her that she could help President Bush's new war on terror. She could help by going to Baghdad on a secret mission for the CIA. Chris explained

---

47 Risen credits inspiration for the reaching out to U.S.-based relatives of Iraqi scientists to then Associate Deputy Director for Intelligence for Collection Charlie Allen, now intelligence Chief for the Department of Homeland Security. But another former CIA official says the program was coordinated by the CIA's National Resources Division and that Allen, a veteran intelligence analyst, was filling in a collection hole using a target set used in other eras and conflicts. "We do this in every war," says a former senior CIA official.

that the CIA wanted Sawsan . . . to travel to Iraq and become a spy. The CIA had identified Saad Tawfiq, Sawsan's brother, a British-trained electrical engineer living in Baghdad . . . as a key figure in Saddam Hussein's clandestine nuclear weapons program.[48]

After flying to Baghdad and talking surreptitiously with her brother on late-night walks and with the TV turned up and phones unplugged to avoid surveillance, Sawsan was stunned to learn from her brother, Saad Tawfiq, that there was no longer an Iraqi nuclear program. "Sawsan tried to continue with her list of questions, but they all seemed to Saad to be the product of some fantasy," Risen reports.[49] "We don't have the resources to make anything anymore, he told her. We don't even have enough spare parts for our conventional military. We can't even shoot down an airplane. We don't have anything left."

But when Sawsan shared her findings with her CIA debriefers in a Virginia hotel room upon her return from Iraq, they didn't believe what her brother had told her, Risen reports. *"We think that Saad is lying to Sawsan,* Chris told Sawsan's husband. *We think he knows much more than he is willing to tell her. . . .* The CIA man smiled, nodded, and left. Sawsan Alhaddad's debriefing report was filed along with all the others from the family members who had agreed to return to Baghdad to contact Iraqi weapons scientists. All of them—some thirty—had said the same thing. They all reported to the CIA that the scientists had said that Iraq's program to develop nuclear, chemical, and biological weapons had long since been abandoned."

---

48 Risen, *State of War*, pp. 85–88.
49 Risen, *State of War*, p. 103.

CIA officials "ignored the evidence and refused to even disseminate the reports from the family members to senior policymakers in the Bush administration," Risen concluded.[50]

A similar dynamic prevailed in the relationship between the White House and the intelligence community on most every matter concerning intelligence on Iraq and alleged weapons of mass destruction—the subject of Valerie's all-consuming work in this period. As multiple accounts indicate, the administration was only inclined to listen to the CIA when it produced evidence that supported its desire to invade Iraq. And the CIA's top leadership, internalizing that intensely politicized environment, tended to highlight the intelligence the White House appreciated, and got exhausted trying to tamp down the hyping of discredited intelligence that the White House sought repeatedly to use to sell the war to the American public, such as the Niger uranium claims.[51] "When it comes to information supporting the invasion of Iraq, the bar was low," a former senior CIA official says. "When it comes to intelligence that doesn't say Iraq has weapons of mass destruction, the bar was incredibly high. . . .

"The interpretation of the intelligence was cherry-picked by officials in the White House to produce the conclusions they wanted, right from the beginning. The CIA could never produce a

---

50 Risen, *State of War*, pp. 105–6.

51 Tyler Drumheller, the former Chief of CIA Clandestine Operations, Europe, and co-author journalist Elaine Monaghan describe another such case, that of "CURVEBALL," an Iraqi defector to Germany, and how his bogus claims on mobile Iraqi biological weapons labs ended up being cited by then secretary of state Colin Powell despite Drumheller's warnings to Tenet that CURVEBALL was a fabricator, in their book *On the Brink: An Insider's Account of How the White House Compromised American Intelligence* (New York: Carrol & Graf, 2006). For a detailed newspaper account of CURVEBALL see also Bob Drogin and John Goetz, "How the U.S. Fell Under Curveball's Spell," *Los Angeles Times*, November 20, 2005.

piece of intelligence that the administration would accept as conclusive that Iraq doesn't have WMD."

Journalists Michael Isikoff and David Corn write in their book on prewar intelligence, *Hubris:*

> The Joint Task Force on Iraq would write up reports detailing the denials they were getting from Iraqi scientists and shoot them into the CIA bureaucracy. But . . . CIA operations officers handling these Iraqi assets were never sure if they could believe their we-have-nothing pronouncements. "The working theory," said one CIA officer involved with the JTFI, "was that we were dealing with a similar mentality we had seen in Soviet scientists. These people were living in a society where lying was a way of life, a way to survive. We didn't take their first answer when they said there was nothing or they themselves hadn't been involved in WMDs." Wilson and other JTFI officers couldn't tell whether they were actually getting the correct answer or whether they weren't doing their job well enough to find Saddam's WMDs. "The fact that we were not getting affirmation of the WMDs did not mean they were not there," this CIA officer recalled.[52]

But as Corn and Isikoff report, Valerie Wilson's CPD group's job was information collection—not analysis. And it was the CIA's analysts primarily in the CIA's Weapons, Intelligence, Nonproliferation and Arms Control Center—WINPAC—that repeatedly called Iraq intelligence the wrong way.

> . . . Valerie Wilson and the others were merely ops officers.
> It was their job to mount operations, ascertain whether

---

52 Isikoff and Corn, *Hubris*, p. 167.

sources were blowing smoke or telling the truth, and bring in whatever data they could. The analysts in the Directorate of Intelligence—such as WINPAC analysts—were supposed to figure out what it all meant.

But on the Niger deal, Curveball, and the [aluminum] tubes, WINPAC analysts were making one profoundly wrong call after another—and consistently fending off challenges from other experts and even their own CIA colleagues. Their conclusions were exactly the material the White House wanted—and would soon use in the two final (and disastrous) acts of its sales campaign: the president's State of the Union speech and a historic presentation by the secretary of state at the United Nations.[53]

Journalists Peter Eisner and Knut Royce, in their book on the Niger yellowcake forgeries, *The Italian Letter*, came to a similar conclusion: WINPAC served as a secret cheerleading faction inside the CIA for the administration's most stretched Iraq intelligence claims. They concluded that while parts of the CIA were collecting intelligence that showed an unclear picture about Iraq's weapons programs, WINPAC had a different agenda. As Eisner and Royce report:

> One day in December 2002, [WINPAC director Alan] Foley called his senior production managers to his office. He had a clear message for the men and women who controlled the output of the center's analysts: "If the president wants to go to war, our job is to find the intelligence to allow him to do so." The directive was not quite an order to cook the books, but it was a strong suggestion that cherry-

---

53 Isikoff and Corn, *Hubris,* pp. 167–68.

picking and slanting not only would be tolerated, but might even be rewarded. . . .

With Foley's stated approval, the sycophantic WINPAC staff fed the Bush administration's war plan. . . .[54]

There's an undeniable irony to Valerie Wilson later being exposed by the White House in a subterranean tussle over politicized pre-war intelligence. As her account makes clear, Valerie was not one of the intelligence community dissidents arguing against the threat posed by Saddam Hussein and whose dissents were relegated to the footnotes of the October 2002 National Intelligence Estimate on Iraq. Her CPD Iraq group's work was predicated on the assumption that Iraq was continuing to try to procure materiel for its presumed unconventional weapons programs. As Valerie writes, "Writing these pages in 2007, four years after the invasion of Iraq, and the evidence of the manipulations of intelligence and failures of the intelligence community prior to the war, it is easy to surrender to a revisionist idea that all WMD evidence against Iraq was fabricated. While it is true that powerful ideologues encouraged a war to prove their own geopolitical theories, and critical failures of judgment were made throughout the intelligence community in the spring and summer of 2002, Iraq . . . was clearly a rogue nation that flouted international treaties and norms in its quest for regional superiority." And yet, though her group shared the working assumptions of the White House, it was not immune to contrary evidence or reality, and its work was not undertaken with the desire to cook the books. Nor were its assumptions ones from which even the administration official

---

54 Peter Eisner and Knut Royce, *The Italian Letter* (New York: Rodale Press, 2007), pp. 18–21.

considered most wary of the consequences of an Iraq invasion was immune. "It was a powerful presentation," Valerie writes of then Secretary of State Colin Powell's February 2003 appearance at the United Nations, "but I knew key parts of it were wrong."

Valerie's work was being conducted in an environment in which the administration elevated the intelligence that justified invasion, and suppressed that which would call it into doubt. But the CIA clearly made its own mistakes as well, chiefly in not sufficiently challenging its basic assumptions: Iraq's opacity and seeming subterfuges might not be evidence that it was hiding banned weapons stockpiles and programs, but the reactions of a tyrant desperate to hide the fact he had no unconventional weapons deterrent and therefore was vulnerable. "We were prisoners of our own beliefs," said a senior U.S. weapons expert to the *Los Angeles Times*'s Bob Drogin.[55] "We said Saddam Hussein was a master of denial and deception. Then when we couldn't find anything, we said that proved it, instead of questioning our own assumptions." Valerie reiterates this point: "As the summer went on, our anxieties gradually shifted from fears that our troops would be subjected to a surprise WMD attack . . . to bewilderment over why we weren't finding any WMD caches at all. I began to have a sinking feeling in my stomach that Saddam pulled off one of the greatest intelligence deceptions of all time: he had made the world believe he had significant stashes of WMD that he would use . . . when in fact, he had nothing."

Such was the atmosphere in which the CIA asked Joseph Wilson to undertake a trip to Niger in February 2002 to investigate one such claim: that Iraq was contracting to purchase a huge amount—over a million pounds—of yellowcake uranium from Niger. Joe Wilson investigated and found the report wasn't

---

55 Bob Drogin, "U.S. Suspects It Received False Iraq War Tips," *Los Angeles Times*, August 28, 2003.

credible, and told the Agency so. Time would prove that Joe Wilson was right. And repercussions of the trip would reveal the fault lines in the administration's case for war, and a U.S. intelligence community conditioned to elevate the intelligence that justified going to war and suppress that which offered a murkier picture.

The White House fury over being confronted publicly with Ambassador Wilson's findings would lead it to retaliate by outing Valerie Wilson as a CIA operative—effectively ending her career. The White House and its surrogates would orchestrate a highly organized campaign to try to discredit Joe Wilson by whispering in journalists' ears, "Don't get too far out" on Wilson because the reason he had been sent to Niger was that his wife was a weapons of mass destruction operative at the CIA, and the (unpaid) Niger fact-finding mission had been some sort of junket or boondoggle arranged by his wife.[56]

It's not easy to understand how an unpaid week interviewing ex-officials in the second-poorest country on earth could be construed as a boondoggle by even the most avid political operative, and the nepotism talking point did little to neutralize Joe Wilson's fundamental and still-compelling claim: that the White House exaggerated the case for war to the American public. It's a claim that teams of CIA-led Iraq weapons hunters did nothing to dispel when they delivered their findings to Congress shortly thereafter that there were no weapons of mass destruction in Iraq.

---

56 See Libby trial defense exhibit DX846.1, note from *Time* magazine's Matt Cooper to colleagues (http://wid.ap.org/documents/libbytrial/jan31/DX846.pdf).

6. EXPOSED (2003–2007)

When Valerie Wilson was exposed in the summer of 2003, she was contemplating an offer to move from an operational to a more managerial role within the Directorate of Operations Counterproliferation Division. While she had initially turned down the offer to become the CPD's Chief of Personnel Evaluation Management, she accepted in the fall of 2003, just as the Justice Department was undertaking an investigation of the outing of her identity. "No sooner had I begun to get my arms around a branch . . . than the FBI paid me a visit," she writes.

At the same time, the Senate Select Committee on Intelligence was undertaking an investigation of prewar intelligence. The Republican chair of the committee, Pat Roberts, a Kansas Republican with close ties to the White House and in particular Cheney, demanded that the first part of the committee's investigation on prewar intelligence focus exclusively on the mistakes of the intelligence community. Only *after* the 2004 presidential election, Roberts insisted, would the committee investigate other factors, including the role of a Pentagon intelligence shop, the Office of Special Plans, Iraqi exile leader Ahmad Chalabi, and the Iraqi National Congress in influencing policy makers' misjudgments and misstatements about what would be found in Iraq. But

Roberts stalled the second phase of the investigation for over two years, and argued for releasing it in pieces, diminishing its impact.[57]

As Valerie Wilson and many colleagues from the CIA who testified before the committee would soon learn, some of its Republican members considered them fair game as well—for character and professional assassination and for attempted retaliation for offering testimony to the committee. Roberts would later be reported to have let the Office of the Vice President intervene repeatedly to influence and reduce the scope of the investigation, in order to prevent the White House and the Office of the Vice President itself from ever coming under any congressional oversight scrutiny.[58] Cheney "exerted 'constant' pressure on the Republican former chairman of the Senate Intelligence Committee to stall an investigation into the Bush administration's use of flawed intelligence on Iraq, the panel's Democratic chairman charged Thursday," McClatchy newspapers' Jonathan Landay reported in January 2007. In an interview, the committee's new Democratic chairman "[Jay] Rockefeller said that it was 'not hearsay' that Cheney . . . pushed Sen. Pat Roberts, R-Kan., to drag out the probe of the administration's use of prewar intelligence. 'It was just constant,' Rockefeller said of Cheney's alleged interference. He added that he knew that the vice president attended regular policy meetings in which he conveyed White House directions to Republican staffers."

●   ●   ●

57 See Laura Rozen, "The Report They Forgot: The Fitzgerald Probe Reminds Us—Whatever Happened to Pat Roberts' Phase II Intelligence Report?" *American Prospect*, October 19, 2005, and "He's Done," *American Prospect*, December 2005.

58 See Jonathan Landay, "Rockefeller: Cheney applied 'constant' pressure to stall investigation on flawed Iraq intelligence," McClatchy newspapers, January 26, 2007.

After Valerie was exposed in Robert Novak's July 14, 2003, newspaper column, her colleagues, some from her Career Trainee class days who had only known her as Val P., were horrified—and outraged. They began contacting one another, to try to think of ways to offer their support. "We all knew somebody from our class had been exposed," says Jim Marcinkowski. "But we didn't know each other's last names and, of course, hers had changed."

Marcinkowski was an unlikely Bush White House antagonist. As the first chairman of the Michigan State University College Republicans, he had received an award from Jack Abramoff—later to be a disgraced GOP lobbyist tight with the Bush White House—for heading the fastest-growing state College Republicans chapter in the country. He had helped run Reagan's 1980 campaign outreach to Michigan college students. Marcinkowski had been a CIA officer, an FBI clerk, a Navy enlistee, a public prosecutor, and by 2003, was deputy city attorney for Royal Oak, Michigan.[59] In 1992, he ran, unsuccessfully, as a Republican for a state office. Marcinkowski later donated to the Bush/Cheney campaign at a 1999 fund-raiser headlined by Laura Bush.

" 'Hey, this is our Val,' " Marcinkowski remembers of an e-mail to their group by fellow classmate Larry Johnson. " 'We have to do something about it.' " A group of her classmates and colleagues wrote a letter to the editor of the *Los Angeles Times*, which was published in October 2003. "The public identification, the 'outing' if you will, of an undercover intelligence operative has never before, to my knowledge, been accomplished by the United States in a deliberate political act," Marcinkowski wrote in the letter published by the *Times*.[60] "The exposure of Valerie Plame—who I

---

59 Author interviews with Jim Marcinkowski and public accounts. In 2006, Marcinkowski ran unsuccessfully as a Democratic challenger to Michigan congressional incumbent Mike Rogers.

60 Letter provided by Marcinkowski to this writer.

have reason to believe operated undercover—apparently by a senior administration official is nothing less than a despicable act for which someone should be held accountable. This case is especially upsetting to me because she was my Agency classmate as well as my friend."

Shortly after that, the group went on ABC's *Nightline,* including a CIA colleague who, like Valerie, had formerly worked clandestinely, and had her voice disguised and face obscured in black shadow.

Nothing in his past experience as an FBI clerk, CIA officer, lawyer, and public prosecutor prepared Marcinkowski for what he faced when he went to testify before Pat Roberts's intelligence committee about the Plame leak. "We sent a letter to the Senate Select Committee on Intelligence, saying we want to tell them something," Marcinkowski recounted. The letter was signed by a half dozen former CIA officers, including three from Valerie's 1985 Career Trainee class, himself, Brent Cavan, Larry Johnson, and Mike Grimaldi. "They blew us off. After that, nothing happened until [then Senate minority leader] Tom Daschle contacted us and said, 'I am going to have a Senate Democratic committee hearing,' " and asked if they would appear.

The Democratic Policy Committee hearing was supposed to take place on Friday, October 24, 2003. Shortly after it was scheduled, Marcinkowski recounts, "my boss here in Detroit got a fax from a staffer on the Senate Select Committee on Intelligence. Basically it said in some snotty way, 'Somebody claims in your office to have information.' [The staffer] made it sound like, 'Who is this punk? If he wants to say anything, he can come in at 1pm on Thursday' "—the day before the policy committee hearing was scheduled, Marcinkowski recounts.

He provided the fax sent October 20, 2003 by then Republican Chief of staff to the Senate Intelligence Committee, Bill Duhnke—strangely, to Marcinkowski's boss. "The Senate Select

Committee on Intelligence has received a fax from your office sent by James Marcinkowski," Duhnke, Roberts's staffer, wrote in his e-mail to Marcinkowski's boss.[61] "Mr. Marcinkowski claims to have 'important information' he wishes to share with the committee. . . . The letter states that '[t]ime is of the essence.' Therefore, I respectfully request that Mr. Marcinkowski contact me at his earliest convenience to discuss an appearance before the Committee." It seems obvious that, under the guise of a backhanded invitation to say something to the committee, Duhnke intended to try to get Marcinkowski in trouble with his boss. But it failed, Marcinkowski says, because his boss is an old friend with whom he had worked for years, who recognized the virtue in Marcinkowski's desire to seek justice for their former colleague Valerie. "Like I told you, it was my classmate they exposed," Marcinkowski says he told his boss. "He said, 'OK great. Go beat the shit out of somebody.' "

"The next evening I was on the plane to D.C.," Marcinkowski continues. As it turned out, various other colleagues were out of town and Marcinkowski ended up facing twelve senators from the Senate Intelligence Committee for the closed briefing on Thursday, October 23, 2003, all by himself.

Marcinkowski told the senators that the exposure of Plame by her own government was "unprecedented. It was our classmate. We had kept a secret for eighteen years. And we were all betrayed by this White House." Marcinkowski had prepared a statement to deliver in open session before the Senate Democratic Policy committee the next day. "I also said she was covert, and I knew it. And they were taking it very seriously."

---

61 E-mail from B. Duhnke, then staff director and Chief counsel, to the Roberts-led Senate Intelligence Committee, obtained by the author.

He took questions after his statement. One of the committee's more moderate Republicans, Chuck Hagel, a Vietnam vet from Nebraska, asked him, do you think this White House can investigate itself?

As Marcinkowski responded that if the attorney general was trying to intimidate federal judges, why would you think they would not be prepared to intimidate a special counsel, a ranking Republican close to the White House, Christopher "Kit" Bond of Missouri, walked in.

"He went off," Marcinkowski said. " 'I am not going to sit here and listen to this guy attack my good friend, the attorney general Ashcroft, of this country.' " A total "food fight" ensued, Marcinkowski said, with committee member Democratic senator Dianne Feinstein accusing Bond of trying to intimidate a witness.

After he finished with his testimony and the senators' questions, Marcinkowski went out the back door of the building and walked over to a little park between the Senate office building and Union Station. He sat down to think about what had just happened and his cell phone rang. It was Tom Daschle's staffer, who was setting up the hearing for the next day's Democratic Policy Committee meeting. "And she told me, 'Jim, Pat Roberts just declared all your testimony to be secret. I don't know what you are planning on saying tomorrow, but he declared it secret.' "

Marcinkowski, the lawyer and deputy city attorney, was stunned. "I sat on the park bench, in a daze. I didn't know what the hell to do. Now it hits me, *that* is why the Senate Select Intelligence Committee had scheduled their testimony for the day before the Senate Democratic public hearing. Until that happened we didn't hear shit from the Senate Select Intelligence Committee. They slapped the secrecy thing on it, that was their intention," to try to prevent Valerie's CIA colleagues from testifying publicly about what had happened to her, and why it was a betrayal of everyone in the CIA.

Marcinkowski called a close friend, an attorney in Detroit, to get legal advice on what he should do, since what he had told the Senate Intelligence Committee was exactly what he planned to tell the Senate Democratic Policy Committee the next day, and Roberts had appeared to try to suppress that testimony by, implausibly, declaring it classified. " 'Jim, I tell you what,' " his friend told him. " 'I already know what you're going to do. I am going to call all your friends and start collecting bond money right now,' " Marcinkowski recounts. "I told him, 'You think this is funny. I'm sitting here in a park, by my lonesome, and they're saying I'm violating all kinds of laws.' And he said, 'Yep, and I know exactly what you are doing tomorrow morning.' "

Gathering courage, Marcinkowski called Daschle's staffer back. "You call Roberts' office and you tell him, I said that he can go straight to hell," Marcinkowski says he told her.

Refusing to be intimidated (a Hill staffer says that Roberts doesn't have the power to classify anything), the hearing proceeded. Marcinkowski showed up to testify with fellow former CIA official Johnson and former CIA Counterterrorism Chief Vincent Cannistraro. They testified publicly before the Senate Democrats, and as Daschle was wrapping things up, Marcinkowski saw ranking Senate Intelligence Committee Democrat Jay Rockefeller whispering in Daschle's ear.

"Daschle says, 'Senator Rockefeller has one more question,' " Marcinkowski recounts. "And Rockefeller looks straight at me. 'I would like to ask Mr. Marcinkowski, who is an attorney, one more question: Do you think the White House can investigate itself?' " Asking the question that had caused the uproar in the closed Senate Intelligence Committee hearing the day before, Rockefeller had a "big-city grin" on his face.

Afterward, Marcinkowski said, Rockefeller grabbed his hand and asked, smiling, "What did you think of the food fight yesterday?"

• • •

In January 2007, after Democrats took control of both houses of Congress, Rockefeller became chairman of the Senate Intelligence Committee, and Roberts was replaced as ranking Republican by Christopher Bond.

In the spring 2007 release of "Prewar Intelligence Assessments about Postwar Iraq"—one section of the Senate Intelligence Committee's long-awaited "Phase II" investigation of prewar intelligence that Roberts had gone to such lengths to stall—Bond would continue the campaign against the Wilsons.[62] The report mostly consists of two declassified prewar National Intelligence Council assessments that focused on the postwar environment in Iraq. "The Intelligence Community assessed prior to the war that establishing a stable democratic government in postwar Iraq would be a long, difficult, and possibly turbulent challenge," the SSCI report found. "The Intelligence community noted that Iraqi political culture did 'not foster liberalism or democracy' and was 'largely bereft of the social underpinnings that directly support development of broad-based participatory democracy.' . . . The Intelligence Community assessed prior to the war that al Qaeda probably would see an opportunity to accelerate its operational tempo and increase terrorist attacks during and after a US-Iraq war."

Committee Republicans complained the report was "partisan" and Vice Chairman Bond, joined by senators Orrin Hatch and Richard Burr, set about in the "additional views" to turn their attention once again to the Wilsons. "While not directly related to the subject of the report released today," they wrote, "it is appropriate here to discuss some additional information that has come

---

62 See "Prewar Intelligence Assessments about Postwar Iraq," Senate Select Committee on Intelligence.

to light about an earlier prewar inquiry report . . . that deals with Iraq-Niger uranium intelligence. . . . Additional information . . . supports the Committee's finding that Mrs. Wilson is the one who originally suggested Ambassador Wilson to look into the Iraq-Niger uranium matter. . . ."

The trio offered few thoughts on the report's evidence that the administration apparently ignored the prewar assessments about the difficulties the U.S. would encounter trying to establish a democracy in Iraq.

On July 2, 2007, President Bush commuted Scooter Libby's prison sentence. A pardon, close Libby trial observers note, would have eliminated Libby's ability to declare the right against self-incrimination to avoid testifying before Congress about not only his own role, but the role of the vice president and the president in authorizing the disclosure of Plame's identity to journalists. "If Bush were to pardon Libby, he and Vice President Cheney would give up the rationale they have used successfully for four years to avoid addressing their own roles in the case," wrote Jeff Lomonaco.[63] "And Libby's trial made very clear that the President and Vice President played significant and troubling roles at the very heart of the case. . . . Published reports have indicated that Bush told Cheney something to the effect of 'Get it out,' or 'Let's get this out,' referring to information that would damage the case Joe Wilson was making against the administration. That means that if Bush and Cheney discussed Wilson's wife before the direction was given, the President was effectively authorizing his subordinate to disclose Plame's CIA identity to the press."

---

63 See Lomonaco, Web post, July 2, 2007, http://delong.typepad.com/sdj/2007/07/jeff-lomonaco-p.html.

· · ·

Plame formally resigned from the CIA on January 9, 2006. She had served the Agency and her country for more than twenty years.

In early 2007, as the trial of Libby got under way, she and Wilson moved with their children to New Mexico to try to re-create their lives.

Appendix

Washington, D.C. 20505

Publications Review Board

Telephone:
Facsimile:
E-mail:

22 December 2006

Valerie E. Wilson
c/o Diane Plame

Dear Ms. Wilson:

As we explained in our letter of 21 November 2006 and as we discussed during our recent meeting, pages 1 through 124 of your manuscript, as currently drafted, would reveal classified information primarily because of the context in which the information appears and the timeframes associated with the material. At our recent meeting, you asked us to provide you with line-in/line-out edits to this part of the manuscript. We are committed to working with you and to providing you with constructive assistance in identifying changes that could be made to your manuscript to render it unclassified. However, we are unable to provide you with line-in/line-out edits in an unclassified correspondence.

The first 124 pages of your manuscript are replete with statements that may be unclassified standing alone, but they become classified when they are linked with a specific time, such as an event in your personal life, or are included in another context that would reveal classified information. A detailed description of this information along with how the timeframes and contexts are problematic would be classified. We are available to meet at your convenience to discuss these issues in person. However, we are not able to communicate this information to you in an unclassified correspondence.

Additionally, there is more than one approach to revising the material in the first 124 pages of your manuscript in order to render it unclassified. For example, one approach to revising these portions of your manuscript to make them unclassified might be to separate certain statements and vignettes from the timeframes in which they currently appear in your manuscript and incorporate them into other parts of the manuscript. Another approach might be to remove the references to the times and events in your personal life.

We recognize that these options might not be feasible in some instances and that the only way to avoid revealing classified information in those cases would be to recast that information or fictionalize it. The approach that you prefer to take to revising the material in your manuscript would significantly affect the line-in/line-out changes that would be required to render it unclassified.

We look forward to hearing from you in the near future regarding how you wish to proceed. Please do not hesitate to contact me if you have any questions or if we can be of further assistance.

Sincerely,

R. Puhl
Chairman, Publications Review Board

NKFURT KURNIT KLEIN & SELZ ᴘᴄ

David B. Smalir ᵗᵤ ᵢ
Direct dial:
e-mail:

February 16, 2007

<u>VIA FAX</u>

Ginger A. Wright, Esq.
Assistant General Counsel
Office of General Counsel
Central Intelligence Agency

Dear Ms. Wright:

      I am writing in response to a fax letter from you dated February 9, 2007 ("Agency's February 9 Letter") (copy attached) in response to my letter of January 31, 2007 ("January 31 Letter"). Quite frankly, I was surprised and dismayed to receive official correspondence from the Agency containing such obviously false and self-serving assertions – as described below – which distort unfairly Ms. Wilson's numerous good faith discussions with CIA's Publications Review Board ("PRB") during the past year. While Ms. Wilson looks forward to receiving from the Agency on or before February 24 the promised list of proposed revisions, Ms. Wilson reserves all of her rights and remedies with respect to the Agency's dilatory conduct and any related actions resulting in improper censorship or restraint of publication of her manuscript by the Agency and/or other parts of the Executive Branch, including, for example, the Office of Vice President, in possible violation of the Constitution and the laws of the United States.

      As an initial matter, the Agency's February 9 Letter fails to provide the information requested in connection with Central Intelligence Agency's official acknowledgement and disclosure of Ms. Wilson twenty year employment affiliation with CIA in an unclassified letter dated February 10, 2006, which was published in the Congressional Record on January 16, 2007 ("Published February 10, 2006 Letter") (copy attached). In order to respond properly to the letter Ms. Wilson received from Ms. Tumolo on January 19, 2007 ("Tumolo January 19 Letter") (copy attached), I am reiterating my request that the Agency send to me as soon as possible a revised and remarked version of the February 10, 2006 letter (with any ostensibly classified information redacted) that complies in good faith with the applicable provisions of Executive Order 12958, as amended ("E.O"), § 1.6. If the Office of General Counsel

Ginger A. Wright, Esq.
February 16, 2007
Page 2 of 2

CIA is unable or unwilling to provide a redacted version of the letter indicating the information that it believes to be classified, please provide to me at your earliest convenience the Agency's legal basis for seeking reclassification of the Published February 10, 2006 Letter and confirmation that all required actions have been undertaken by the Agency in connection with seeking reclassification. Ms. Davis and I also are available to meet with you and the Agency's Acting General Counsel, Mr. Rizzo, to discuss these matters.

In order to ensure an accurate record, I must also note that the Agency's February 7 Letter incorrectly describes the actual history of Ms. Wilson's meetings with PRB staff to discuss her manuscript. Contrary to the flatly wrong assertion that "Ms. Wilson has declined to meet with PRB staff," the opposite is true: Ms. Wilson met with PRB staff *three times* at the Agency's headquarters, on November 6, 2006, December 1, 2006, and December 13, 2006, and also had numerous email exchanges and telephone conversations with them. Furthermore, the Agency's February 9 Letter fails to explain adequately the now six month delay in completing a review that should have, as a general matter, been completed within thirty days of submission by Ms. Wilson of her manuscript to PRB in September 2006.

Finally, the Agency's February 9 Letter mischaracterizes our response to the Tumolo January 19 Letter set forth in my January 31 Letter. In order to correct that mischaracterization, I am again advising you of the following: please be assured that Ms. Wilson and her counsel intend to comply fully with all applicable obligations regarding "Classified National Security Information" pursuant to E.O. 12958, and any other applicable law, and, while fully reserving her rights and without prejudice to or otherwise waiving any rights she may have, Ms. Wilson will provide a copy of the February 10, 2006 letter to Ms. Tumolo.

I will look forward to hearing back from you regarding the above matters at your earliest convenience, and will expect the Agency to provide Ms. Wilson with a list of any proposed revisions to the first 124 pages of her manuscript no later than February 24, 2007.

Sincerely,

David B. Smallman

Attachments
cc: Lisa E. Davis, Esq.
    Elisa Rivlin, Esq.

**UNITED STATES DISTRICT COURT
SOUTHERN DISTRICT NEW YORK**

VALERIE PLAME WILSON;   ᵖ)
SIMON & SCHUSTER, INC.,   )
)
     Plaintiffs,   )
)
          v.   )   Civil Action No.:
)
J. MICHAEL MCCONNELL,   )   **COMPLAINT FOR**
IN HIS OFFICIAL CAPACITY AS DIRECTOR)   **DECLARATORY**
OF NATIONAL INTELLIGENCE;   )   **AND INJUNCTIVE RELIEF**
CENTRAL INTELLIGENCE AGENCY;   )
GEN. MICHAEL V. HAYDEN, IN HIS   )
OFFICIAL CAPACITY AS DIRECTOR OF)
CENTRAL INTELLIGENCE AGENCY,   )
)
     Defendants.   )
)

PRELIMINARY STATEMENT

1.   This is an action by Valerie Plame Wilson and Simon & Schuster, Inc., the

publisher of Ms. Wilson's forthcoming memoir entitled "Fair Game" (the "Manuscript" or

"Memoir"), seeking a declaratory judgment that the Executive Branch of government cannot

restrain publication of previously unclassified or currently unclassifiable information

documenting Ms. Wilson's dates of federal service disclosed in 2006 by the Central Intelligence

Agency ("CIA") in an official, authorized, and unclassified letter now in the Congressional

Record and available world-wide on the Library of Congress website.

2.   Valerie Wilson's decades of dedicated service to the United States ended

prematurely when she was "outed" as an undercover officer for the CIA by senior government

officials entrusted to protect that classified information. Following the initial "outing" in the

media in July 2003, Valerie Wilson's prospects as a covert CIA operative evaporated and her

long career was effectively destroyed. Ultimately, Ms. Wilson formally resigned her position on

January 9, 2006. She now seeks to tell the story of her career in public service and its premature termination.

3.   Well before any publishing agreement was entered into, or any manuscript was written, Ms. Wilson grappled with the consequences of a completely unexpected and involuntary conclusion to her CIA career. Suddenly facing unemployment and an uncertain future, Ms. Wilson also learned that she did not meet the statutory age requirements necessary to begin receiving her government annuity.

4.   Ms. Wilson's inquiries about her retirement benefits at the end of 2005 resulted in a February 10, 2006 letter from the CIA which provided official, unclassified confirmation of her precise years of service and confirmed that due to statutory age requirements she would only be eligible to receive a deferred annuity years after her resignation. The letter was executed by the CIA's "Chief, Retirement and Insurance Services," and was delivered by regular mail on official CIA letterhead.

5.   Certain members of Congress were also concerned that as a result of calculated leaks by government officials at the highest levels of the Executive Branch and through no fault of her own, Ms. Wilson would lose her career as a covert CIA operative and suffer significant financial consequences. Accordingly, a member of Congress approached Ms. Wilson during 2005 to propose a legislative remedy to her annuity predicament, and draft legislation was prepared.

6.   With the change of Congressional control, the "Valerie Plame Wilson Compensation Act," H.R. 501, was finally introduced in Congress in January 2007. Congress reprinted in the Congressional Record a partially redacted copy of the CIA's February 10, 2006 letter to document that Valerie Wilson had achieved the necessary 20 years of service for a

2

government annuity. (The redacted version of the official CIA February 10, 2006 letter published in the Congressional Record is hereinafter called the "Agency Annuity Letter"). Thus, since January 16, 2007, Ms. Wilson's actual dates of service have appeared in the Congresional Record and have been available worldwide on the Internet at http://www.thomas.gov.

7.   Despite official and unclassified acknowledgment of her decades of service in the Agency Annuity Letter and no effort for almost a year to retrieve that letter or to suggest that it be treated as classified – and notwithstanding the fact that the CIA's own letter appears in the Congressional Record as part of pending legislation and is unquestionably irretrievable – the CIA now purports to classify or reclassify Ms. Wilson's pre-2002 federal service dates. Further, it demands that significant portions of Ms. Wilson's Manuscript be excised or rendered "fiction," purportedly to protect the "secret" of Ms. Wilson's government service prior to 2002. By unreasonably interfering with Valerie Wilson's Memoir in violation of the First Amendment, the Executive Branch seeks to prevent information relating to its own misconduct from reaching the American public.

8.   A loyal former CIA officer, Valerie Wilson is not seeking *carte blanche* to discuss her entire government service or to reveal any classified information in her Memoir. On the contrary, for more than ten months, she has diligently worked with the CIA's Publications Review Board ("PRB") to comply fully with her secrecy agreements and to avoid any possibility of divulging national security information with which she has been entrusted.

9.   But the Executive Branch cannot have it both ways. In 2003, senior government officials leaked information to the news media identifying Valerie Wilson's covert affiliation with the CIA; defendant CIA subsequently disclosed in its 2006 unclassified letter her *exact dates of service* when providing official information relevant to her ability to receive a

government annuity after 20 years of service. Yet, now, the CIA seeks to prevent plaintiffs from publishing the exact information it previously confirmed in its unclassified Agency Annuity Letter and which is currently available to the world on the Internet through the Library of Congress.

10.   Improper classification or reclassification of information officially released to the public by the very federal agency responsible for controlling the information imposes a prior restraint that violates the First Amendment. Defendants' position cannot withstand scrutiny as a matter of logic and is unsupported as a matter of law.

INTRODUCTION OF THE VALERIE PLAME WILSON COMPENSATION ACT

HON. JAY INSLEE
OF WASHINGTON

IN THE HOUSE OF REPRESENTATIVES

Tuesday, January 16, 2007

Mr. INSLEE. Madam Speaker, I rise today to bring to the attention of Congress one of the human impacts caused by the indiscretion of government officials regarding the covert identity of Central Intelligence Agency operative Valerie Plame Wilson.

As nearly every American knows, and as most of the world has heard, the covert CIA identity of Valerie Plame Wilson was exposed to the public as part of an Administration response to a critical op-ed published in the New York Times by Mrs. Plame Wilson's husband, Joe Wilson.

The national security ramifications for this act have been discussed thoroughly on this floor, in the news media, and I am quite certain behind CIA's closed doors. Today I intend to call my colleagues' attention to the human toll that this "outing" has had on one, often overlooked, individual. That person is Valerie Plame Wilson.

While the media, Congress, and the judiciary have gone to great lengths to discuss the impact of this unfortunate act on politicians, bureaucrats, agents in the field, and the suspected perpetrators of the outing, few have looked at the impact that the outing has had on Mrs. Plame Wilson and her family.

On July 14, 2003, Mrs. Plame Wilson's professional life was forever altered, and her CIA career irrevocably ruined by the syndicated publication of a column, which revealed Mrs. Plame Wilson's identity as a covert CIA officer. Since this time, numerous reports on Mrs. Plame Wilson's personal history have surfaced in the press, official government documents, and by government officials.

Following the initial outing in the media, Mrs. Plame Wilson's future as a covert CIA operative ceased to exist and her career of two decades was destroyed. On January 9, 2006, Mrs. Plame Wilson resigned from the CIA, recognizing that any future with the Agency would not include any work for which she had been highly trained. For these reasons, and under these distressing conditions, Mrs. Plame Wilson voluntarily resigned from the Agency.

Despite Mrs. Plame Wilson's 20 years of federal service, she does not meet the minimum age requirement to receive her retirement annuity. She has been left without a career.

I am introducing legislation to allow Mrs. Plame Wilson to qualify for her annuity, as one who has served her country for two decades, and waive the age requirement for collecting it. To best demonstrate the annuity for which Mrs. Plame Wilson may qualify if this legislation were to pass, I am submitting for the record a document sent to Mrs. Plame Wilson by the CIA. It outlines her deferred annuity and testifies to 20 years of service. The document bears no indications of classified material as required by CIA procedures, and was sent via regular postal mail after Mrs. Plame Wilson was no longer in the employ of the CIA. Legal experts have assured me that this is not a classified document.

I believe that this is one small measure to help send a message that we must stand up

Please let me know if I can be of any further assistance.

Sincerely,

TRIBUTE TO THE REVEREND JAMES D. PETERS

HON. DIANA DeGETTE
OF COLORADO

IN THE HOUSE OF REPRESENTATIVES

Tuesday, January 16, 2007

Mr. DeGETTE. Madam Speaker, I rise to honor the extraordinary life and exceptional accomplishments of The Reverend James D. Peters, Pastor of New Hope Baptist Church. This remarkable gentleman merits both our recognition and esteem as his spiritual leadership, service and lifelong devotion to civil rights have done much to advance the lives of our people.

While many have made notable contributions to our community, few have left a legacy of progress as has Reverend Peters. He is a powerful champion of social justice and has led with those who fought for civil liberty and whose deeds changed the very fabric of our nation. Reverend Peters has touched countless lives and he has built a ministry that joins faith with equality. He is a dynamic pastor whose teaching and counsel is infused with a spiritual fervor that constantly entices us and moves us to do what is right.

Reverend Peters' journey began in Wash-

ished a reputation as a powerful advocate for inclusion and expanding opportunity for all people. He served as a volunteer member of the Denver Housing Advisory Board for approximately ten years assisting the twenty-two thousand public housing residents in changing the quality and image of public housing.

He served as a member of the Colorado Civil Rights Commission for nine years, serving as its Chairman from 1987 to 1988, during which time he traveled throughout Colorado and held countless civil rights hearings to secure justice and equality for all citizens.

Reverend Peters has received service recognitions from numerous organizations including the Southern Christian Leadership Conference, Martin Luther King Jr., the Anti-Defamation League, the Denver Post and the NAACP. He is also the recipient of the Carle Whitehead Award, the highest award given by the American Civil Liberties Union.

Reverend James Peters is an unwavering advocate for the causes that elevate the human condition and his immeasurable contributions to the spiritual life of our community merit our gratitude. He has led in the struggle for freedom, justice and equality for all people. But Reverend Peters' leadership goes to the heart of what it means to be a leader. At New Hope Baptist Church, remembers how he helped homeless people himself, not delegating it to a deacon. [He] would get into his own car, and use his own money to get someone a hotel room. And then there was a Christmas season one year, when a woman and her chil-

for public service officers, such as Mrs. Plame Wilson, who have been treated wrongly despite their loyalty and sacrifice to country. For those who have been, for all practicable purposes, pushed out of public service for reasons unrelated to performance, but instead seeded in politics, we should not turn our backs.

CENTRAL INTELLIGENCE AGENCY,
Washington, DC, February 10, 2006.
Mrs. VALERIE WILSON

DEAR MRS. WILSON, This letter is in response to your recent telephone conversation with regarding when you would be eligible to receive your deferred annuity. Per federal statute, employees participating under the Federal Employees Retirement System (FERS) Special Category, who have acquired a minimum of 20 years of service, are eligible to receive their deferred annuity at their Minimum Retirement Age (MRA). Your MRA is age 56, at which time you'll be eligible to receive a deferred annuity.

Your deferred annuity will be based on the regular FERS computation rate, one percent for every year of service vice the FERS Special rate of 1.7% for every year of service. You will receive 1.7% for each year of overseas service, prorated on a monthly basis, after January 1, 1987 in the calculation of your annuity. Our records show that since January 1, 1987, you have acquired 6 years, 1 month and 29 days of overseas service.

Following is a list of your federal service: Dates of Service: CIA, CIA (LWOP), CIA (P/T 40), from 11/9/1985 to 1/9/2006—total 20 years, 7 days.

Based on the above service and your resignation on January 9, 2006, your estimated deferred annuity is $21,541.00 per year, or $1795 per month, beginning at age 56.

The above figures are estimates for your planning purposes. The Office of Personnel Management, as the final adjudicator of creditable service and annuity computation, determines final annuity amounts.

---

grew up poor but he grew up in church. He was a gifted student and grew to recite Longfellow, Keats and Kipling. He served full time at the Navy Annex near the Pentagon and struggled to get an education, attending night school for ten years. Reverend Peters recently noted that "I couldn't eat in restaurants, I couldn't sleep at a hotel or go to the movies, I could never go to school with white children. All the way though high school I never sat in a classroom with white people, not until I went to college." Many of us in the country forget how far we've come. Although civil liberties were deep roots in our republic, there was a time when businesses, clergy and equality for all people were not a part of our shared experience. The courage and the work of Reverend Peters during the dark days of the Civil Rights Movement helped make families and equal rights part of our shared values. Reverend Peters was at the founding meeting of the Southern Christian Leadership Conference and he worked closely with Dr. Martin Luther King, Jr. He faced guns and dogs during the marches and civil rights demonstrations in Albany, Georgia, in Selma and in Birmingham, Alabama. He was part of the March on Washington that led to the historic site of the Lincoln Memorial where Dr. King gave his unparalleled "I Have a Dream" speech.

Reverend Peters' work, ethic and his service to the Civil Rights Movement molded a life of enduring accomplishment and a vocation that included ministering to congregations in Connecticut and Virginia. He became pastor of Denver's New Hope Baptist Church in February of 1979 and during his twenty-eight year tenure, he led his congregation through construction of a new church home and the expansion of services for an ever growing congregation. As a spiritual leader, he has be-

come suddenly homeless. We don't just get her connected with housing but also supplied her with gifts and food." Reverend Peters leads by example.

In a recent Denver Post article, Reverend Peters expressed "concern that young people don't understand what it was like before the Civil Rights Act and that some believe King's message is now irrelevant." At some level, I think, we all share his concern. But I would submit that Reverend Peters' legacy provides a powerful example that not only affirms Dr. King's undertaking, but inspires all of us to remember the struggle and keep faith with those who have gone before.

Reverend Peters' tenure as pastor of New Hope Baptist Church is quickly drawing to a close. His leadership has been exemplary and his contributions are rich in consequence. On behalf of the citizens of the 1st Congressional District of Colorado, I want to express our gratitude and look forward to his continued involvement in the life of our community.

Please join me in paying tribute to Reverend James D. Peters, a distinguished spiritual and civic leader. The vision, leadership and commitment he exhibits set the mark and compel us to continue the work that distinguishes us as Americans.

OPPORTUNITY KNOCKS IN TURKMENISTAN: IS ANYONE LISTENING?

HON. JANICE D. SCHAKOWSKY
OF ILLINOIS
IN THE HOUSE OF REPRESENTATIVES
Tuesday, January 16, 2007

Ms. SCHAKOWSKY. Madam Speaker, the Administration's crusade to spread democracy

Postpartum Depression Resources

BOOKS

Beyond the Blues: A Guide to Understanding and Treating Prenatal and Postpartum Depression by Shoshana Bennett & Pec Indman (2006)

A Daughter's Touch by Sylvia Lasalandra (2005)

A Deeper Shade of Blue: A Wonan's Guide to Recognizing and Treating Depression in Her Childbearing Years by Ruta Nonacs (2006)

Depression in New Mothers: Causes, Consequences, and Treatment Alternatives by Kathleen A. Kendall-Tacket (2005)

This Isn't What I Expected: Overcoming Postpartum Depression by Karen Kleiman and Valerie Raskin (1994)

WEB SITES

www.postpartum.net (Postpartum Support International). Largest worldwide network of education, support, advocacy, and referral information.

www.janehonikman.com.

www.mededppd.org New NIMH-sponsored PPD Web site from MediSpin.

www.womensmentalhealth.org From Massachusetts General Hospital Women's Mental Health Center.

www.state.nj.us/health/fhs/ppd/index.shtml From former New Jersey First Lady Mary Jo Codey.

Acknowledgments

This book has my name on the cover, but it is unquestionably the work of many. *Fair Game* could not have been published without the heroic efforts of my lawyers, David Smallman and Lisa Davis, who guided both me and this book through the entire process, from contract to lawsuit to publication. Their unstinting professionalism, ironclad belief in the rights and remedies granted under the Constitution, and impeccable judgment in navigating the tremendous and sometimes frightening hurdles on the way to publication made it all possible.

At Simon & Schuster, I owe publisher David Rosenthal a great debt of gratitude. Without his support, leadership, creative (and sometimes crazy) ideas, and occasional hand-holding, I could not have continued when this book seemed like a very dim prospect. My editor, Ruth Fecych, patiently went through each line word by word, many times. Her fortitude, sharp eye, and active pencil made this a much better book than it would have been without her. Thanks are also given to Simon & Schuster's corporate management, Jack Romanos and Carolyn Reidy, for their courageous decision to allow Simon & Schuster to be a coplaintiff in my suit against the CIA. Victoria Meyer and Tracey Guest of Simon & Schuster's publicity department deserve special medals for shepherding this project and its unique needs through the media gauntlet with professionalism and grace.

My literary agent, Elyse Cheney, has been called upon to do

far more for a client than is typical or expected. I have come to rely heavily on her exquisite judgment, coaching, and, indeed, her friendship. Melanie Sloan, intrepid leader of Citizens for Responsibility and Ethics in Washington, has served as a trusted sounding board for the many legal issues swirling around *Fair Game*, and her colleagues—Anne Weissman for her legal acumen and hard work, and Naomi Seligman—are also due a heartfelt thank-you for all their assistance. Joe Cotchett and Frank Pitre are valiant knights, ready to fight for what they think is fair and right. Erwin Chemerinsky, First Amendment superstar, has been an unfailingly thoughtful participant in this project as well, giving generously of his time. Chuck and Justyn Winner have been by our sides from nearly the beginning of this saga to offer their time, expertise, and friendship. We are lucky to have them on our team. Don Epstein, of Greater Talent Network, has waited patiently and understood the many challenges placed in our path.

In times of trouble, it is essential to have friends. It is even better when those friends are smarter than you and can serve as mentors with sage counsel. Melody Miller and Bill Wilson are worth their weight in gold and the sort of friends with whom we can laugh until we cry. Ellen and Gerry Sigal never faltered through good times and bad, ever ready with empathy, good advice, a drink, and, perhaps most important, a good laugh about the foibles of life. Jackie and Sidney Blumenthal extended their friendship to Joe and me in the darkest of times and are our heroes in many respects for their personal and political courage. Nancy and Marty Edelman have helped us navigate many unknown waters and Joe and I are grateful and better for having known them. Trudy and Jay Inslee have been true friends and supporters throughout. Janet and Jerry Zucker have believed in the truth from the early days and provided us with unforeseen opportunities that have opened new doors for us. David and Victoria Tillotson are the most generous and kind next-door neighbors we could have asked for, from invitations to swim on a hot day to watching our children in a pinch. Thank you all.

During the course of writing this book, I relied heavily at times upon former CIA colleagues for their moral support and insights and I am deeply indebted to them. Whether for checking facts, names, background, experience, or a wry laugh at the absurdity of it all, I sincerely thank you for all you've done and salute your service to our country: Larry Johnson, Jim Marcinkowski, Tyler Drumheller, Bob Baer, Melissa Mahle, Michael Grimaldi, and Brent Cavan. To those who put their names and reputations on the line in open letters to Congress about the implications of the leak of my name—Vince Cannistraro, Ray Close, Mel Goodman, Patrick Lang, David Mac-Michael, John McCavitt, Ray McGovern, Marc Sageman, James Smith, William Wagner—you all have my respect and gratitude. There are others, who continue to serve their country proudly and loyally and whom I obviously cannot thank by name, but who have been of tremendous help.

My girlfriends of long standing are like sisters to me. Without their unfailing friendship, acceptance, and ability to make me laugh, I would have lost my sanity at a number of points in the last few years. They are Janet Angstadt, Duffy Asher, Leigh Cassidy, Jane Cibel, Sheri Clark, Marty Compton, Tulu Gumustekin, Sue Mazza, Molly Mullally, Maria Pelucio, Tillie Ranich, Sue Seiff, Kathy Tone, and Ruth Weissel. Thank you, from the bottom of my heart; you are all my foundation. I am so much richer having you all in my life. My friend Jane Honikman, who helped compile the postpartum depression resource section, is a constant source of wisdom and soothing calmness. A sincere thank-you, too, to Wendy Hookman and Susan Stone, president of PSI.

Sharing in the joys and sorrow of life is a family's destiny. I am blessed with parents who gave me everything I need to survive and ultimately emerge on the other side of this experience a better person. To my father, Samuel Plame, who can always be counted upon to be calm in times of crisis, and my mother, Diane McClintock Plame, who gave nothing short of her constant, unconditional love, I wish us all some smoother sailing in the years ahead. My respect, gratitude, and love for my big brother, Robert Plame, and his wife, Christie, only grew deeper as their sterling characters were revealed during tough times. It has been an honor to help guide and a deep pleasure to see the fine young adults that Joe's children, Joe V and Sabrina, have become. I look forward to sharing with you many happy family times together in the future.

At age seven, Samantha and Trevor have only the vaguest notion of what this book is about. Which is as it should be. When they are older, they will have plenty of time to learn what was at stake during their youngest years. Perhaps then they will forgive their mother for the many hours on the telephone or at the computer, shushing them, when all they wanted was for her to play with them or answer an important question. I pray they will understand why their parents were away so much and less than patient with their concerns. They are truly the light of my life; they are two of the reasons Joe and I fought for the truth and what we thought was right.

Finally, there is Joe, whom I fell for, hard, at first sight. You have my enduring respect and love. It has been a journey, and will continue to be so, and there is not a day that goes by that I don't feel blessed to have you at my side. Thank you for your courage, passion, and deep love.

Afterword Acknowledgments

I would like to thank many who contributed insights, information, memories, and advice for the reported afterword. Particular thanks on this project to Simon & Schuster's Ruth Fecych and David Rosenthal, who gave me the opportunity if a short deadline, attorney Henry Lanman, who reviewed the contract, the *New Yorker*'s Jeff Frank for the plug, and for particular expertise on subjects relevant to Valerie's life and career: Daniel Tompkins, Brady Kiesling, Diane Plame, Janet Angstadt, Joe Wilson, Larry Johnson, Brent Cavan, Jim Marcinkowski, Melissa Mahle, Janine Brookner, Bob Baer, and others unnamed. Colleagues and friends generously provided a sounding board at various points, chief among them: Jeff Lomonaco, Jason Vest, Richard Byrne, Karen Buerkle, Sharon Fisher, Rachel Rubin, Rachel Vile, Shana Burg, Serif Turgut, Nora Ahmetaj, Dan Trantham, Dave Wagner, Ken Silverstein, Jeet Heer, Bara Vaida, John Judis, and Knut Royce. Editors Monika Bauerlein, Mike Tomasky, Sam Rosenfeld, Tara McKelvey, Rachel Morris, Paul Glastris, Joe Conason, and Pat Pexton supported my work. I am particularly grateful to my parents, Jay and Sandra Rozen, my sister, Natalie Rosenberg, and family, my in-laws, Beverley and Larry Evans, and family, and to Lena Gladstone. Most especially, my love and gratitude to Mike and Zoe.

About the Author

Valerie Plame Wilson, the former CIA Covert Operations Officer, was born on Elmendorf Air Force Base in Anchorage, Alaska, in 1963. She holds a bachelor's degree from Pennsylvania State University and two master's degrees, from the London School of Economics and Political Science, and the College of Europe in Bruges, Belgium. Her career in the CIA included extensive work in counterproliferation operations to ensure that enemies of the United States could not threaten America with weapons of mass destruction. She and her husband, Ambassador Joe Wilson, are the parents of seven-year-old twins. Mrs. Wilson and her family live in New Mexico.

Laura Rozen reports on national security from Washington, D.C. Her work frequently appears in *Mother Jones*, *National Journal*, and *Washington Monthly*. She has also written for *The Boston Globe*, the *Los Angeles Times*, and *The Washington Post* and reported for six years from Russia, the Balkans, and Turkey. She earned a master's degree from Harvard's Kennedy School of Government. She lives in Washington, D.C., with her husband and daughter.